PLYMOUTH AT WORK

ERNIE HOBLYN

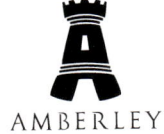

ACKNOWLEDGEMENTS

In the text of this book I have made numerous acknowledgements to the authors of various books I have quoted. It would be difficult, if not impossible, to write a book like this without referring back to the huge amounts of research that others have done before, especially those from long ago, and my thanks goes to them all. Next a general thank you to Brian Mosely for his Old Plymouth, Old Devonport and Old East Stonehouse websites, which are always a source of interesting and useful facts. Similarly my thanks to Steve Johnson of Cyberheritage for helping me with my research into the Palmerston forts for the Military chapter and for allowing me to use some of the pictures from his enormous collection. Another general thank you to the Devon Archives for allowing me to use sections from their online tithe maps, and also to the National Library of Scotland for allowing me to use sections from their wonderful historic Georeferenced 25-inch OS maps.

I would like to thank Brian Lewarne, Honorary Science Officer of the Devon Karst Research Society, for all his assistance in helping me understand the history and complexities of limestone quarrying in Plymouth, for allowing me to use material from their huge website and finally for proofreading the Quarrying chapter for me. I must also thank David Boden for allowing me access to his extensive collection of books and pictures, which helped me enormously in writing the chapter on the Dockyard. Finally, a big thanks to my old mate Dave Davies, retired master boatbuilder, for helping me with the chapter on Fishing and Boatbuilding.

Thanks to you all. Without your help this book could not have been written.

First published 2019

Amberley Publishing
The Hill, Stroud
Gloucestershire, GL5 4EP

www.amberley-books.com

Copyright © Ernie Hoblyn, 2019

The right of Ernie Hoblyn to be identified as the Author of this work has been asserted in accordance with the Copyrights, Designs and Patents Act 1988.

ISBN 978 1 4456 8565 6 (print)
ISBN 978 1 4456 8566 3 (ebook)

All rights reserved. No part of this book may be reprinted or reproduced or utilised in any form or by any electronic, mechanical or other means, now known or hereafter invented, including photocopying and recording, or in any information storage or retrieval system, without the permission in writing from the Publishers.

British Library Cataloguing in Publication Data.
A catalogue record for this book is available from the British Library.

Typesetting by Aura Technology and Software Services, India. Printed in the UK.

Introduction	4
Expansion from the Early Days	7
Fishing and Boatbuilding	19
The Dockyard	36
Quarrying	50
The Military	66

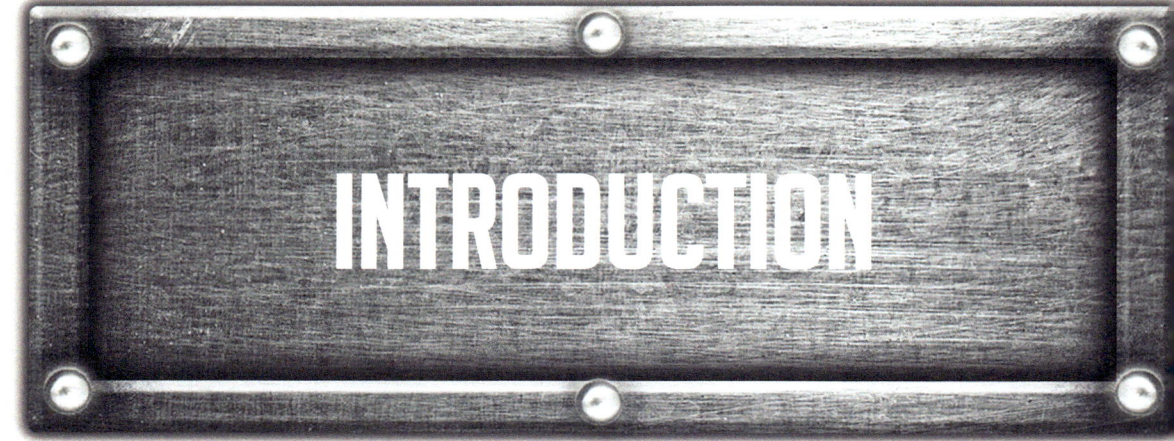

INTRODUCTION

Every settlement needs to have a reason, or more likely several reasons, for its inception. Obviously it needs access to a supply of fresh water, but it also needs a reason to be there. This could be access to minerals that could be traded, a nearby forest to supply building materials and more importantly a source of food. This will explain why a settlement comes into being, but it then needs long-term reasons to continue to exist and possibly to expand.

Some seemingly ideal situations never expand beyond being a hamlet or a village. Others wither and die when the reason to be there disappears: the supply of minerals or wood gets used up, the needs of the people change and they no longer want to be there. For a village to become a town, a town to become a city, it needs a continuous reason to survive, or better still a series of reasons that keep it going as times and tastes change. Many towns and villages that were hugely important centuries ago are now mere collections of ruined buildings because the industry or mineral source that made them important died out.

In Plymouth's case the original reasons why our forebears decided to set up home here were good soil for growing crops, the presence of fresh water (two rivers plus several streams) as well as sheltered access to the sea to provide food. The sea has continued to be a major and expanding source of work for the city in many ways, not just as a food source. Before our forebears started filling in the inlets, the area we know as Plymouth was a spider's web of tidal creeks, some of which provided sheltered places where people could build boats and from which they could go fishing or, as the boats they built grew bigger, embark on trading voyages.

Plymouth also had other assets apart from the sea that could be exploited and I will be exploring those as well in my story of Plymouth at work over the centuries.

Before I start I need to define what I mean by Plymouth. The place has grown from a tiny fishing village or two possibly dating back to the Bronze Age into the city of today with a population of over a quarter of a million, stretching all the way from the Sound to the foothills of Dartmoor. It is hemmed in on both sides by rivers – the Tamar to the west and the Plym to the east. The modern city of Plymouth also includes the towns of Plympton and Plymstock, both independent, thriving towns until 1967 when they were swallowed up by their larger neighbour.

As both Plympton and Plymstock have seperate, well-documented histories and are only recently part of Plymouth, I intend to leave them out of my story, so the area I will be covering is the post-war, pre-1967 Plymouth, which includes the housing and industrial

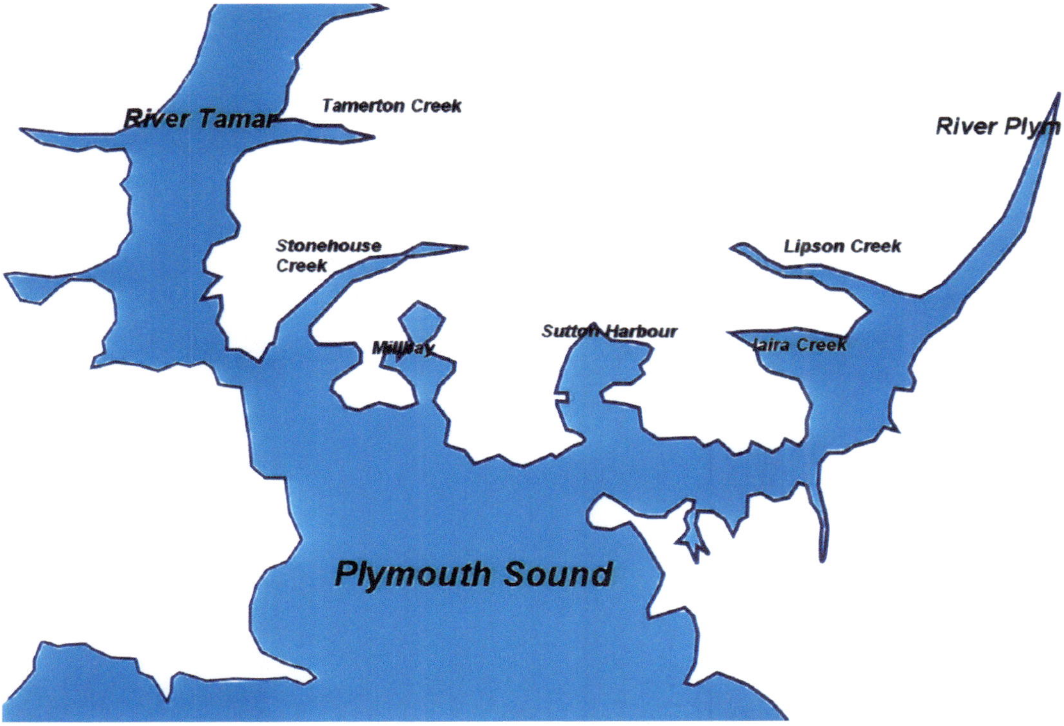

Introduction

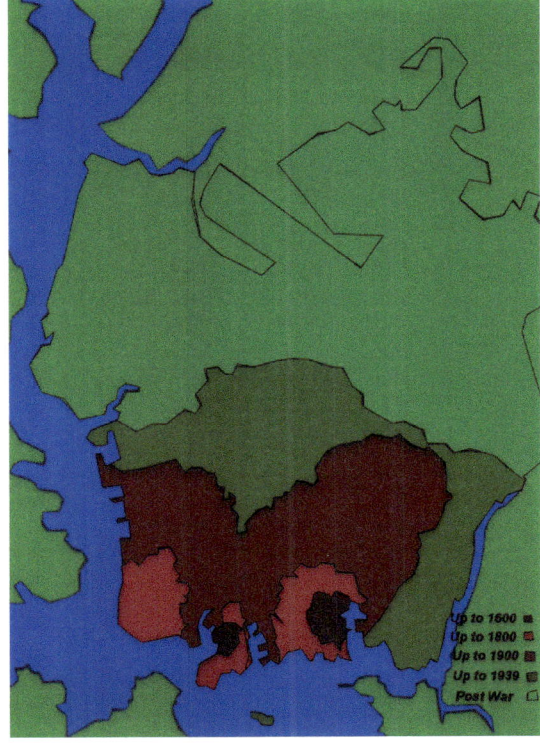

Above: Plymouth as shown in a 1643 map.

Right: Growth from 1600 to post-war.

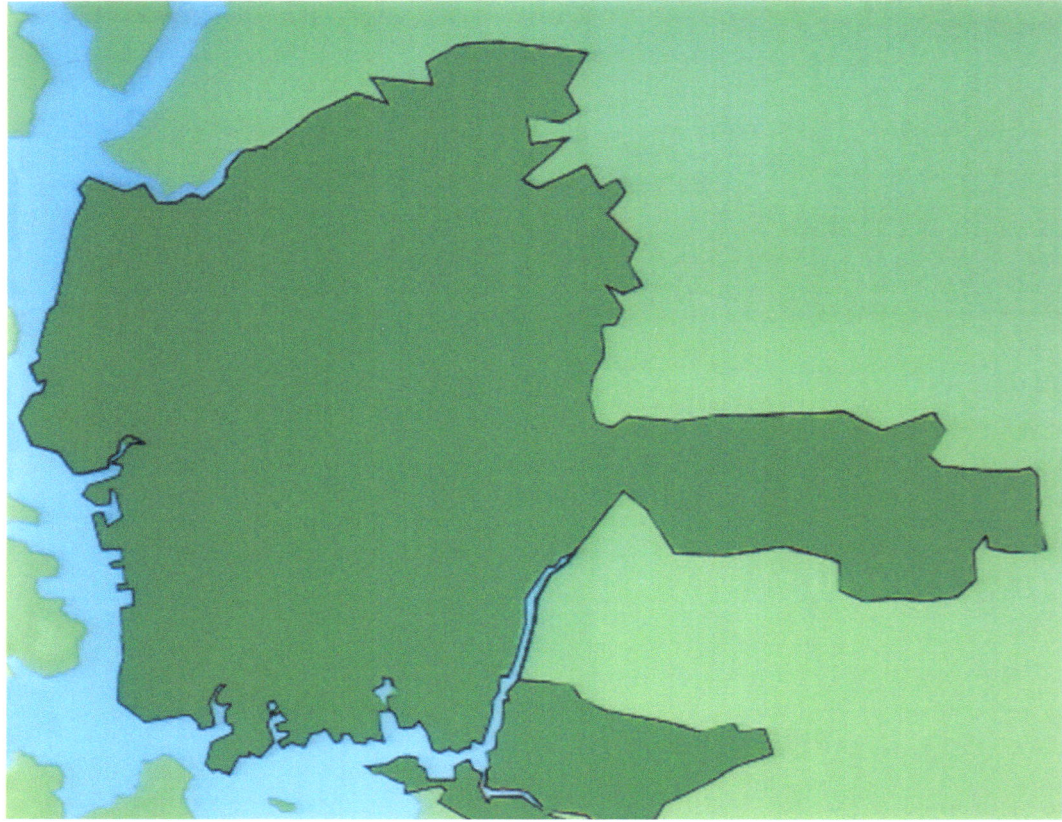

Plymouth city today.

estates to the north of the city where so many of the modern population now live and work since the post-war building boom to replace what had been destroyed in the Blitz.

My growth map in my Introduction shows the way Plymouth has grown over the centuries and the outline of the area I mean to explore. The second map, in comparison, shows the whole of modern Plymouth including the housing and industrial estates on the northern edges near to Roborough, plus Plympton and Plymstock.

I would also like to clarify another point. Plymouth, of course, has hundreds if not thousands of jobs, trades and professions. Extrapolating data from a *Western Morning News*' Annual Business Guide 2018 gives the top fifteen businesses in Plymouth and only two of them will get a mention here. Of course, as this is a list of businesses it does not include employers like the NHS and local and national government organisations, nor does it include the military. The Plymouth Hospital's NHS Trust websites tells me that they employ 'circa 7,000 staff', which would make them the second largest employer behind The Range shops at 8,846 and ahead of the dockyard on 5,127. Obviously, nowadays the vast majority of Plymothians work for large organisations and do hugely important work – for instance working in shops, manufacturing and retailing or in the NHS – but many of those jobs would not have existed 100 years ago. I only intend to cover those jobs that, over the city's history, may have only employed hundreds rather than thousands but I feel have had a lasting impact on the city.

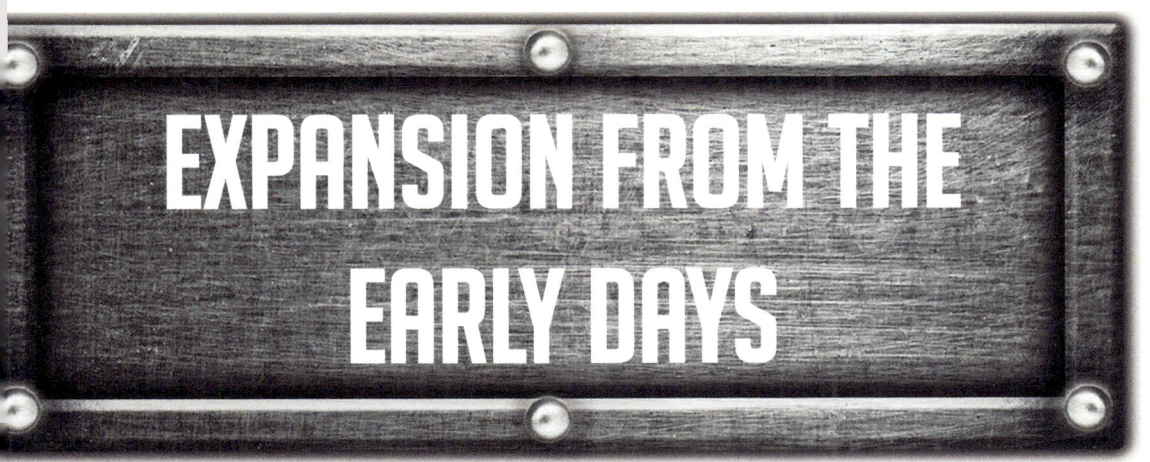

EXPANSION FROM THE EARLY DAYS

The place we know as Plymouth has been home to people since the Bronze Age, as the nineteenth-century discovery of a Bronze Age cave containing both human and pre-historic animal remains shows. More recently we have to rely on written history to trace Plymouth's early days.

The Domesday Book entry for Sudtone or Sutona (what we now call Sutton Harbour) in 1085–86 is as follows:

> The King holds Sudtone. TRE (At the time of King Edward) it paid geld for 1 virgate of land. There is land for 6 ploughs. In demesne is half a plough with 1 slave; and 4 villains and 2 bordars with 5 ploughs. There are 2 acres of meadow and 20 acres of pasture. It renders 20s by weight.

The total population including the slave, four villains (unfree peasants who farmed for themselves but worked for their lord part time) and two bordars (less well-off unfree peasants), plus their families, was thirty according to R. N. Worth. Interestingly the village of Tambreton (the place we now call King's Tamerton) was of similar size and paid the same tax of 20 shillings. Of course landownership and the amount of tax owed by the landowner was what the Domesday Book was all about, rather than historical accuracy. Above all it was certainly not a population census but what is interesting is that it should have listed fisheries and none are mentioned.

The next information we find about this area comes from John Leland, writing in the mid-sixteenth century, who said:

> The town of Plymmouth [sic] is very large and divided into four Wards and there is a Capitaine [sic] in each Ward and under each Capitaine three Constables.
>
> This town, about Henry II's time (1133–1189), was a meane thing as an habitation for fischars, and after increased by litle and litle [sic].
>
> The oldest Part of the Toun [sic] stoode by North and West somewhat, and this part is sore decayed and now come to the leaste of the four.

Tristram Risdon, writing a little later in the early seventeenth century and referring to Leland's comment, said:

It is not long since Plymouth was accounted a mean fishing town, until the convenience of the haven, which (without striking sail) admitteth into its bosom the tallest ships that be, where they ride safe in either of two rivers, to take the opportunity of the first wind. The commodious situation and healthful habitation was vulgarly known and allured many to resort thither; whereby it is so increased with beautiful buildings that the two parts conjoined, is made one populous Plymouth; and now so greatly grown that it may be held comparable to some cities.

Risdon's comparison with 'some cities' has to be taken in context: in the early seventeenth century the population of London was around 200,000. In their book *Plymouth: Maritime City in Transition*, Brian Chalkley, David Dunkerley and Peter Gripaios, writing in the late twentieth century, state that in 1600 the population 'grew to more than 4,000 and Plymouth was established as England's premier western port'. R. N. Worth, whose *History of Plymouth* was published in 1890, estimates the population in 1560 as around 7,000, although he says it changed little over the next few centuries, being 8,400 by 1740.

The Domesday Book paints a picture in 1086 of an area of farmland beside the sheltered inlet, which was little more than a hamlet where a few people, possibly an extended family, scraped a living. Given its position beside a natural harbour, it is unthinkable that the inhabitants did not make use of that natural asset; possibly it was not included because it was subsistence fishing to help feed the family rather than commercial fishing, although the Domesday Book is known to contain errors.

Judging by Leland's comments about the time of Henry II, we can see that Sutton had increased little in the century after Domesday and had still been little more than a fishing village surrounded by good farming land. As time went by and the size of vessels increased, the advantages of the large sheltered harbour became more and more useful. The name changed, with the place starting to be called Plymouth in late fourteenth-century documents.

Of course the area we know as Plymouth was in those days a very different place from the modern city, a spider's web of tidal inlets running up through each of the valleys that make up the area. We can get some idea of what it was like from the map that I included in my introduction, which is based on a 1643 map.

As you can imagine, getting around would have been very difficult. The low-lying areas not filled with water at high tide would have been marshy and there was more high ground as well (as we shall see in later chapters), so getting anywhere would have involved much climbing and descending of hills and fording of streams. As an illustration of this, in 1642 during the Civil War the Royalist forces attacked Plymouth's Parliamentary forces at Laira Point and fought as far as what is now called Freedom Fields. The defenders of Plymouth fought back and drove them down over what we now call Lipson Hill. Unfortunately for them the tide had come up Laira Creek, more or less where Alexandra Road is today, and hundreds of Royalists drowned, showing just how deep that tidal inlet was at that point. Not far away from that point, just the other side of Mutley Plain, the area now known as Pennycomequick marked the end of the tidal Stonehouse Creek, so the two almost bisected Plymouth.

Of course, Drake's famous defeat of the Spanish Armada in 1588 would also have helped to establish Plymouth as 'England's premier western port'. It was during this period of Tudor prosperity that the town, and particularly the port, expanded. The following century saw the military expansion as well, with the Royal Citadel being built in the 1660s on the orders of Charles II as an army garrison and possibly to allow the army to subdue the Parliamentarians of Plymouth who had fought against his father!

Expansion from the Early Days

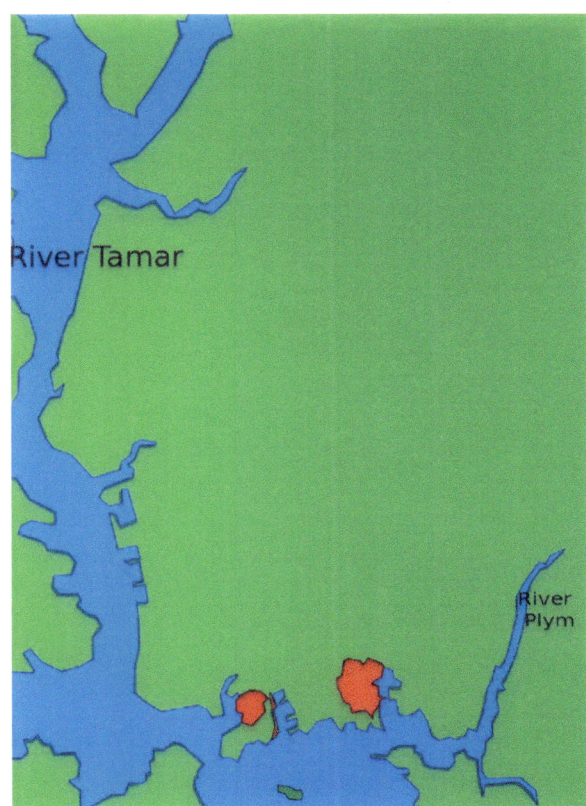

Right: Plymouth in 1600.

Below: The Citadel centre right with modern Plymouth stretching into the distance behind.

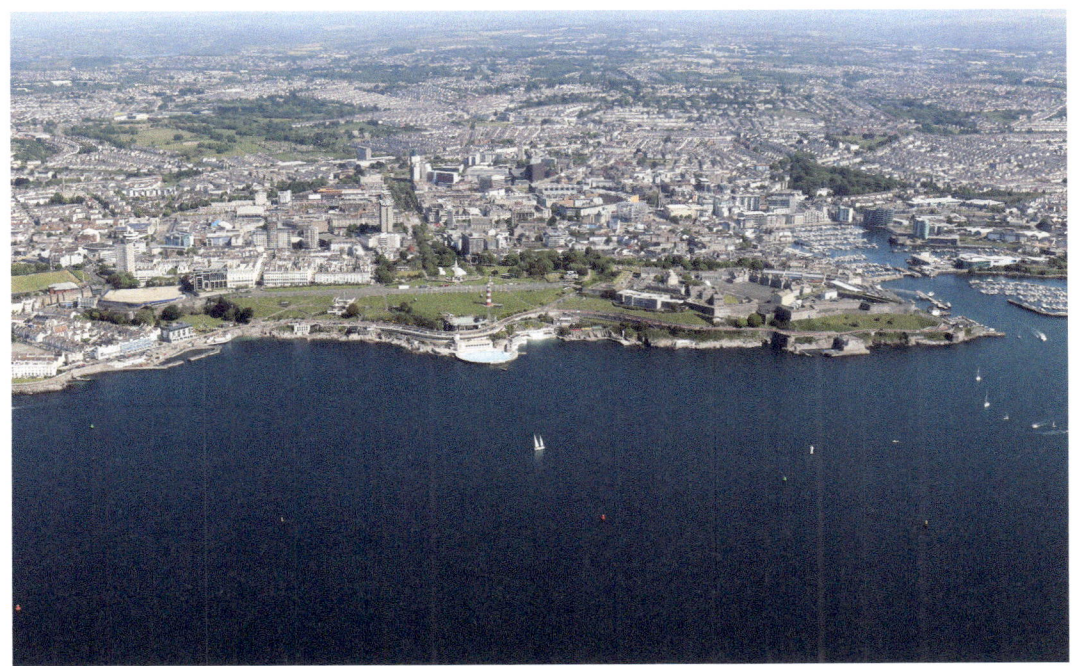

In 1689 William III ordered a dock to be built on the eastern bank of the River Tamar as a western base for the Royal Navy, where even the largest ships of the time could be repaired in dry dock. Large numbers of houses were built around this new dock to house the workers there and as the area then was far outside the town of Plymouth it simply became known as Dock. Between the two was the smaller area known as Stonehouse, built around the end of Stonehouse Creek.

If we assume R. N. Worth's estimate of population above was correct, we can see that by the beginning of the nineteenth century Plymouth was starting to grow rapidly. The 1801 census shows 16,040 inhabitants, growing to 73,794 by 1881. All these people needed to live somewhere and the town had grown slightly to accommodate them. Much of the growth came from Dock, which by 1800 had a larger population than Plymouth. The area of the dockyard itself had also spread northward as far as Pottery Quay to include Morice Yard, with the resultant housing growth to the north and east as well.

Despite all this growth some modern Plymothians might find it surprising that following the New Poor Law Act of 1834, which allowed parishes to join together to form a union with one large workhouse rather than the small parish poorhouses that had previously existed, Eggbuckland, Pennycross, St Budeaux, Tamerton and Compton joined the Plympton St Mary Union because they were not a part of Plymouth. All these parishes were rural, agricultural areas consisting mainly of farms with few parishioners. Laira Green also joined that union in 1861, prior to which it was not even a parish. Plymouth consisted only of Stoke Damerel (which included the burgeoning Devonport), Stonehouse, St Andrews and Charles. According to the tithe maps of the 1840s all of these apart from the smaller Stonehouse, which was mainly built-up, still largely consisted of farmland, although they did have some built-up areas. The Lipson area East of Mutley Plain, for instance, had just two large houses shown on the tithe map for Plymouth Charles and Tothill, north of Embankment Road, had five. Apart from some houses east of the Sutton Harbour area and the wharves and quarries of Cattedown most of the rest of that area was listed as pasture or garden.

By the time the tithe maps were drawn Dock had officially been renamed and was since 1837 the municipal borough of Devonport. Given the fact that Devonport was larger than Plymouth, it is

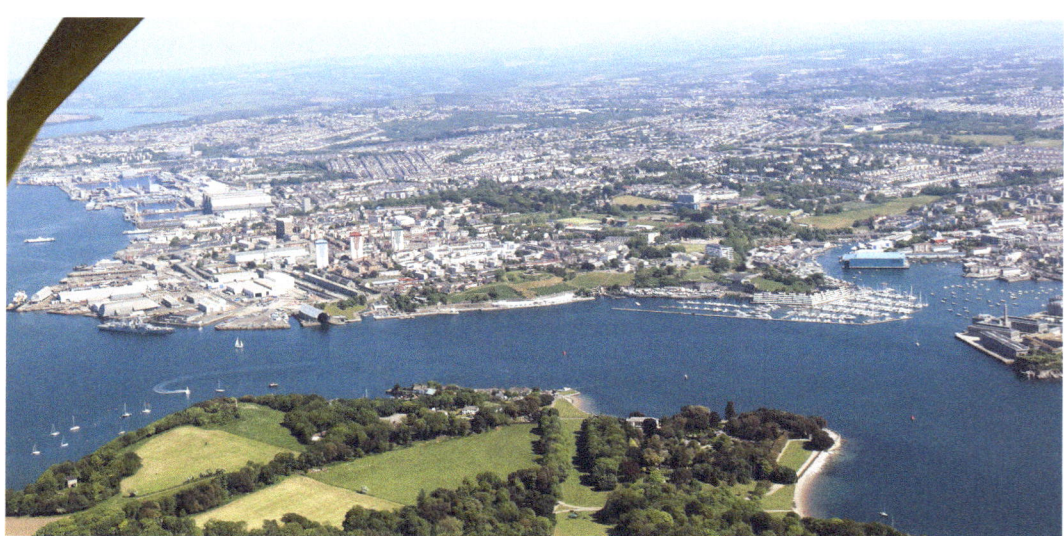

Stonehouse Creek centre right with the dockyard stretching up the river on the left.

Expansion from the Early Days

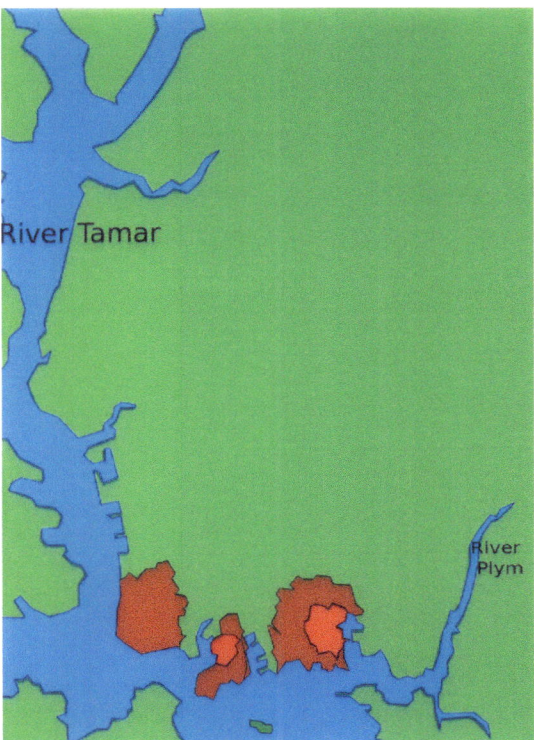

The three towns of Dock, Stonehouse and Plymouth in 1800.

no surprise to find that the Stoke Damerel tithe map shows much more housing. Everything within the Devonport lines, the fortified wall that surrounded the dockyard, the army barracks and the streets of Devonport itself as far north as Morice Square and Granby Green, then running from what is now the entrance to Devonport Park down to Stonehouse Creek and Devonport Hill, was very built up. Lower and Upper Stoke had a few streets as did Morice Town, but Keyham was a Barton (a large farm) and Swilley, now known as North Prospect, was a private estate.

A century later the growth was accelerating. By this time the three towns, which had previously made up Plymouth, had joined together, in fact if not politically. It took the First World War to force the amalgamation of the three towns into the city of Plymouth.

As can be seen from the 1900 map the three parishes that made up the central part of Plymouth had spread until they physically joined and much more of the agricultural land was now covered in houses, although large areas of farmland still remained. Plymouth stretched north as far as Mutley Plain and much more of Stoke, plus the Ford area, were now built on. This growth continued until 1939, by which time Laira, Peverell, Camel's Head, King's Tamerton and St Budeaux had also been absorbed and largely built on.

The Second World War had a huge impact on Plymouth. Most of the centre and much of Devonport were reduced to rubble. Vast numbers were made homeless and the destruction of so many businesses meant many were also jobless. While the centre was being rebuilt post-war, land to the north, which had been farmland, was covered in much-needed houses, mainly council houses. Other areas on the outskirts of the city became industrial estates and this expansion has continued up to the present day.

The following photographs show some of the industrial estates that have grown up surrounding Plymouth.

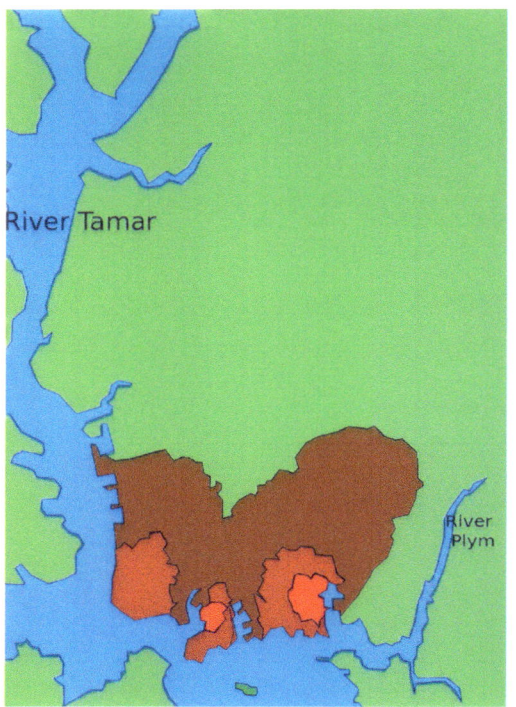
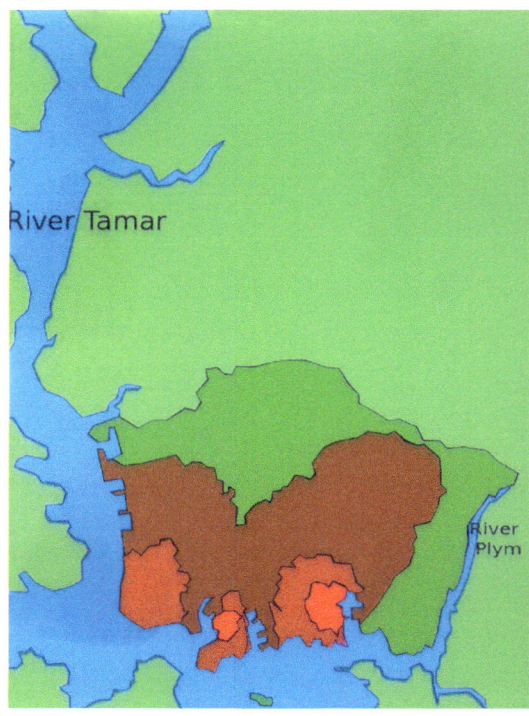

Above left: Plymouth up to 1900.

Above right: The city by the beginning of the Second World War.

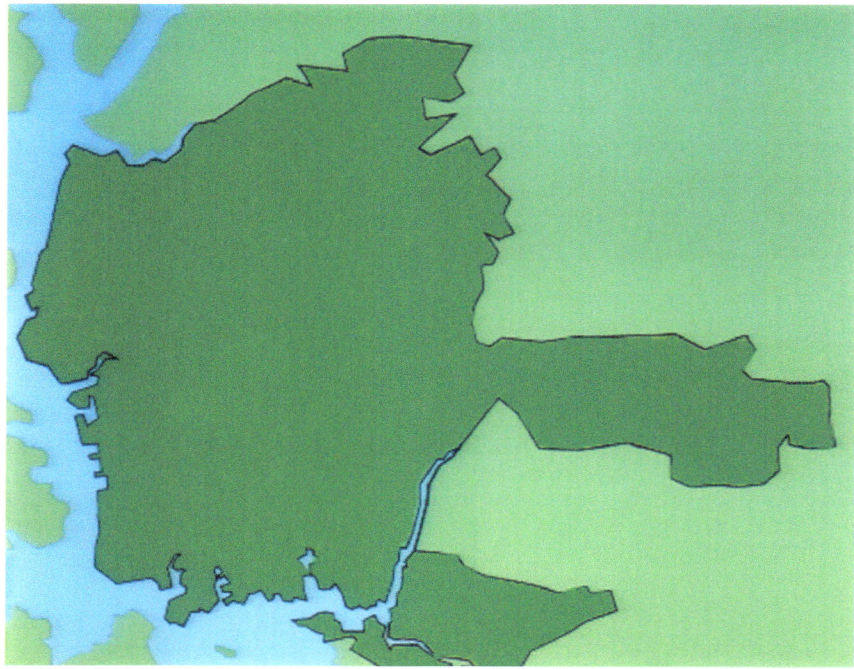

The city today including Plympton and Plymstock.

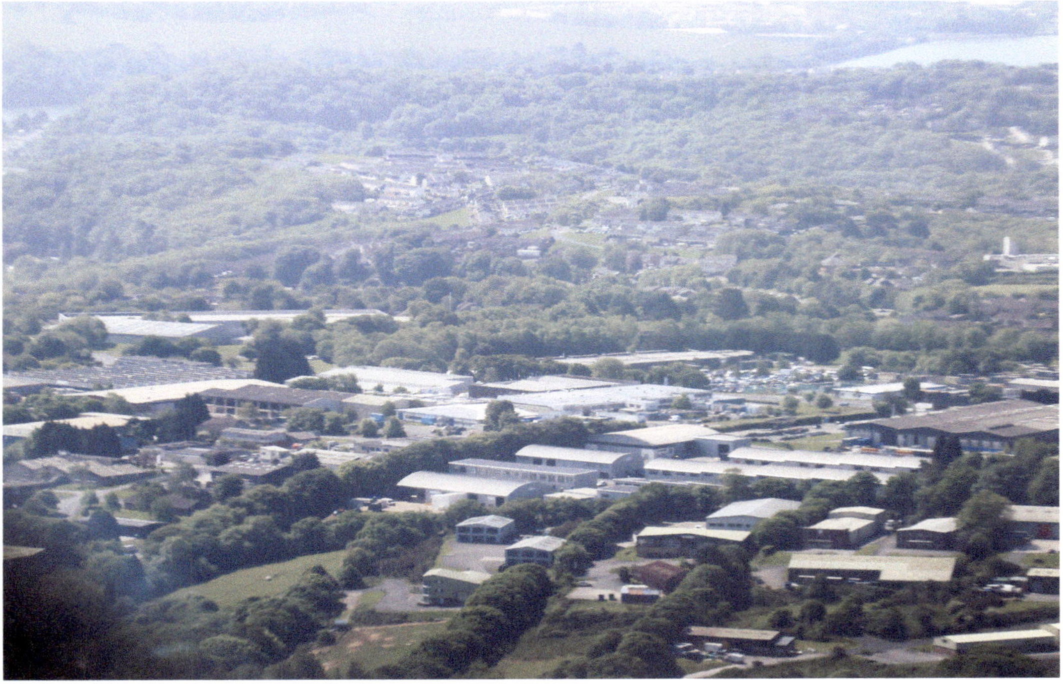

Above: Sisna Business Park, Estover.

Below: Bull Point.

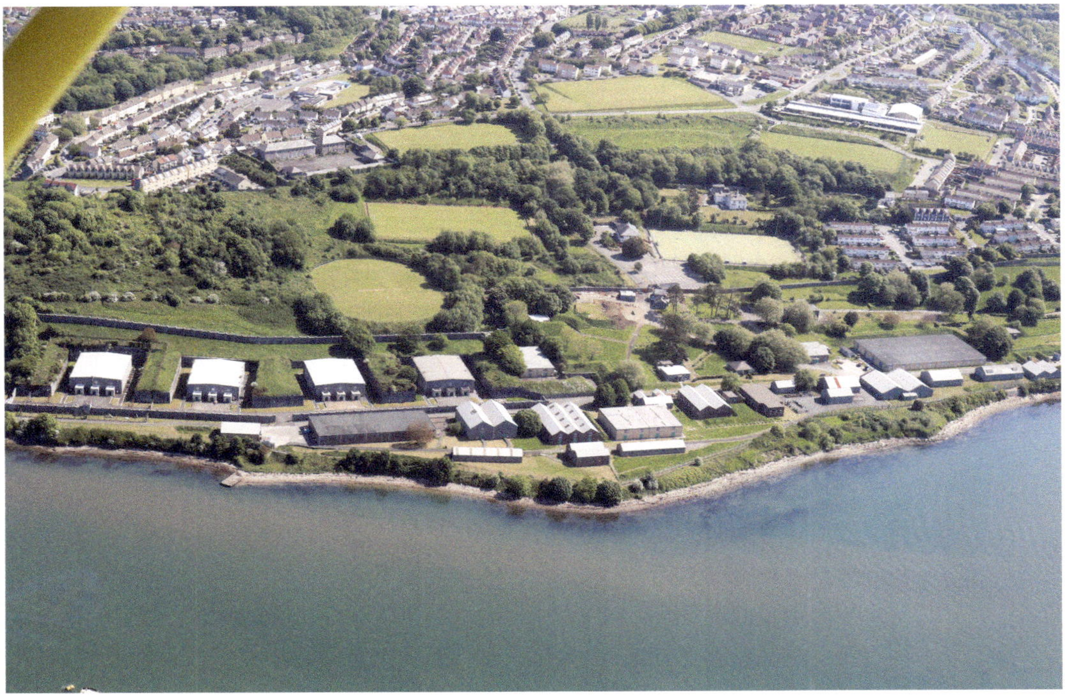

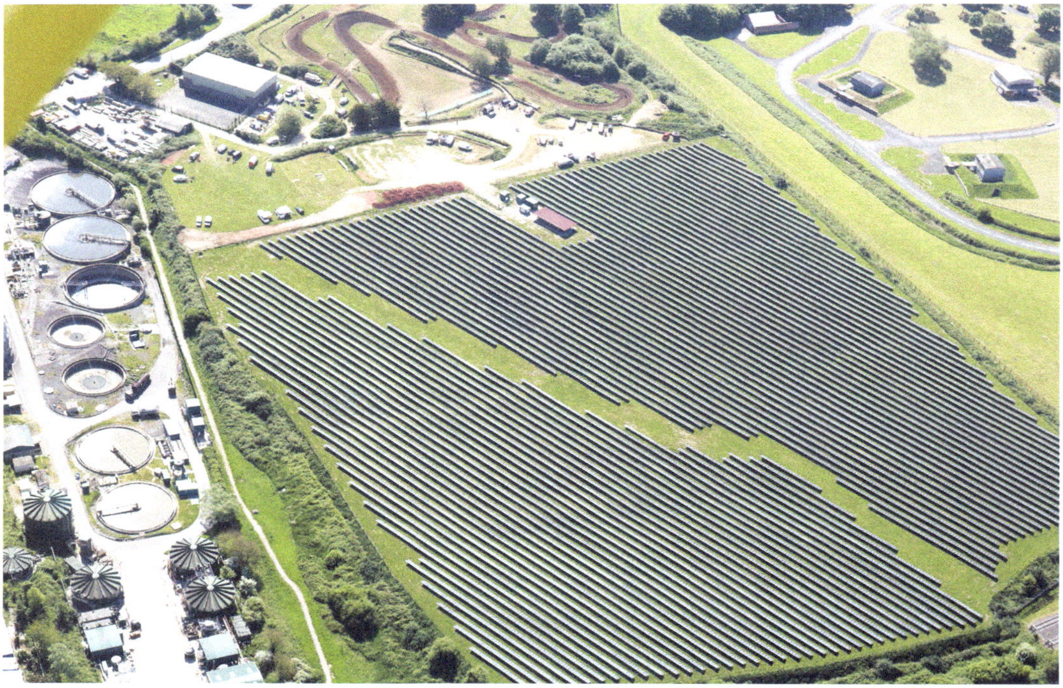

Above: Solar panel array at Ernesettle.

Below: Ernesettle Industrial Estate.

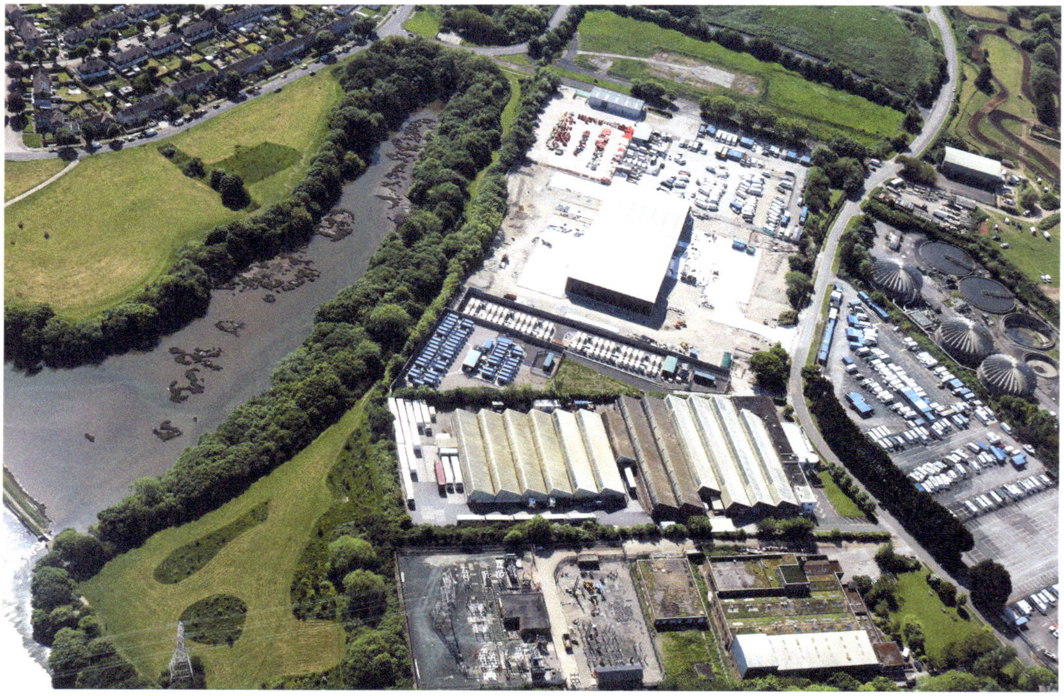

Expansion from the Early Days

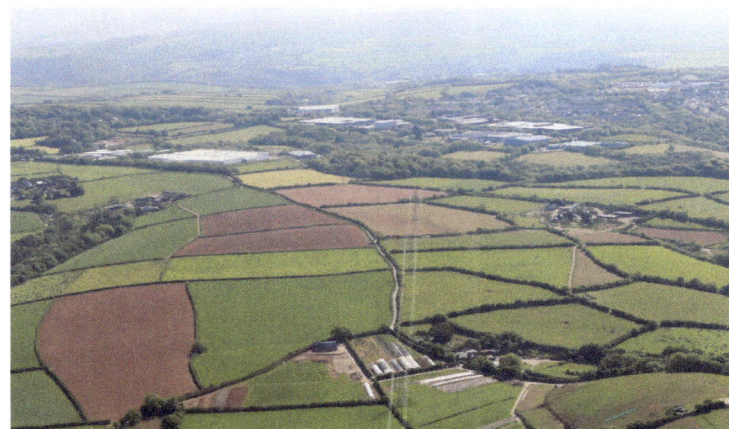

Broadley Industrial Park near Roborough.

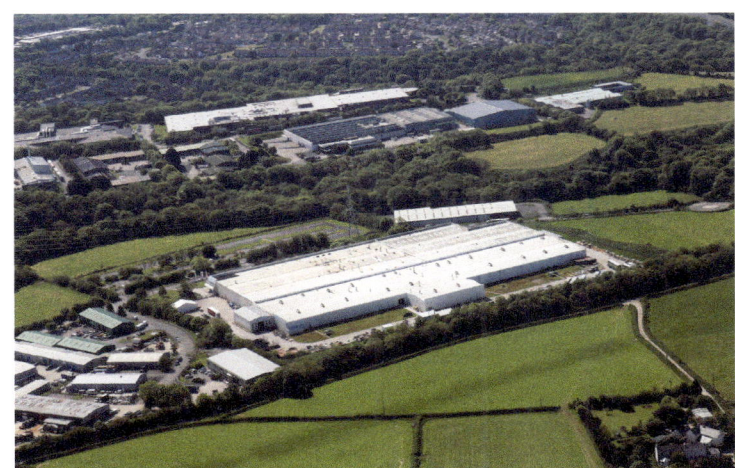

Right: The Rittal building at Broadley Industrial Park.

Below: Looking south over Estover.

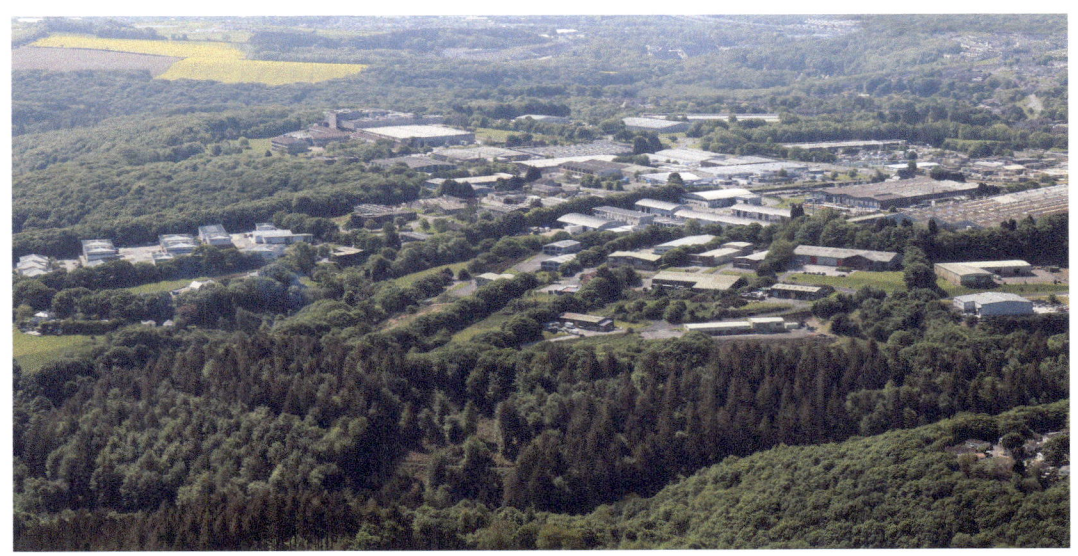

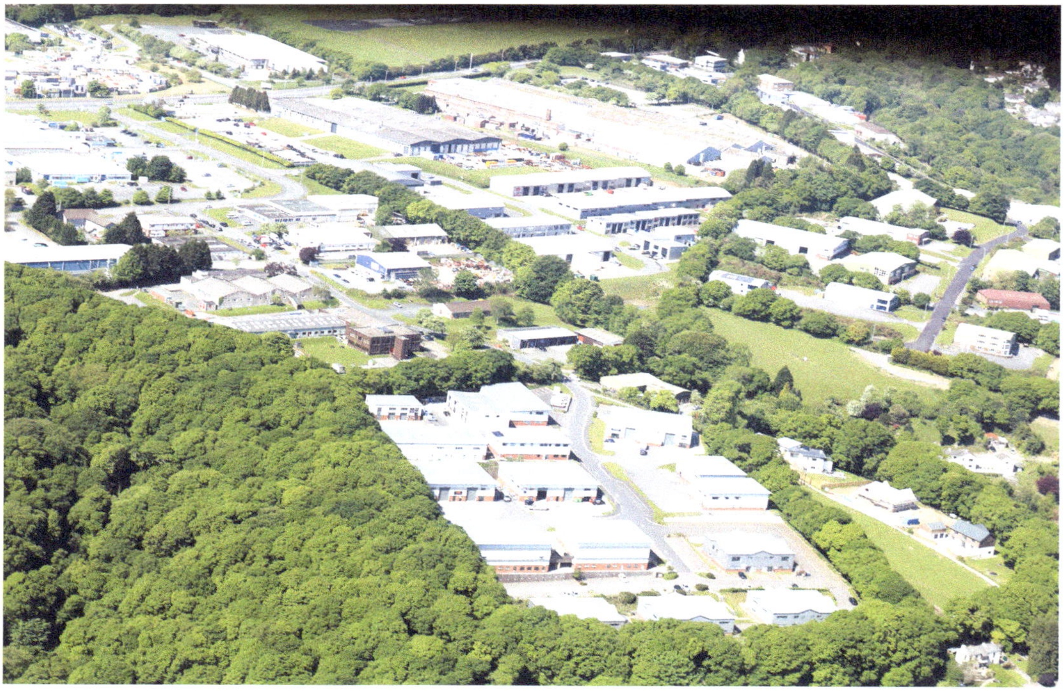

Above: Looking across Estover towards the old airport.

Below: The Wrigley factory at Estover.

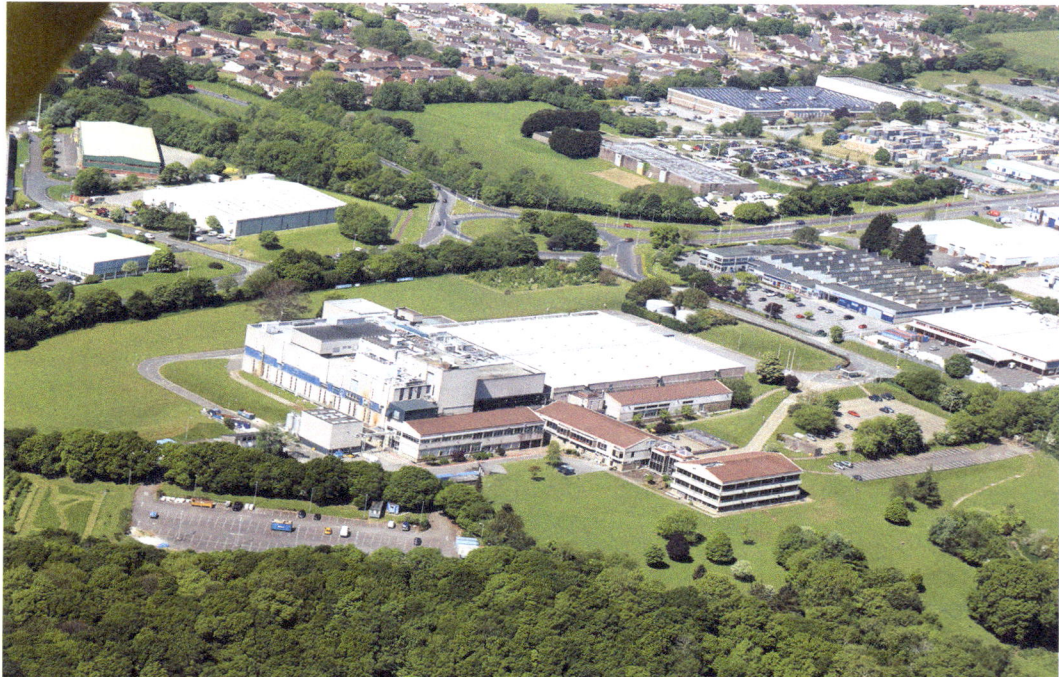

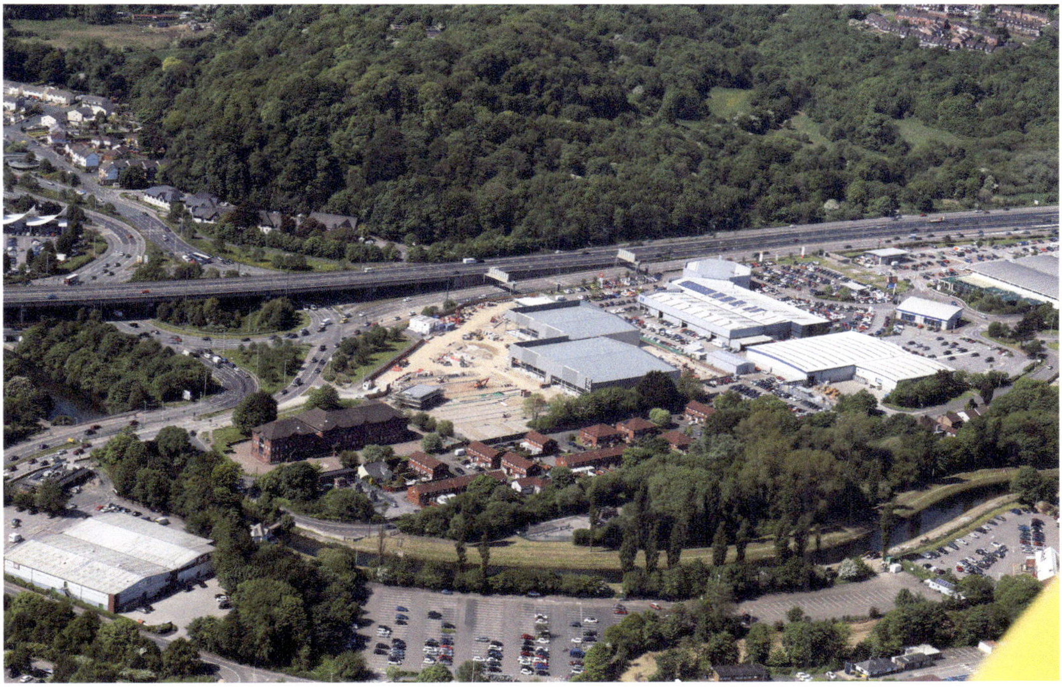

Expansion from the Early Days

Above: Marsh Mills Industrial Estate.

Below: Princess Yachts' Coypool Industrial Estate.

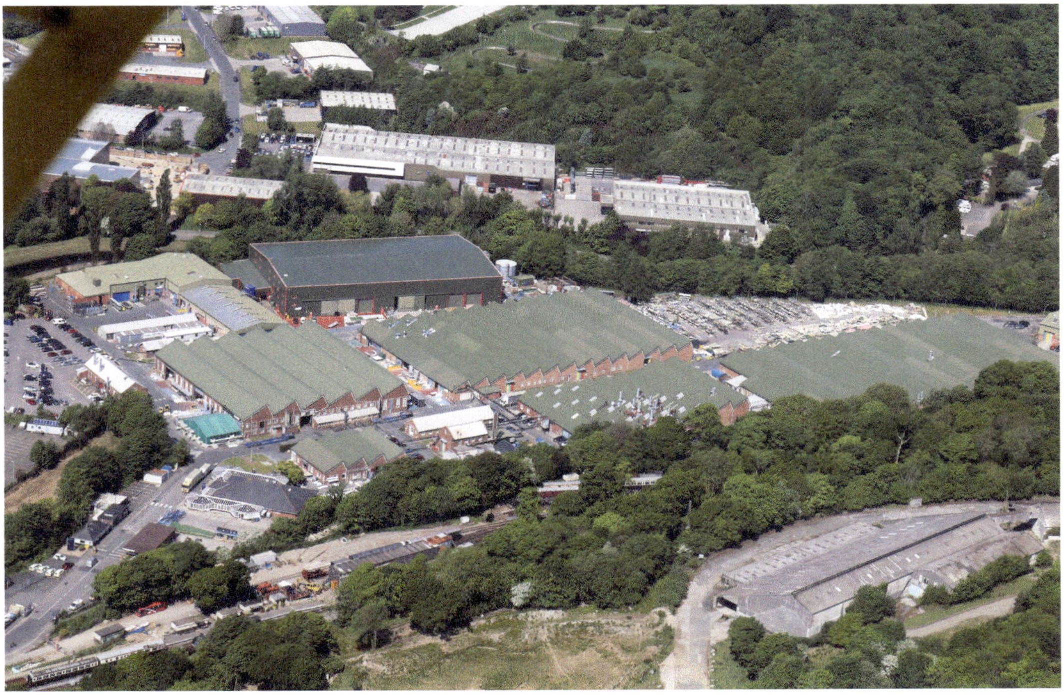

Looking at Plymouth from the air (or on Google maps!) it is now a huge sprawling area stretching from the Sound to Dartmoor, although thankfully there are still large areas of green within the city boundaries, as can be seen from the following photos.

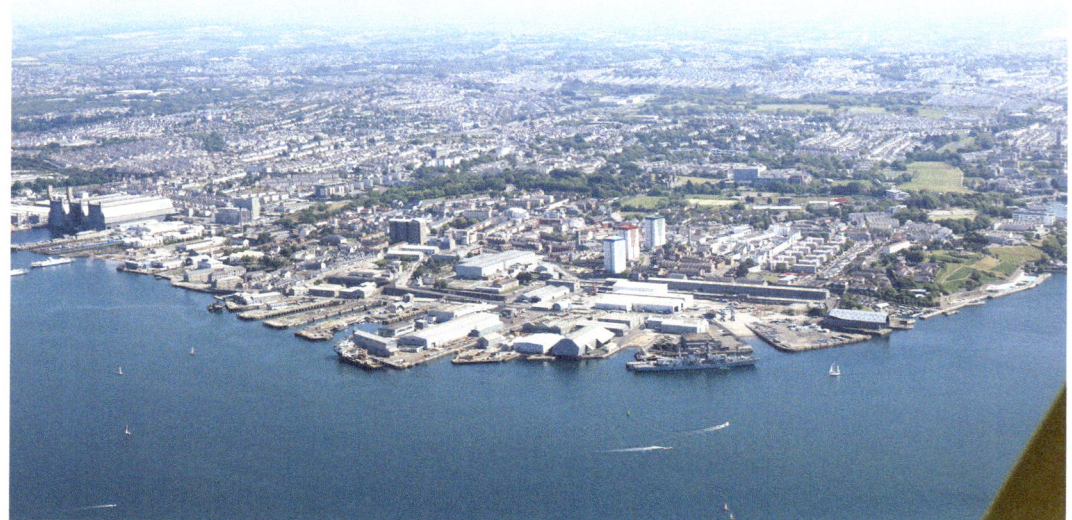

Above and below: Two views from the air showing Plymouth stretching from the Tamar towards Dartmoor.

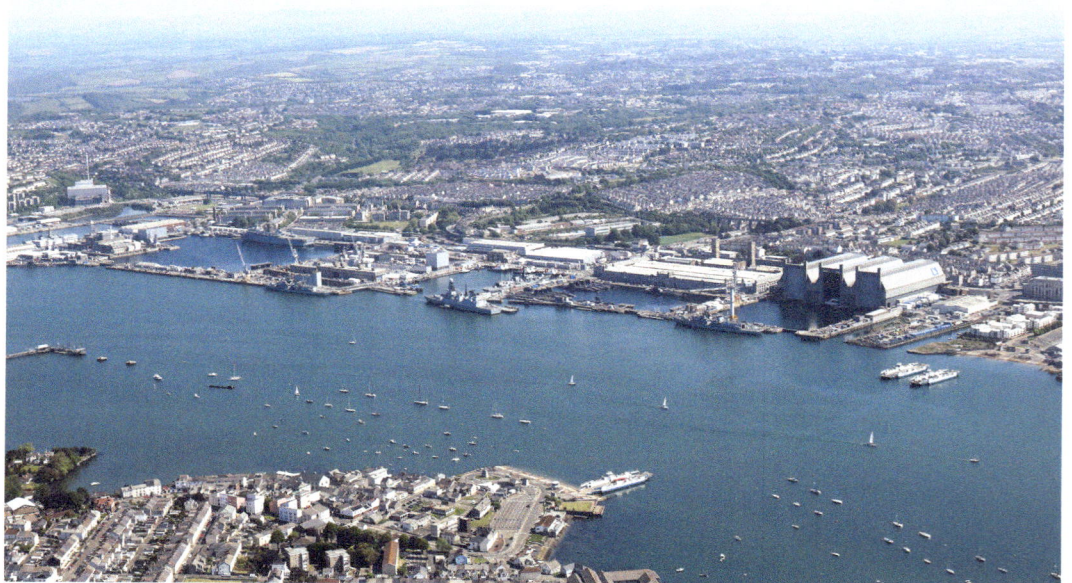

FISHING AND BOATBUILDING

As we have seen, Plymouth developed from small villages clustered around two of the sheltered inlets within the already sheltered Plymouth Sound. Probably the earliest inhabitants were farmers who also caught a few fish from the shore, but soon they would have ventured out onto the water to try to increase their catch, possibly using home-made boats like the ancient coracles still in use.

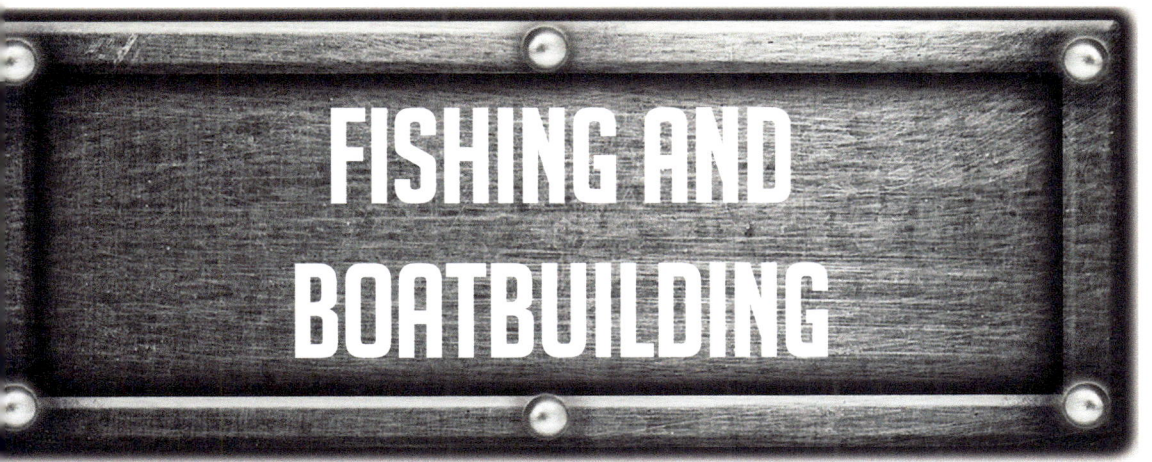

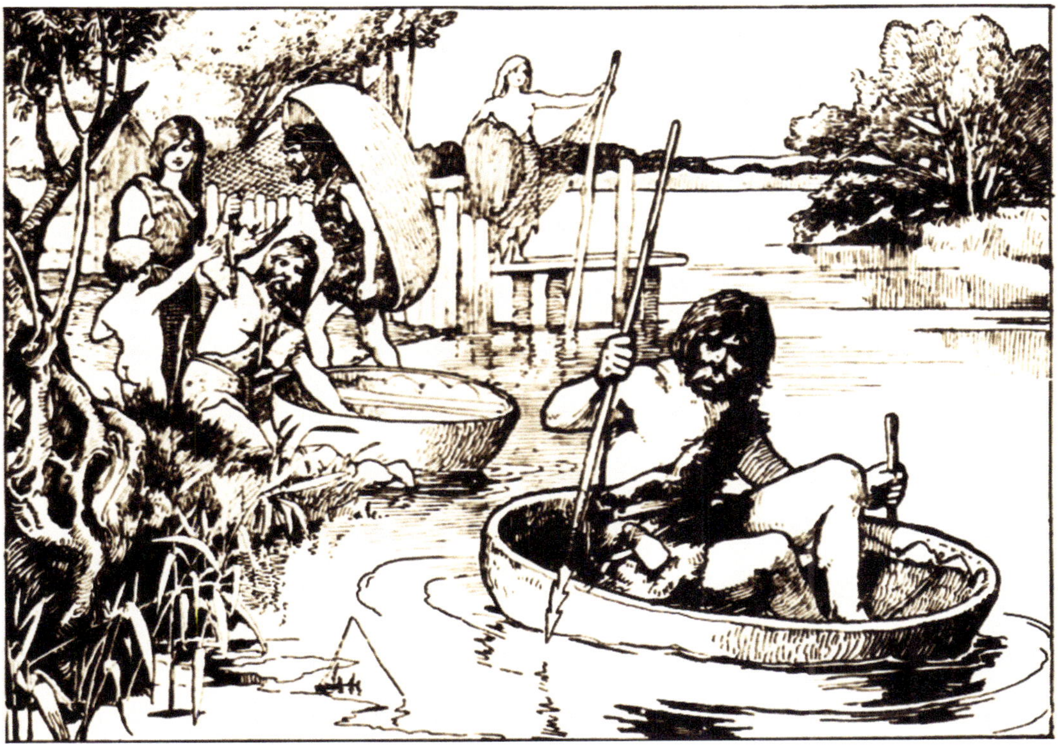

Early Britons using a coracle.

Eventually we can assume they would have started making larger boats that were capable of going out into the rougher waters of the Sound to fish, and the really adventurous people would have gone even further out into the English Channel. Many would have drowned in the storms that even today claim lives, but the more adventuring they did the more they learned about where to catch the most fish, how to make the strongest boats and how to find their way back home afterwards.

Experience is a great teacher and slowly these early inhabitants would have become experienced fishermen and experienced boatbuilders. Boats grew in size and became more seaworthy, capable of voyaging along the coast to other harbours, including those from Fowey to Kingsbridge, to trade. Some adventurous souls even headed south to see what they could find and came back having found their way to a strange land whose inhabitants spoke a different language.

Fishing became more than a subsistence occupation, allowing the fishermen to bring back enough fish to exchange with inhabitants of other nearby villages. The adventurous souls who had sailed along the coast or even visited foreign shores found the locals they met might have useful things they wanted to exchange for things that were more plentiful in Plymouth. In this way trade grew and with it the need for newer and ever larger boats.

Of course back in medieval days most of the trading vessels would have been heading for Plympton, which was a far more important place than Sutton. Eventually the silting caused by the tin works on Dartmoor meant it was impossible for ships to reach Plympton, so they landed at Sutton instead. The Cattewater gave a secure anchorage against the worst of the south-westerly and westerly gales.

Leland talks about Sutton Pool in the sixteenth century, saying 'The mouth of the gulph wherein shippes of Plymouth lyith is walled on each side and chained over in tyme of necessite [sic].'

R. N. Worth quotes from the 1437 customs book in which cargoes imported into Plymouth came from such diverse places as Brittany, Portugal, Norway, Denmark, Holland and Italy, as well as more local ports such as London, Dartmouth, Guernsey, Exmouth, Fowey and Exeter. He also quotes Ralegh [sic] in 1593, saying 'Ordnance could not be carried to Plymouth, the passages will not give leave.' The roads were so bad that anything heavy had to be delivered by ship.

Historical records show that between 1066 and Tudor times fishing and trading vessels were little more than large open clinker-built dinghies, some up to 75 feet long designed to be sailed or rowed, but they were later replaced by the larger, more enclosed galleon type like the *Golden Hinde* of Sir Francis Drake (which of course was sailed around the world) and the carrack type of ship like the *Mary Rose*.

Ships of this size and design, built from locally sourced wood could have been constructed locally on the sheltered banks of the rivers and harbours. These designs are little more than larger versions of rowing boats so their construction could easily have evolved over the years. The villager who built everybody's coracle could have decided to build something a bit bigger and stronger, and being longer and narrower, much easier to handle in rough weather. These were the clinker-built dinghies, which are still very much in use today, and the design could be expanded to make a larger trading vessel. As in all things, someone who gets a name for building good, strong, reliable vessels will become well-known locally and even further afield, allowing a business to grow.

Crispin Gill quotes a written record of the Black Prince ordering a warship to be built on the Cattewater in 1358. Many of the shipbuilders would have been families or small firms building a vessel on the beach, to be slid into the water or floated off at a high tide when it was seaworthy.

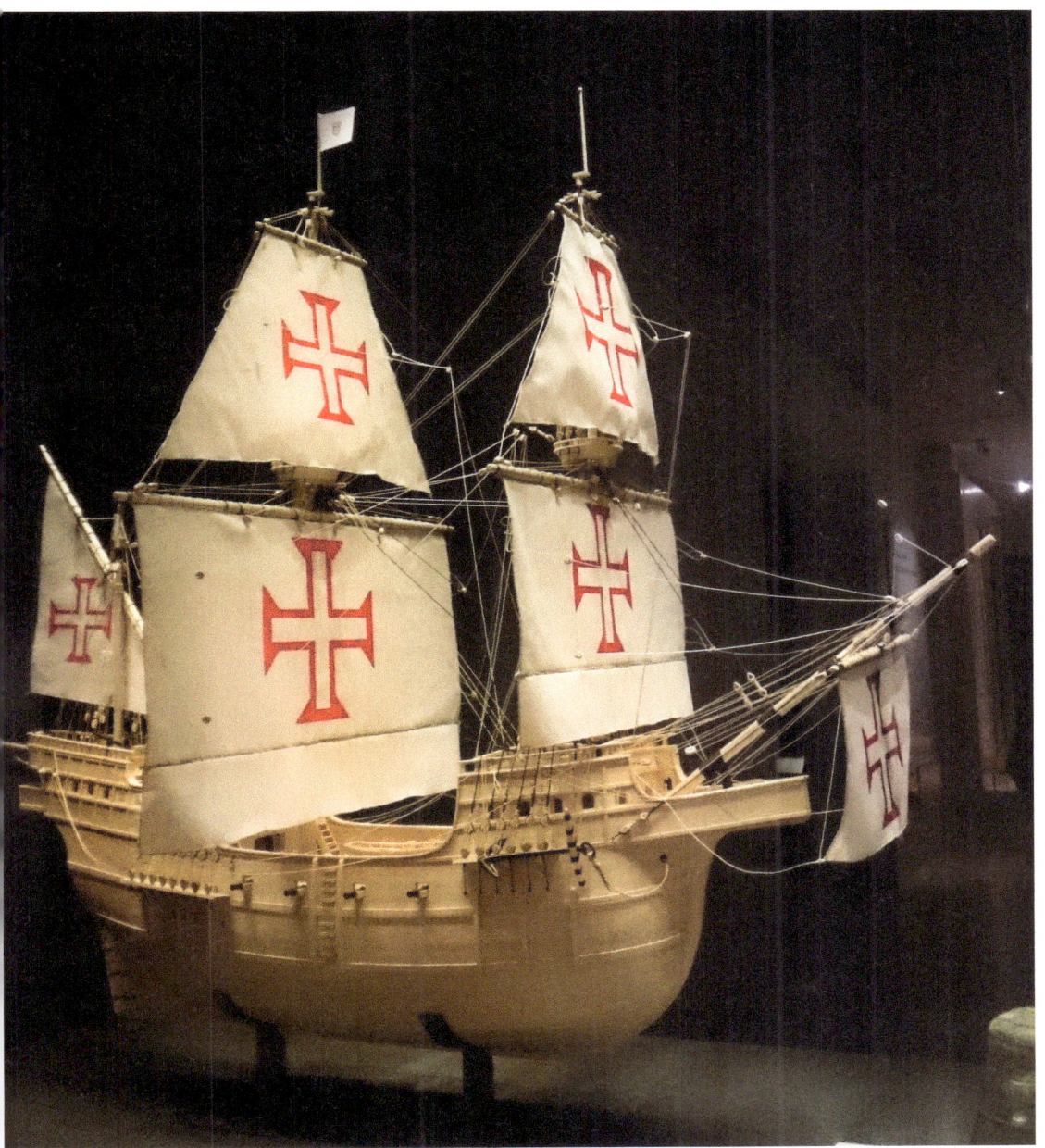

Model of a Portuguese Nau, a type of carrack.

Apart from these trading vessels, disagreements with other nations meant ships were needed to carry soldiers overseas, and from the fourteenth century onwards these armies needed to carry cannon with them as well. From the fifteenth century onwards people had the bright idea of firing some of these cannons from the ships themselves, and as all ships were built from wood a stone or cast-iron ball fired from a cannon could cause devastating damage. Even Columbus's flagship, the *Santa Maria*, carried four bombards, early versions of ship-board cannon in 1492.

With ships rolling and pitching the cannons were almost impossible to fire accurately but even a badly aimed shot could cause a great deal of damage, and a ball hitting on or just below the waterline could sink the ship. Even a ball crashing through all the rigging, masts and sails could render the ship helpless. Of course a ship needed to be fairly large to be capable of carrying such heavy weapons, especially if it was going to carry many of them, so ships were steadily getting bigger. The above-mentioned *Santa Maria* was around 100 tons, and Henry VIII's *Mary Rose*, whose fate in 1545 made her probably one of the most famous ships in history, carried eighty to ninety guns of varying types, had a displacement of about 700–800 tons and was over 100 feet long.

By the late eighteenth century what were called First Rate ships like HMS *Victory*, which carried 104 cannon including thirty 24-pounders weighing 2.7 tons each, had a displacement of 3,500 tons and was 186 feet long, so ships were growing in size.

The traders who bought ships and ventured far afield in search of goods that could be sold at a profit needed wharves and warehouses to store these goods, and obviously the ideal place for the warehouses was right at the waterside so their ships could tie up alongside and unload their cargoes.

Worth also states that in the eighteenth century Plymouth merchants traded with Virginia, the Sugar Islands (the islands of the Caribbean) and Newfoundland, although I presume these trades were disrupted during the American War of Independence (1775–83) and the French Revolution (1789–99). There were some benefits even from these though; Worth mentions that Plymouth was 'the greatest emporium in the country for prize ships and goods' because the privateers were doing very well – but then Plymouth generally did well in times of war!

Following the defeat of Napoleon trade took a nosedive and according to Worth 'it was emphatically asked, Can it be contended that a state of peace is to consign to decay a large and flourishing town and inhabitants, placed in the immediate vicinity of harbours which appear to be designed by Nature to invite Man to the pursuits of commercial industry?'.

The Sutton Harbour Company was formed by Act of Parliament in 1811. Crispin Gill quotes figures from the 1808 *General View of the Agriculture of Plymouth*, which said that Plymouth had 245 ships totalling 15,574 tons and employing 1,105 men. By 1815 there were seven shipbuilders around Sutton Pool, six in the Cattewater and six in the Hamoaze employing 300 men, with fourteen ropewalks and a dozen sailmakers.

Millbay grew in importance as the port of preference during the nineteenth century, the Great Western Docks Company being formed by Act of Parliament in 1846, with Brunel as engineer. This had a 460-foot-long graving (dry) dock on the western side and extensive warehousing as well as a railway line connecting it to the GWR by 1874.

Before the Breakwater was built (1812–44) both Sutton Pool and Millbay were dangerous places in a southerly gale and most ships sheltered either in the Hamoaze (even before the dockyard was built there) or in the Cattewater. Worth records that 'Shipbuilding was a very important local industry; and the yards were either in Sutton Pool or Cattewater'. 'The largest merchant ship built in the port was launched from the yard at Queen Anne's

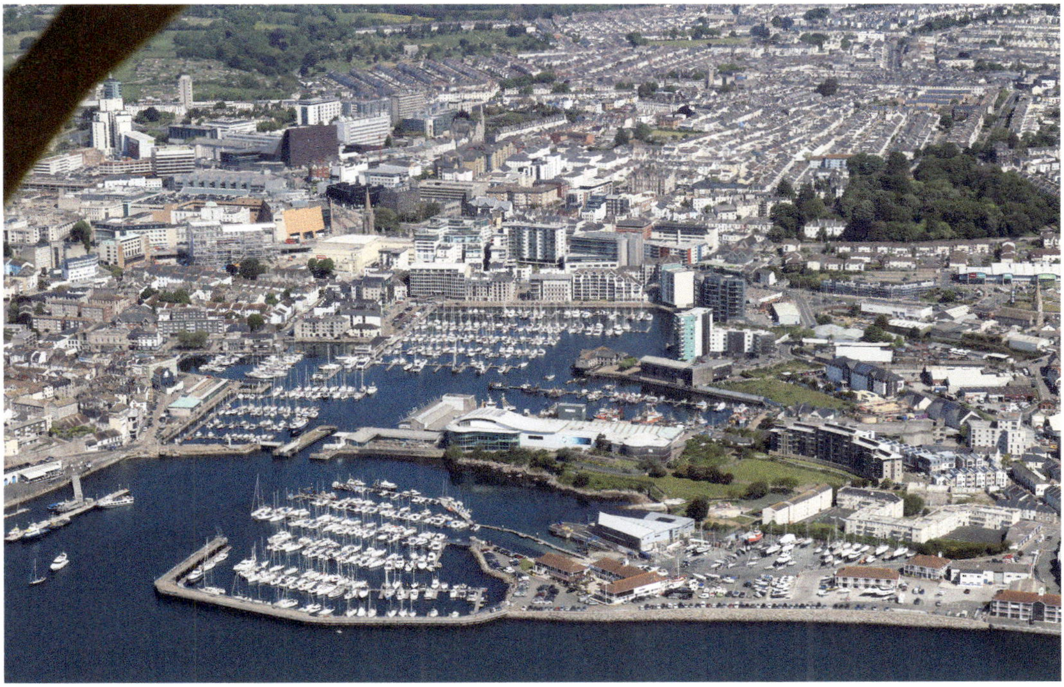

Fishing and Boatbuilding

Above: Sutton Harbour and Queen Anne's Battery today.

Below: Millbay with West Hoe behind.

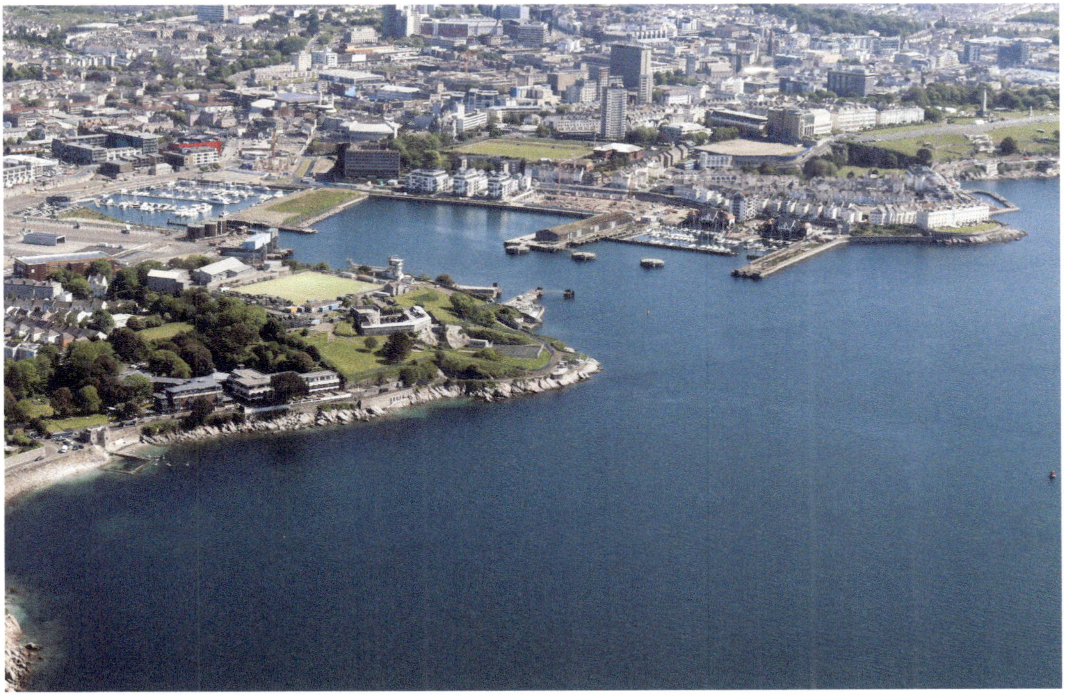

Battery in 1870, she was of 1,127 tons burthen [sic]'. Richard Hill took over the pre-existing shipyard beside the Cattewater in the 1820s and according to Crispin Gill had 'a wet dock, building slip and a patent or railway slip that could take ships up to 1,000 tons'. He built the first steamship launched in Plymouth there in 1824. All this is now lost under the modern Cattedown Wharf.

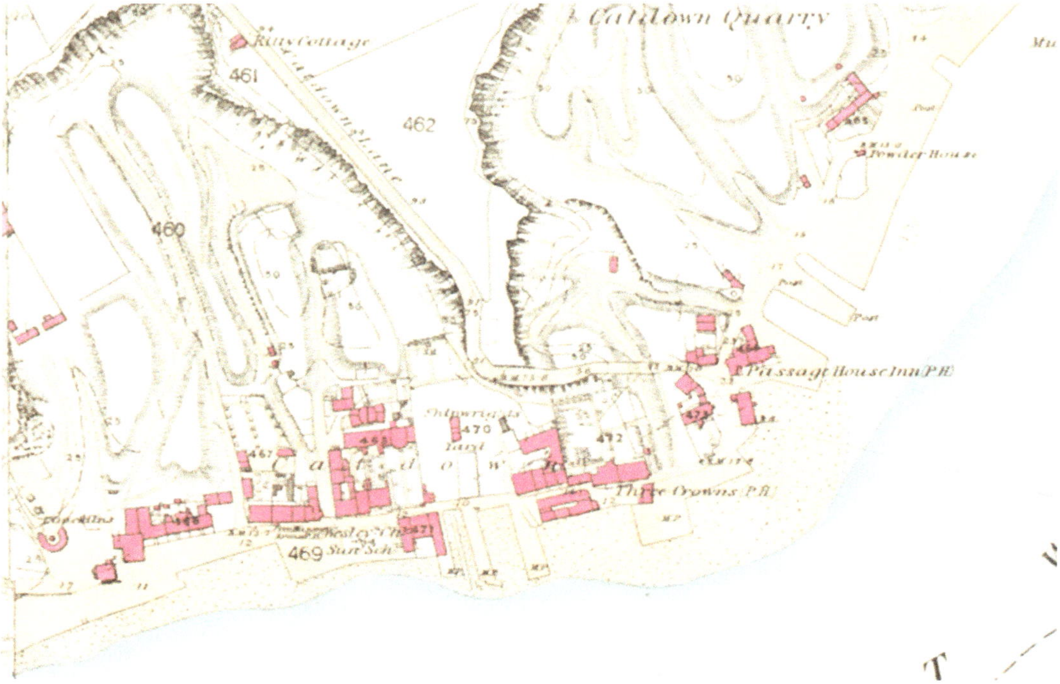

Cattedown Wharf from an 1866 OS map. (Courtesy of the National Library for Scotland)

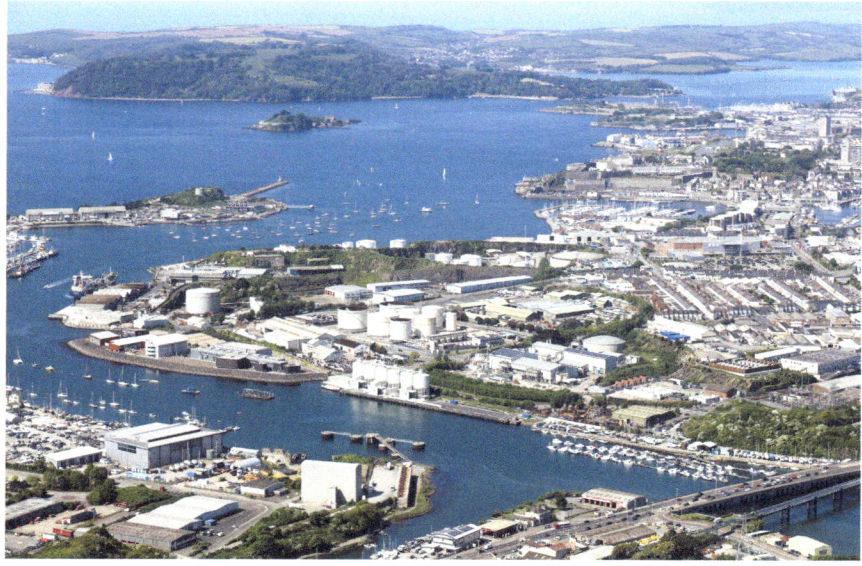

Cattedown Wharf today.

Just around the corner at the entrance to Sutton Harbour is Queen Anne's Battery where various people including Joseph Banks built ships. The 1866 OS map shows a slipway and a large graving (dry) dock that was right in front of what is now the University of Plymouth Marine Station. The slipway is still there, although the graving dock is long gone.

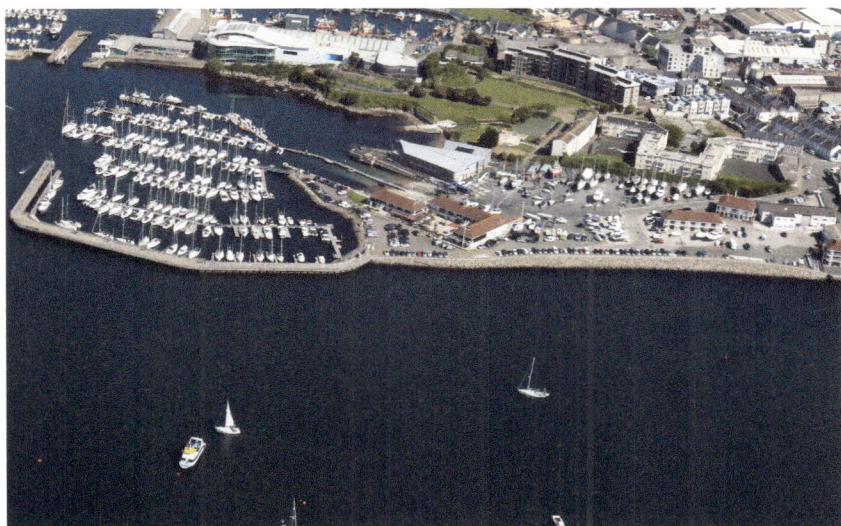

Queen Anne's Battery today.

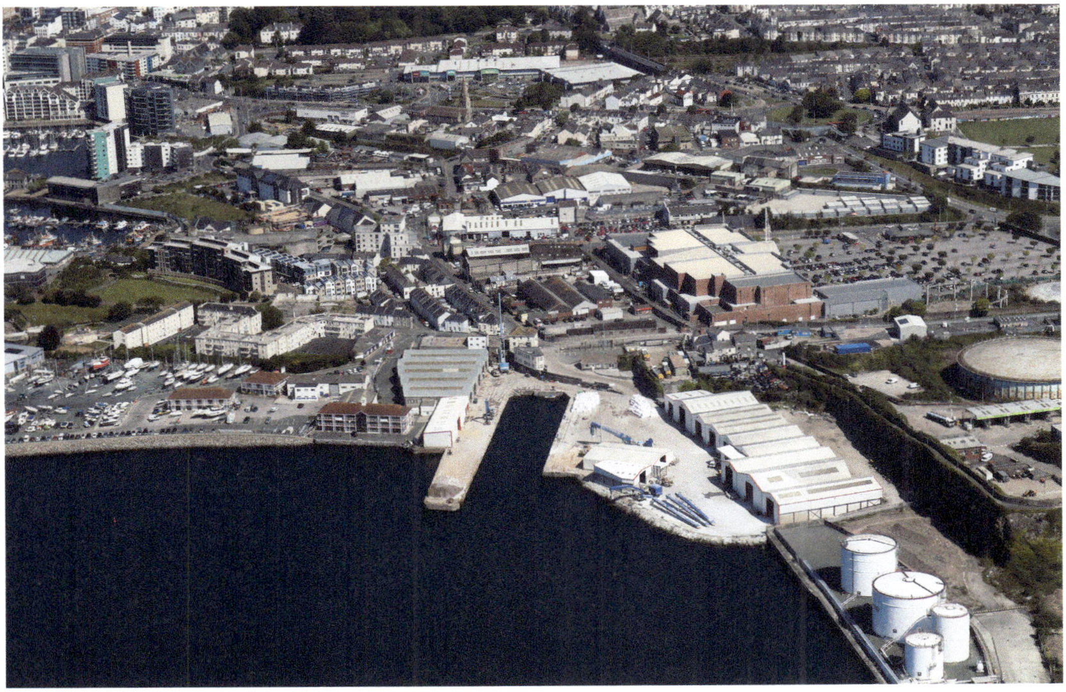

Victoria Wharf between Queen Anne's Battery and Cattedown Wharf where large ships can dock.

As well as shipbuilding there was money to be made in ship breaking, and old ships of the line, containing hundreds of tons of useful wood, would be sold for breaking. There must be many late nineteenth- and early twentieth-century houses locally containing timbers salvaged from old naval vessels. Deadman's Bay, by Queen Anne's Battery, was the site of Edred Marshall's breaker's yard where, among others, in 1867 they broke the eighty-four-gun 200-feet-long second-rate warship *Sans Pareil*. Edred Marshall was listed as a timber merchant of Vauxhall Street in the 1852 Directory of Plymouth, Stonehouse and Devonport.

Further along towards Laira Bridge was Castles, a long-established ship-breaker originally from Rotherhithe, who unlike Edred Marshall was breaking both wooden and steel ships, including the old torpedo training ship HMS *Defiance* in 1931, which had been anchored off Wearde Quay on the Lynher since 1884. The Castles firm, amazingly, was still operating in Plymouth – as Castle's Kitchens – until 2013.

Probably the best-known ship-breaker was Davies and Cann. Originally established at Cremyll Street, Stonehouse, between the Cremyll Ferry slip and the Royal William Yard, the firm was taken over by Eddie Smith in 1951 and moved to Martin's Wharf beside Laira Bridge. For many years anyone driving across Laira Bridge would see ships in the process of being broken including tugs, submarines and frigates.

In 1874 the Cattewater Harbour Commissioners were formed to regulate its affairs. They oversaw the construction of the breakwater at Mount Batten to protect the entrance to the Cattewater, the deep-water wharves at Cattedown and the railway.

The earliest detailed map I have is the 1840 tithe map and the striking thing is the number of shore-side slips, timber yards, wharves and shipbuilders shown at that time, especially around Stonehouse and on Stonehouse Creek, quite apart from the large commercial docks like the Great Western Dock (now Millbay), Sutton Pool and Cattedown Wharves, to make no mention of the dockyard!

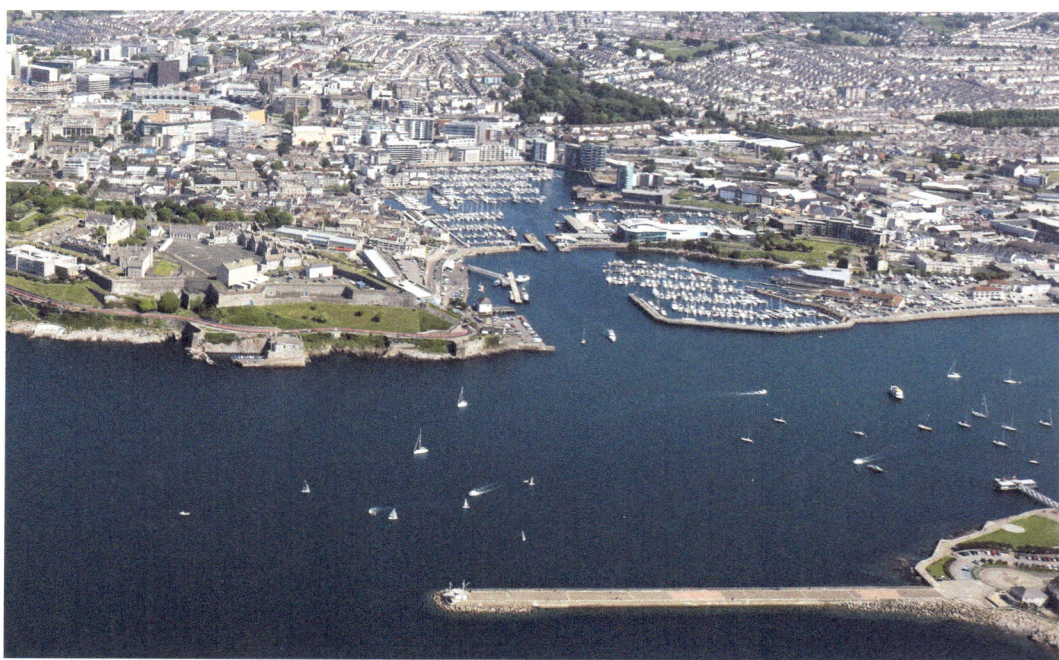

Mount Batten Pier sheltering the entrance to Sutton Harbour.

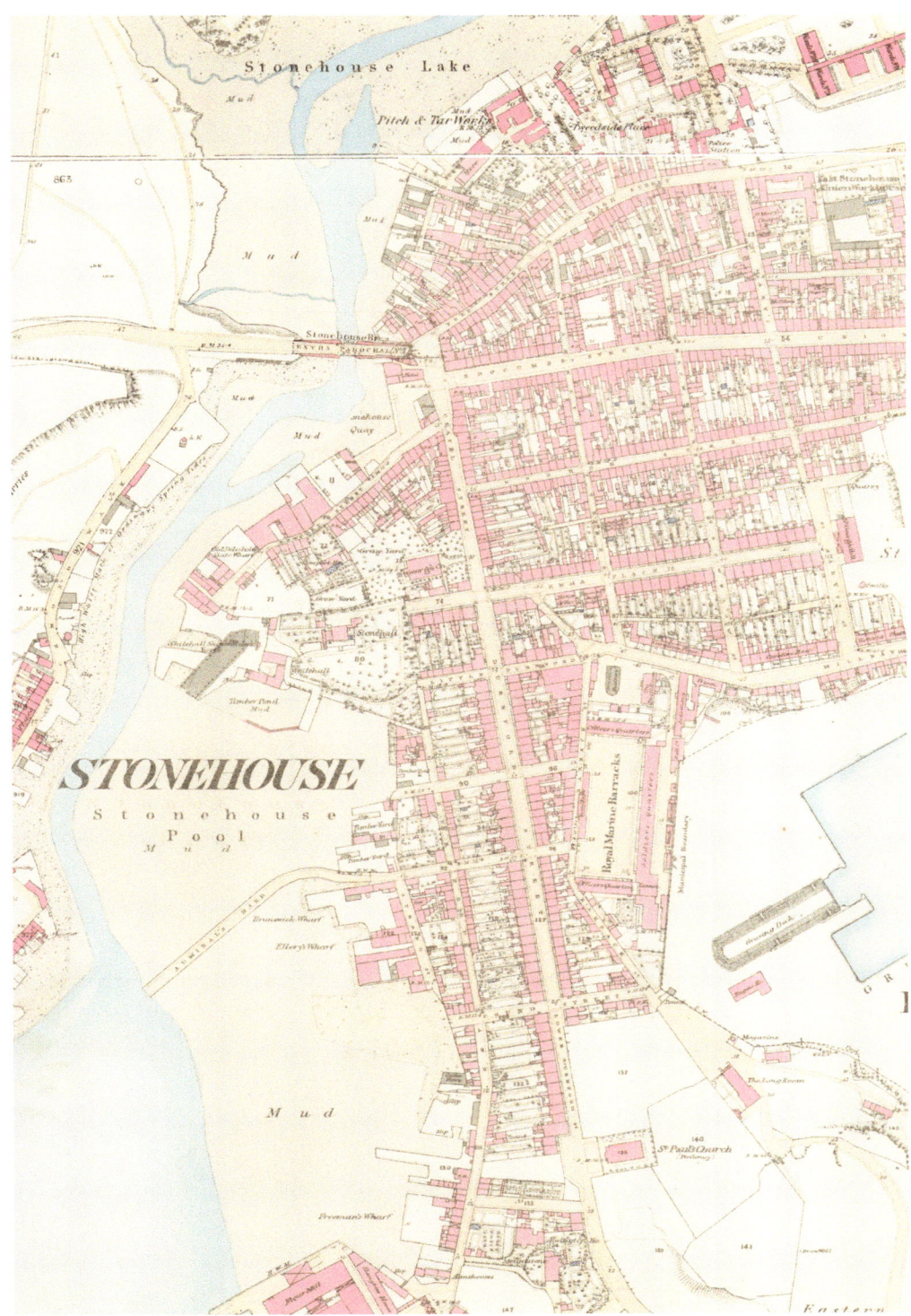

Stonehouse Creek from an 1866 OS map. (Courtesy of the National Library for Scotland)

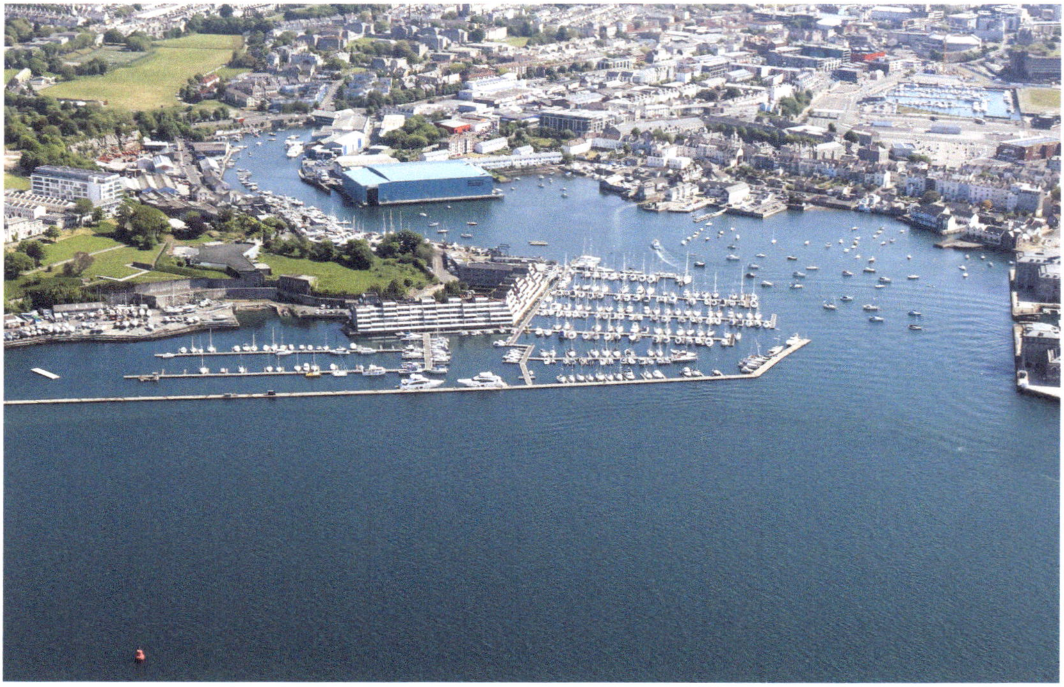

Stonehouse Creek today with the creek drained and filled in above Stonehouse Bridge.

Worth stated in 1890 that 'the coasting trade is large giving Plymouth the sixth position in England and Wales. As a fishing port it stands about tenth. Sutton Pool is the harbour for the fishermen and is often crowded with fishing craft'.

A fine example of a late nineteenth-century fishing boat is the 1895 Brixham Sailing Trawler Pilgrim with her distinctive red sails and old fishing number BM45, similar vessels to which would have sailed out of Plymouth. Still sailing, she is the newest addition to a small fleet of historic vessels sailing out of Brixham. This 74 feet wooden sailing ship was once part of a fleet of over 2,000 deep sea sailing trawlers that revolutionised the way fish were caught in Europe. Today only a handful of these wooden sailing trawlers have survived.

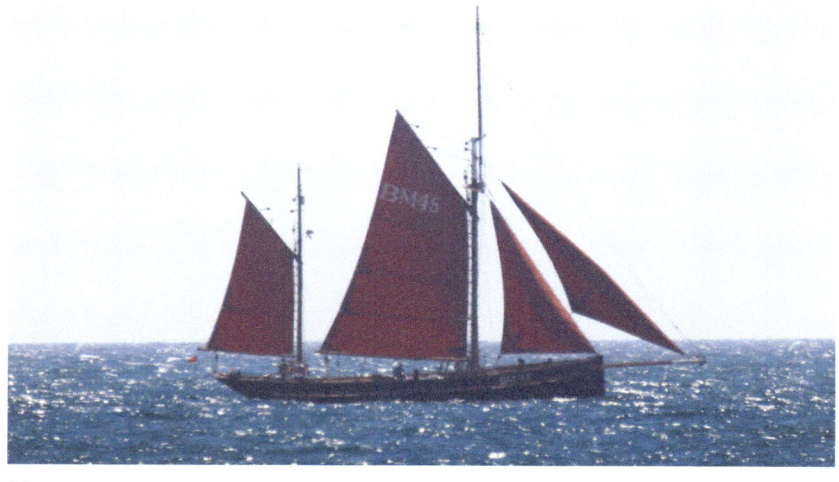

Pilgrim.

Worth also quotes from various directories that in 1783 there were seven shipbuilders listed, rising to thirteen by 1830. The 1852 Directory of Plymouth, Stonehouse and Devonport lists twelve ship agents and brokers, three ship biscuit bakers, seven shipbuilders, one ship carver, eight ship chandlers, fourteen shipowners, five ship smiths and three ship surveyors.

As well as all these there were ten sailmakers. I think it's fair to say that shipbuilding and allied trades were flourishing at that time.

In order to help boost the trading after the Napoleonic wars, Edmund Lockyer proposed 'the forming of an association to build or purchase vessels to engage in the coal, Baltic, Greenland and Colonial trades; for the working of a sugar refinery; for the conversion of Sutton Pool into a wet dock and for the establishment of East India packets'.

Alan Kitteridge mentions the boatyards operating around Plymouth in the late nineteenth and early twentieth centuries in his book *Sail and Steam*. Probably the largest and one of the longest-lasting was Willoughby Brothers, iron founders and marine engineers, founded in 1844 originally at the Central Foundry and Engineering Works in Rendle Street. I assume this was the foundry shown on the 1866 OS map near the Manor Street end of Rendle Street, across the road from the building marked as Central Hall.

In 1890 they became a limited company and took over the Phoenix Foundry at the Millbay Road end of Phoenix Street. At around this time they also bought a large building shed adjacent to the graving dock in Millbay. Here they could now construct iron ships,

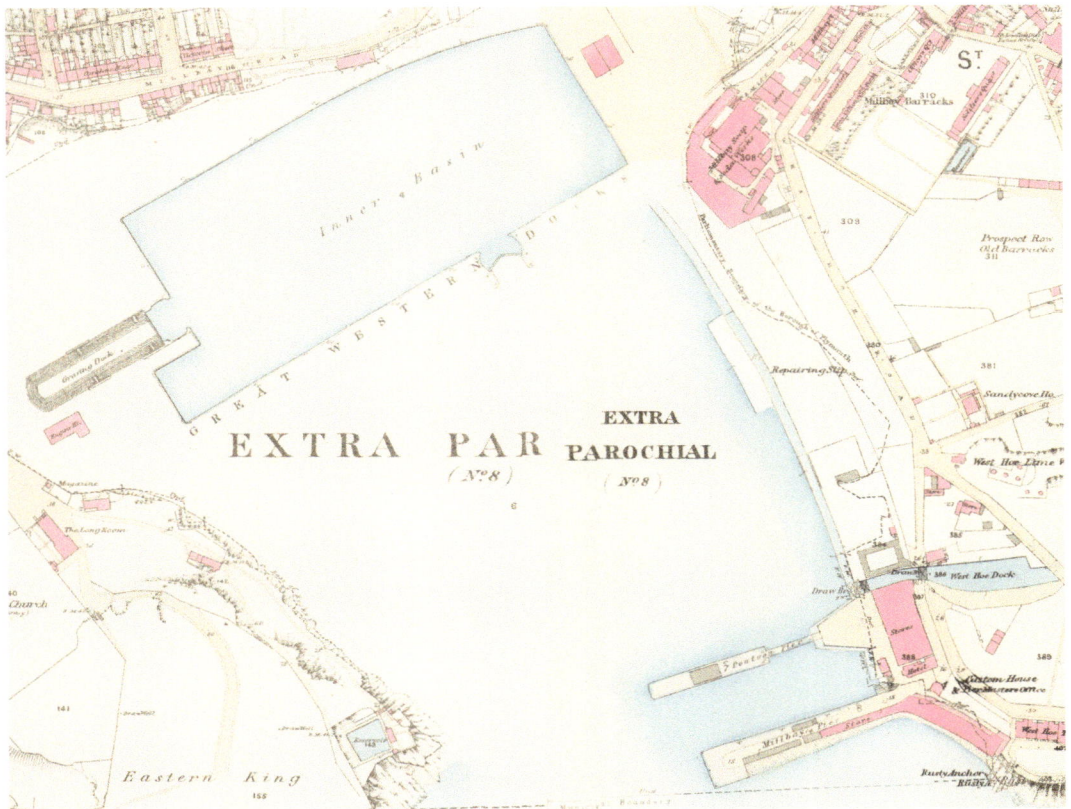

Millbay showing the graving dock from an 1866 OS map. (Courtesy of the National Library for Scotland)

whereas previously they had needed to cast the parts for both ships and/or steam engines and then transport them to Richmond Walk for assembly.

They built iron ships complete including two Torpoint Ferries, the first in 1871, the second in 1878. They also built a Saltash ferry in 1892 and a second one in 1911. Many of the local iron- and steel-hulled paddle steamers and excursion boats were built by Willoughby's. Although they went into receivership in 1908 a new company, Willoughby (Plymouth) Ltd, was set up in 1915 and, according to Alan Kitteridge, amalgamated with Ellacott & Son, founders and engineers, in 1921. In 1958 they amalgamated with Bickle Engineering, their neighbours beside the graving dock, then in 1969 the company ceased trading after 125 years.

The graving dock opened in 1857 but was extended from 367 feet to 454 feet length in 1887. It was 80 feet wide to allow paddle steamers to be accommodated. When Willoughby's ceased trading in 1969 the graving dock and almost half of Brunel's Inner Basin was filled in to accommodate the new Brittany Ferries terminal.

Among the other boat- and ship-builders in the Plymouth area mentioned in Alan Kitteridge's book were Frederick Hawke of Stonehouse, who built the *Phoenix* for Lewis Sparrow in 1900, sold to F. J. Moore in 1908. He also built the *Shamrock*, which is now preserved at Cotehele. The Shilston shipyard at China House, Sutton Harbour, built ships for F. J. Moore at Cattedown. William Kelly of Turnchapel built *Despatch* in 1885, later used by the Millbrook Steamboat Company. C. F. Williams of Stonehouse built the barge *Silver Spray* in 1880 to carry 'dock dung' from Pottery Quay for manure on Tamar Valley farms.

Outside of my area was the James Goss yard at Calstock, which built a great many boats over the years including the Garlandstone in 1909 for coasting around Milford Haven and which now lives at Morwellham. Anyone wishing to see an authentic locally built historic boat can do so there.

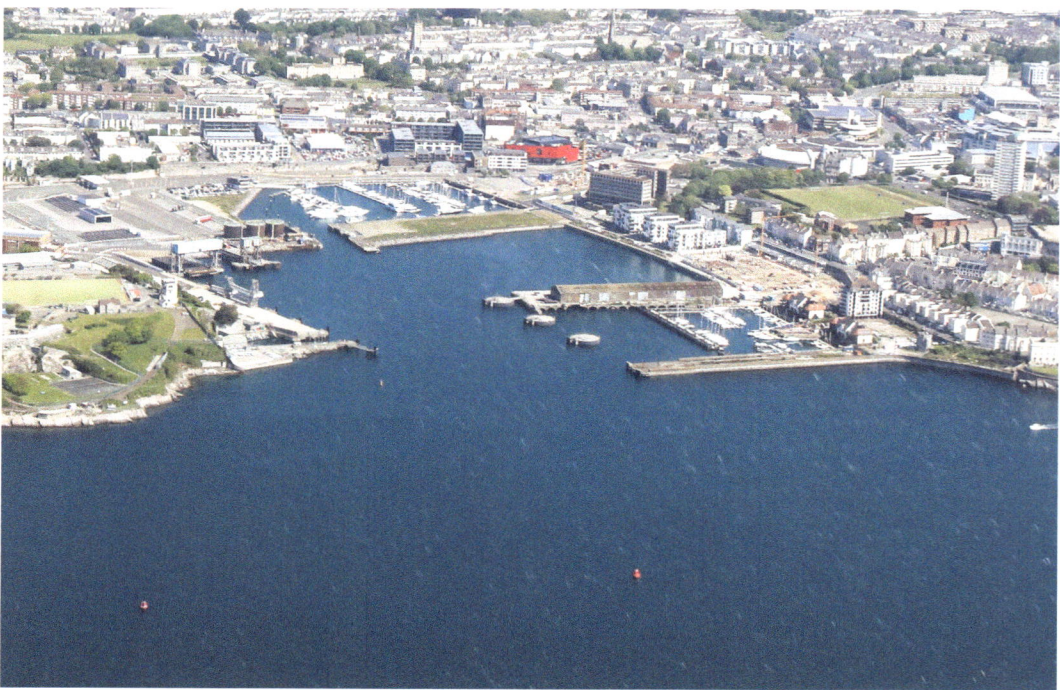

Millbay Docks today showing the much-reduced inner dock and Brittany Ferries terminal on left.

Also outside of my area is Cremyll, home to Mashford's, now UK Docks, at one time famous for repairing and building high-class wooden boats. My father worked there and during the 1960s we lived in a cottage inside the yard so I got to know it very well. They had engineering shops, blacksmith's and specialist woodworking shops, plus two slipways to haul out boats for repair. They employed a small army of specialised people to work there. Looking back it must have been hugely inefficient. Many of the specialists would have spent time labouring because there was no specialist work for them to do and once a boat was on the slipways they could not be used for anything else until it was finished, possibly in months or even years.

With modern equipment it is possible to hoist boats out of the water and park them on the quayside where they can be worked on. If the boat needs specialist work either a specialist firm can come and do it there or it could even be hoisted onto a trailer or low loader and taken to the specialist firm, some of which are many miles inland. It is no longer necessary to be beside the water, nor to provide a full range of services at one boatyard.

And what of the present? There are still many boatbuilders in Plymouth and the best known is the large-scale builders of hugely expensive gin palaces, Princess Yachts. They are the fifth largest employer in Devon and Cornwall according to the most recent figures I have. They have premises all over the city but their office and the main assembly building for smaller craft is at Newport Street, beside Stonehouse Creek. They also lease much of South Yard where they assemble and fit out their larger boats. The old Royal Marines base at Coypool, possibly just outside of my area, is another of their acquisitions, housing their main store plus manufacturing of stainless steel fittings and furniture.

There are still a few old-fashioned builders and repairers, specialising in wooden craft, such as Stirling & Son based in South Yard of the dockyard. There are many others dotted around the city, mainly at Blagdon's Yard, Richmond Walk and Queen Anne's Battery, plus one or two at Camel's Head. Many boats these days are made from GRP rather than wood and there are many people working from home who will repair and refurbish boats, plus others who deal in the marine electronics and engines, chandlery and brokerage.

A look at many of the photos above show hundreds, if not thousands, of privately owned boats tied up at the many marinas dotted around the waterfront. Whereas in centuries past

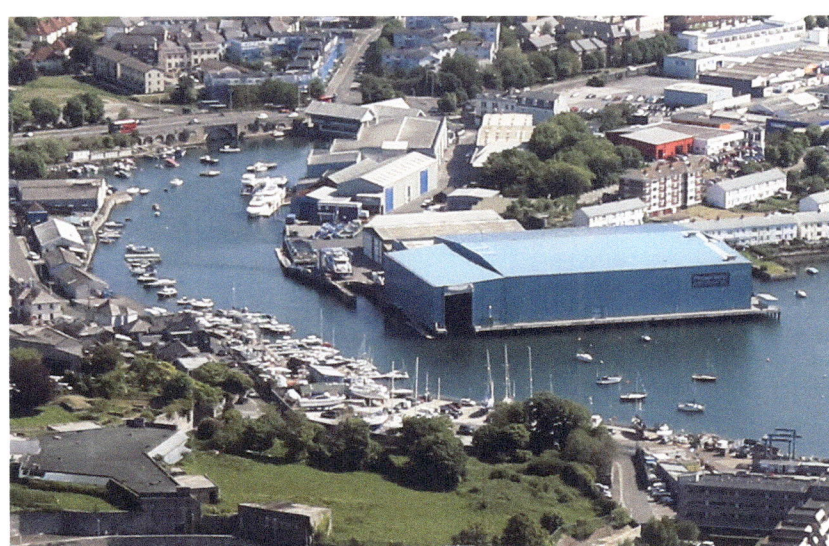

Princess Yachts' Newport Street site.

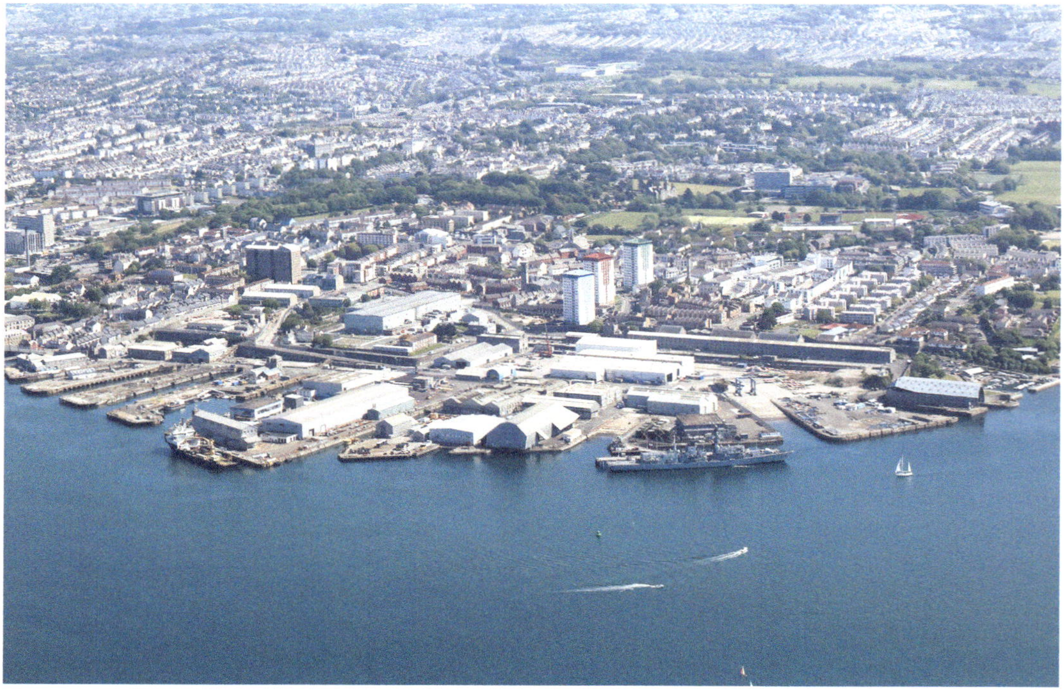

Above: South Yard, now partly owned by Princess Yachts.

Below: Coypool store and manufacturing centre.

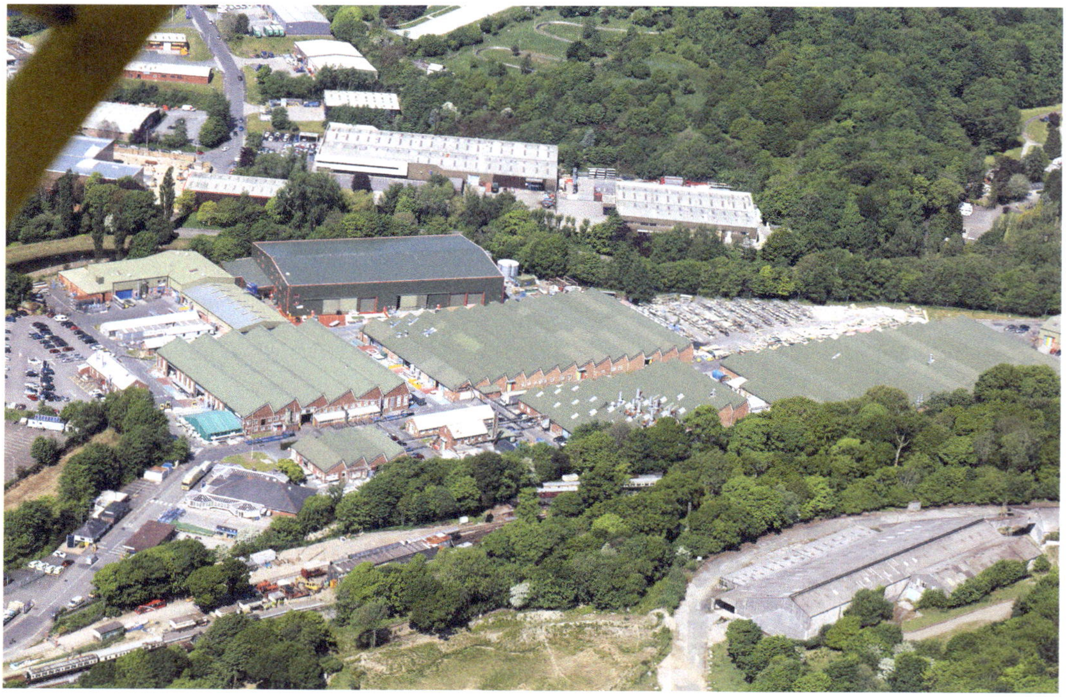

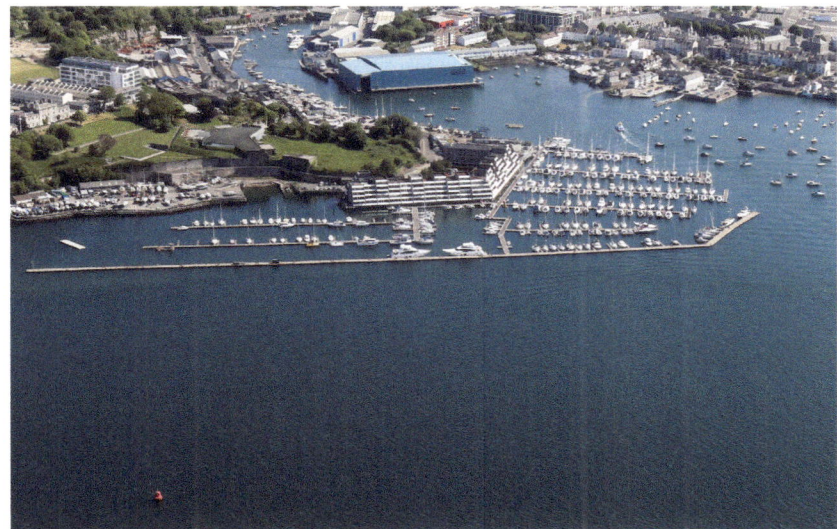

Richmond Walk and Ocean Quay today.

the ownership of a boat, whether for business or pleasure, was the preserve of the rich, nowadays it is something that many ordinary people can afford.

Plymouth City Council has named Plymouth 'Britain's Ocean City' and it still has many connections with the sea. The EU regulations may have done their best to destroy the fishing industry here but some still cling on as fishermen and many make a good living from the sea one way or another.

The following photos all show fishing vessels tied up in Sutton Harbour on a Sunday.

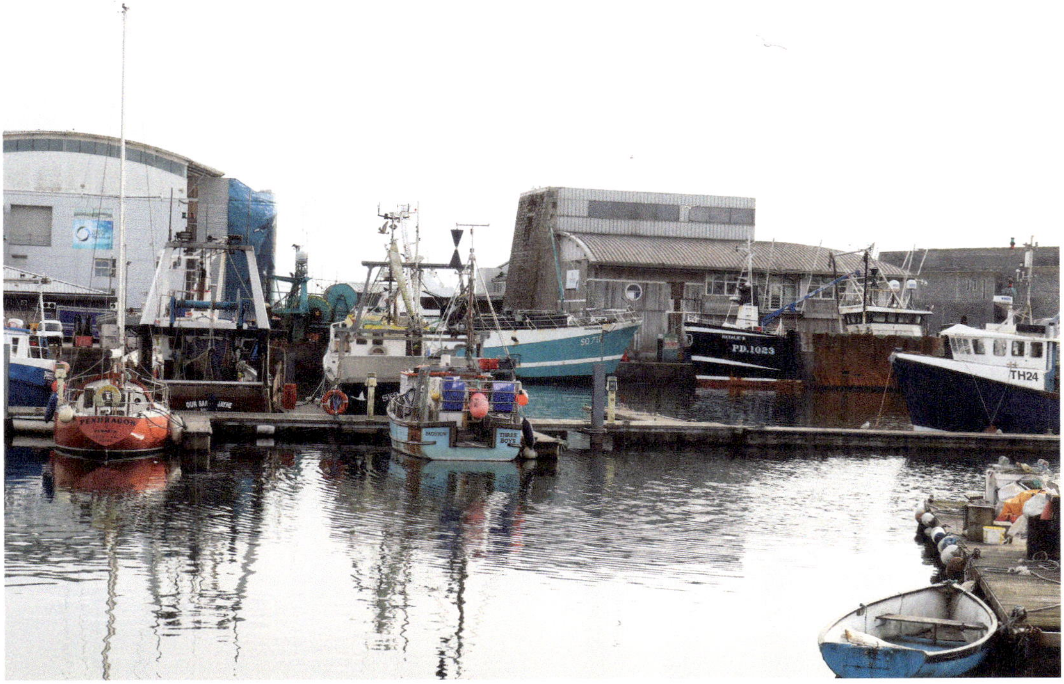

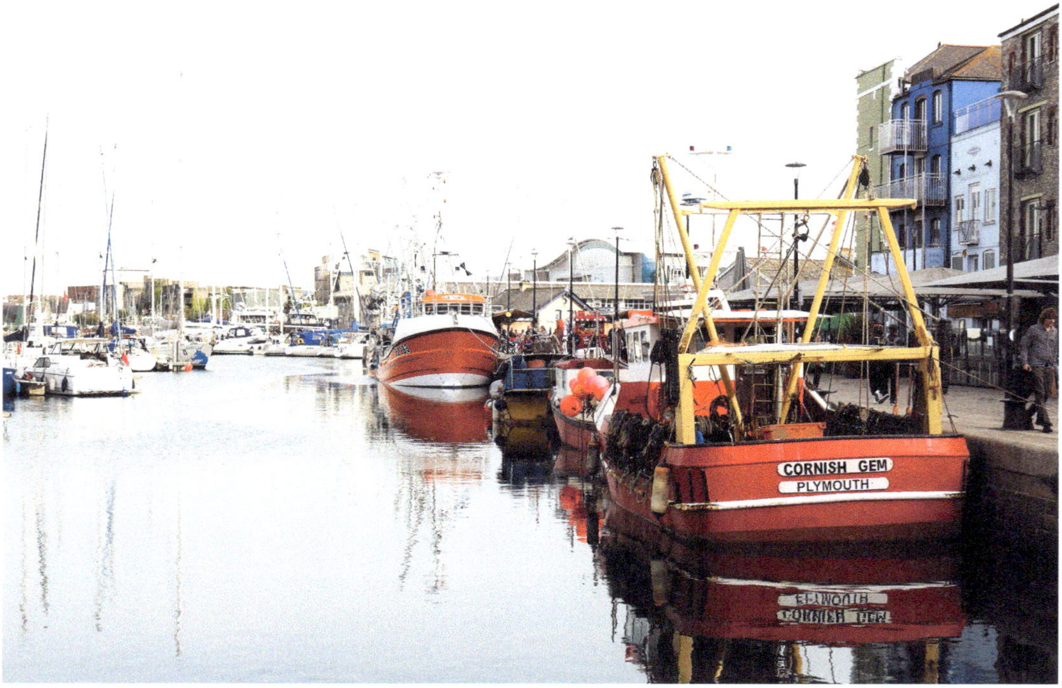

Plymouth at Work

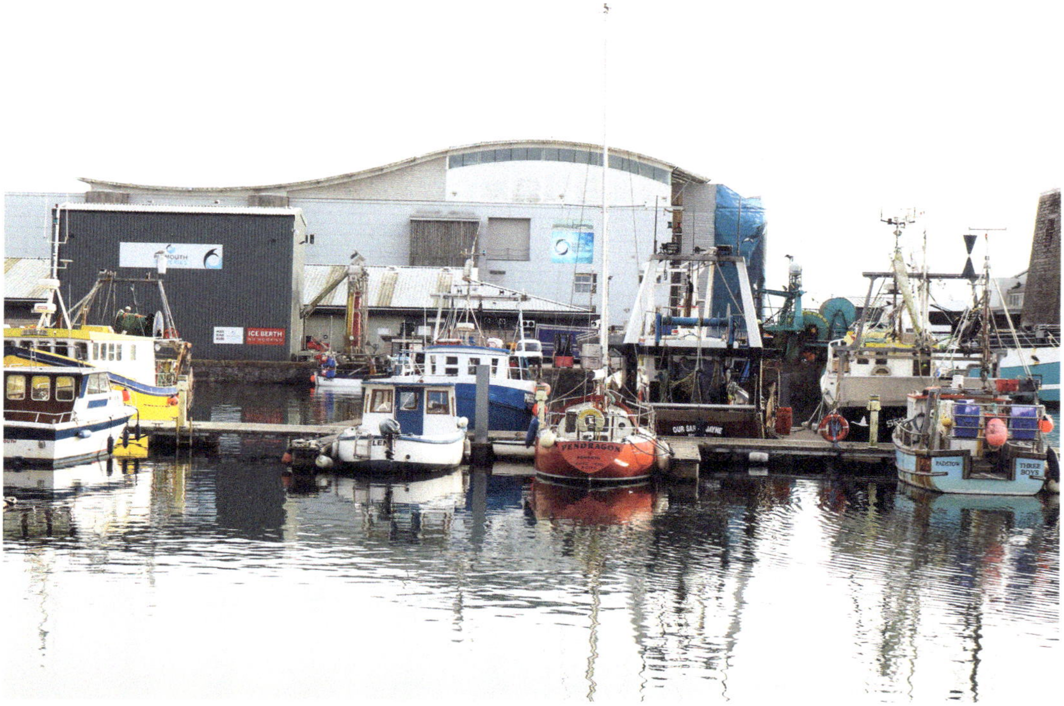

Fishing and Boatbuilding

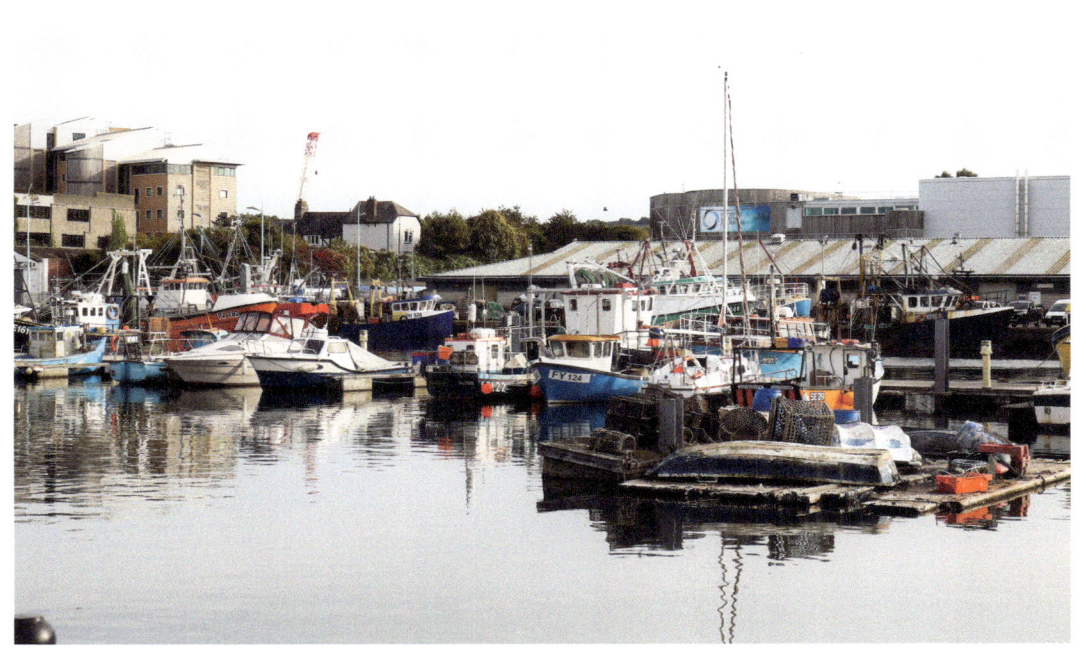

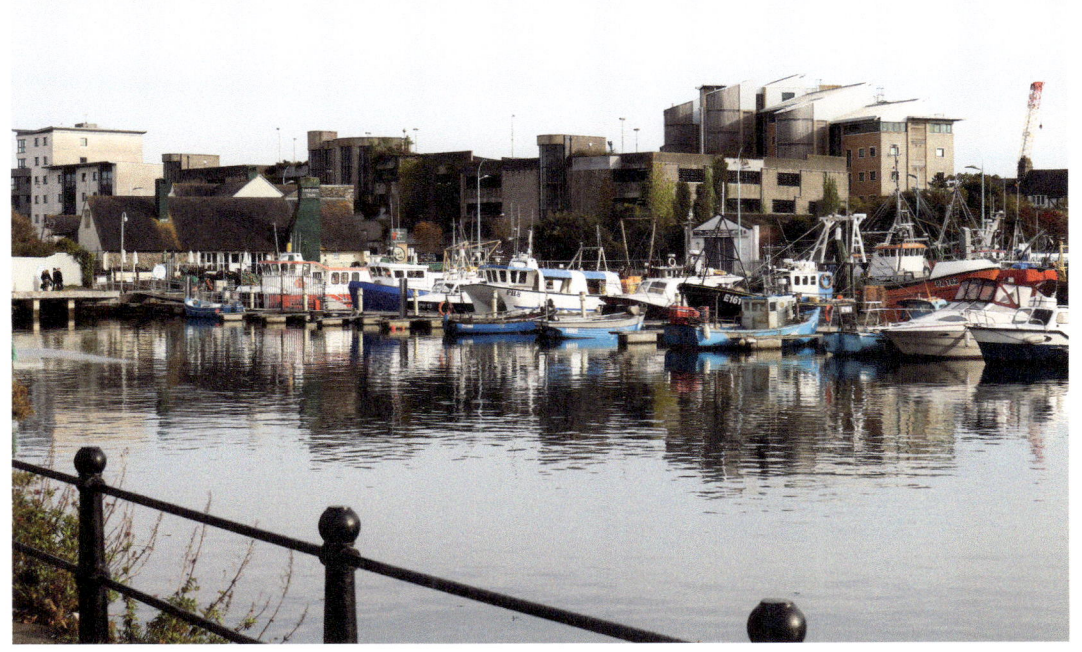

THE DOCKYARD

Having long been used by the Royal Navy as a sheltered harbour to escape the worst of the Atlantic's weather, Plymouth became famous after Drake's renowned battle with the Spanish Armada in 1588. A century later, in 1689, Edward Dummer, Surveyor to the Navy, was sent west to find the most suitable place to build a single dry dock. Having rejected both the Cattewater and Dartmouth as a possible site, planning work started almost immediately at a site by the Hamoaze on the east bank of the Tamar, the area we now know as South Yard.

On 6 January 1690 the Admiralty reported to the Navy Board that:

> His Majesty *(King William III)* having resolved (at our attending him yesterday at the Robes) that he would have a dry dock built of stone at Ham Oze in the Port of Plymouth, wee do herebye desire and direct you to give order that it may be gone in hand with all possible dispatch and good husbandry.

Moving with a speed that seems unimaginable to anyone used to dealing with government departments today, on 11 July 1692 the Admiralty decided to build a fully-fledged dockyard on the site, rather than the simple dry dock originally intended:

> The service of their Majesty's Navy requiring that a yard be made in the place at Hamoze near Plymouth where the new dock is now building and several buildings erected therein as well as for accommodation of the Officers of the Navy that shall be appointed there, as for storehouses and other services ...

By 1700 Plymouth Dock was described as 'the latest thinking on the planning and layout of a substantial naval base'. By the time of its completion the original dry dock, on a site chosen because of an existing small inlet, had been joined by a wet dock, the hugely impressive 400-feet-long Officers' Terrace (sadly mostly destroyed during the Blitz), a 1,056-feet-long ropery and yarn house, the Great Store, mast houses and every kind of workshop necessary to large-scale wooden shipbuilding. The dry dock was 230 feet long and 40 feet wide, large enough to take first-rate ships of the time, with a double dock added in the 1720s and a further dry dock added by 1763. According to Chris Robinson, by 1710 the brand-new dockyard employed 741 men.

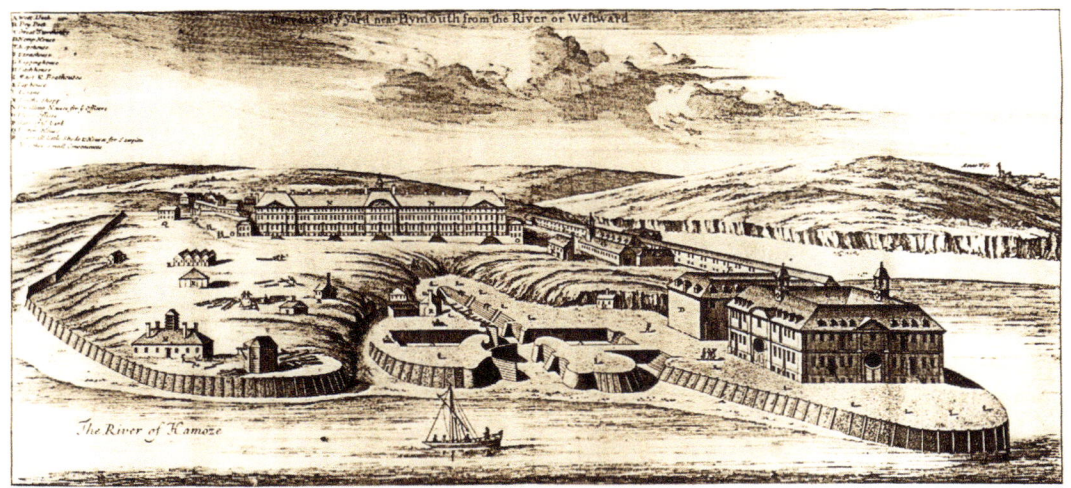

Above: The dockyard, *c.* 1698. (British Library, Lansdowne 847)

Below: The original dockyard area today.

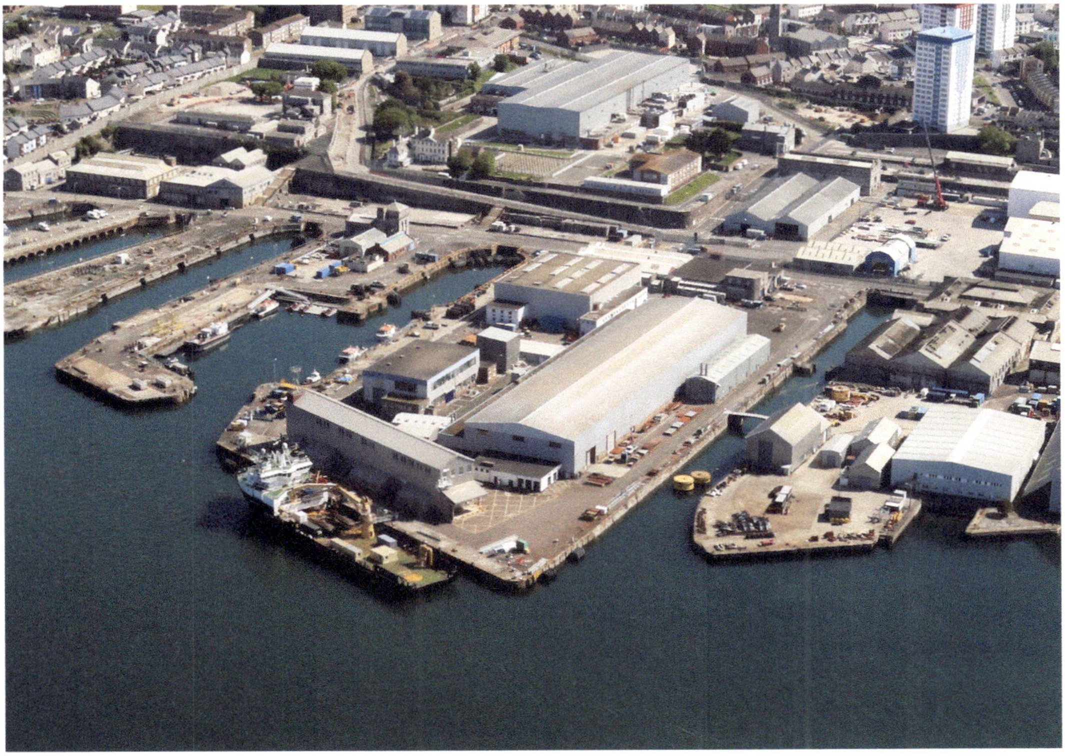

In the 1720s Daniel Defoe wrote in his *Tour Through Great Britain*: 'Plymouth is a town of consideration and of great importance to the public. It is situated between 2 very large inlets of the sea and in the bottom of a large bay, which is very remarkable.'

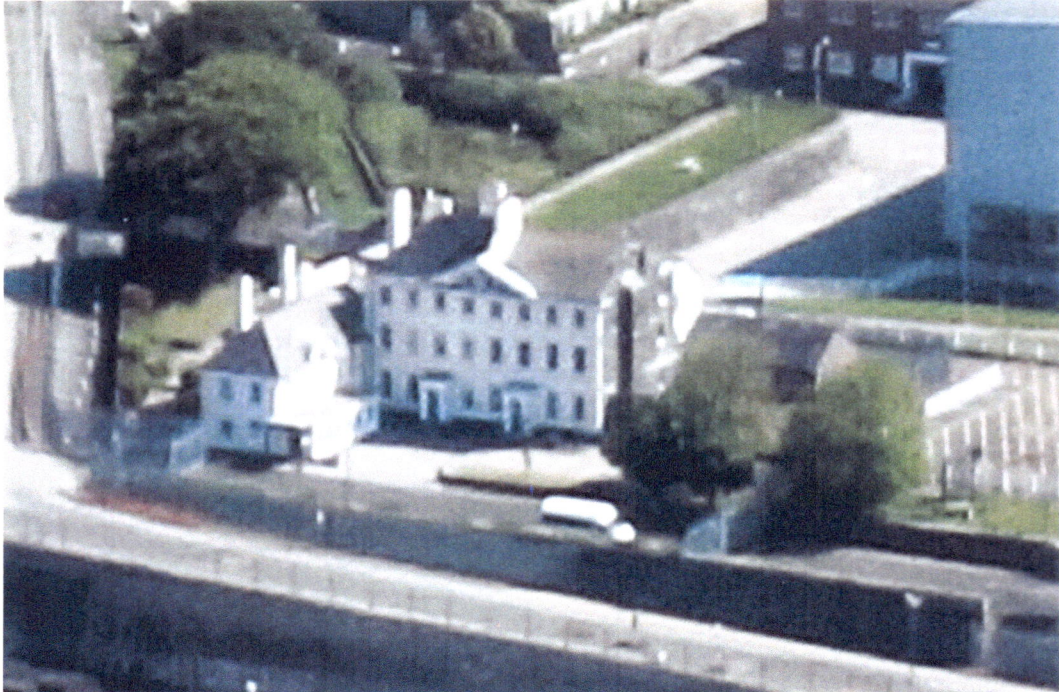

Flotilla House, the sole remaining part of the magnificent Officer's Terrace.

He also wrote of Plymouth Dock:

The late King William order'd a wet dock, with yards, dry docks, launches, and conveniencies of all kinds for building, and repairing of ships to be built; and with these followed necessarily the building of store-houses and warehouses, for the rigging, sails, naval and military stores, &c. of such ships as may be appointed to be laid up there, as now several are, with very handsome houses for the commissioners, clerks, and officers of all kinds usual in the King's yards, to dwell in: It is in short, now become as compleat an arsenal, or yard, for building and fitting men of war as any of the government are masters of, and perhaps much more convenient than some of them, tho' not so large.

The building of these things, with the addition of rope walks, and mast-yards, &c. as it brought abundance of trades-people, and workmen to the place, so they began by little and little to build houses on the lands adjacent, till at length there appeared a very handsome street, spacious and large, and as well inhabited, and so many houses are since added, that it is become a considerable town, and must of consequence in time draw abundance of people from Plymouth itself.

This period (1717–19) also saw the expansion north into the new Ordnance section at Morice Yard (named after the landowner Sir Nicholas Morice), replacing a small gun wharf and storehouse at Mount Wise. This took the dockyard right up to the slipways of the Torpoint Ferry, which at that time ran from the southern end of the modern slip. To the north of this was the Ferry Canal with its associated slipways, long filled in and now the waiting area for the ferries.

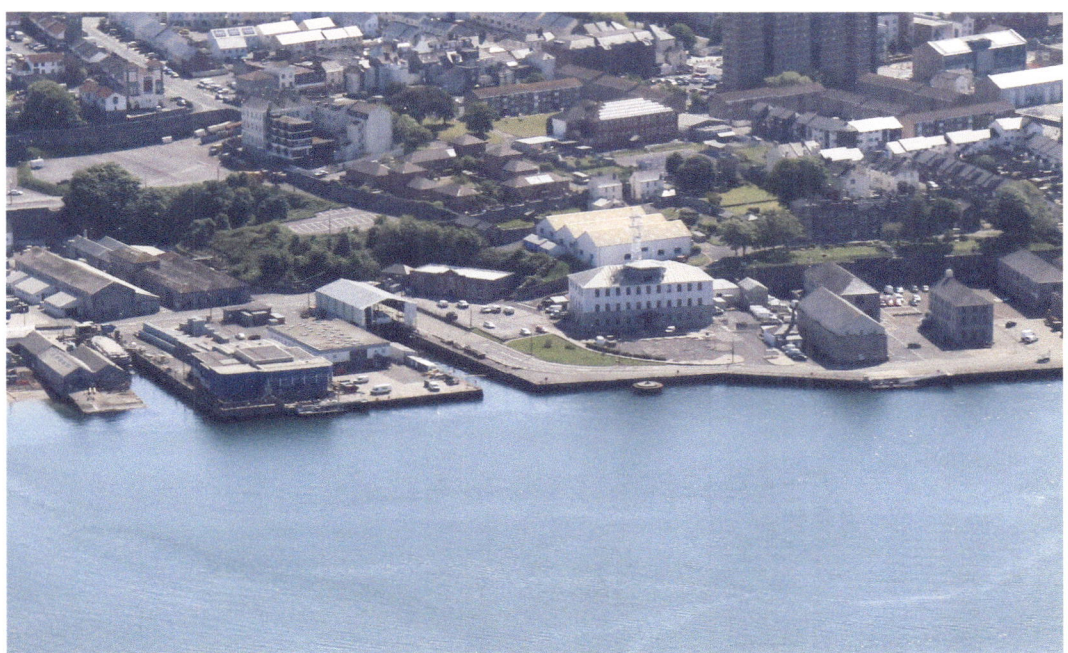

Above: Morice Yard.

Below: South Yard with the streets and houses of Devonport behind.

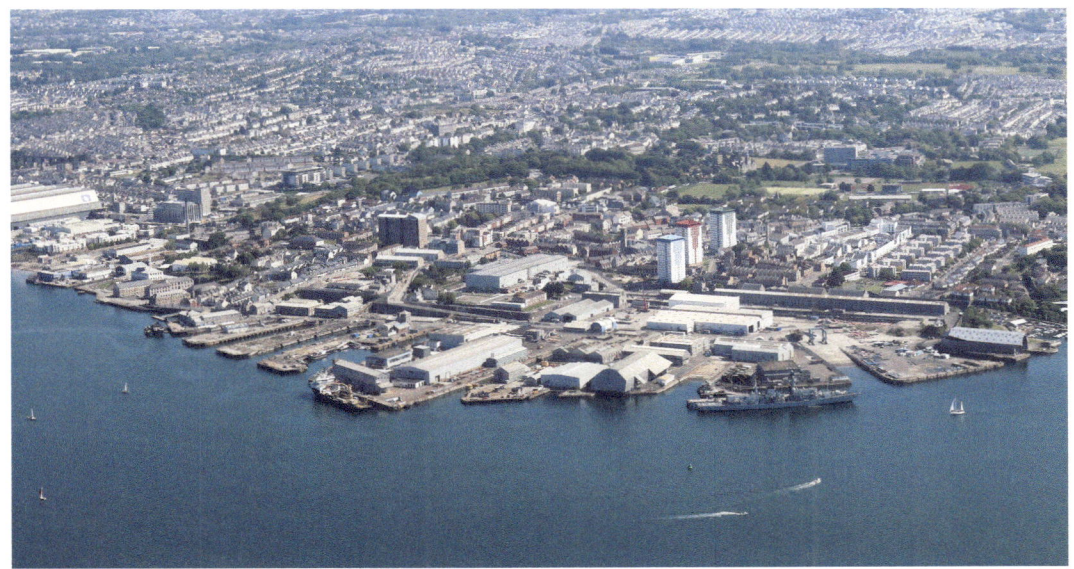

A major modernisation programme began in 1761 following a Navy Board report which said: 'We have met with much difficulty, the yard having been laid out originally upon much too contracted a plan, being confined on the north and east sides by the town and bounded by the harbour to the west, so that it will admit of no enlargement but to the south.'

Thus started an expansion south to use up all available land there including the realignment and extension of the ropery to 1,200 feet and the construction of the impressive No. 1 Building Slip at the extreme southern end, described as 'the last intact eighteenth-century building slip in any Royal dockyard'. One great advantage Devonport had, as also mentioned in the Navy Board report, was it could provide much of its own building material thanks to the local limestone outcrop mentioned elsewhere. The same Navy Board report continued:

> Should it be thought by their Lordships that to the reducing to a level that part of the ground proposed to be taken in, which is a hill of marble rock, may be attended with too great an expence [sic], we pray leave to answer that we apprehend that the force of such an objection will be considerably lessened as that rock will afford an ample supply of stone and lime for all the buildings and wharves ...

The sole remaining part of this limestone is King's Hill with its crowning gazebo, built to commemorate the visit of George III in 1822.

Jonathan Coad's *Historic Architecture of HM Naval Base Devonport, 1689–1850* says that Devonport was 'one of the best planned and equipped dockyards of any naval power' by the end of the eighteenth century and by then had virtually doubled in size from Dummer's original plan. By 1800 the dockyard employed over 1,800 people 'excluding those in the ropery', second only to Portsmouth. This includes only those employed by the dockyard; the almost constant series of improvements and rebuilds would have meant that many hundreds more would have been employed by the civilian contractors who were doing all the building work.

The dockyard workers, who walked to work every day, wanted to live close to the dock. In the eighteenth century new houses were built near the dock and a new town grew up.

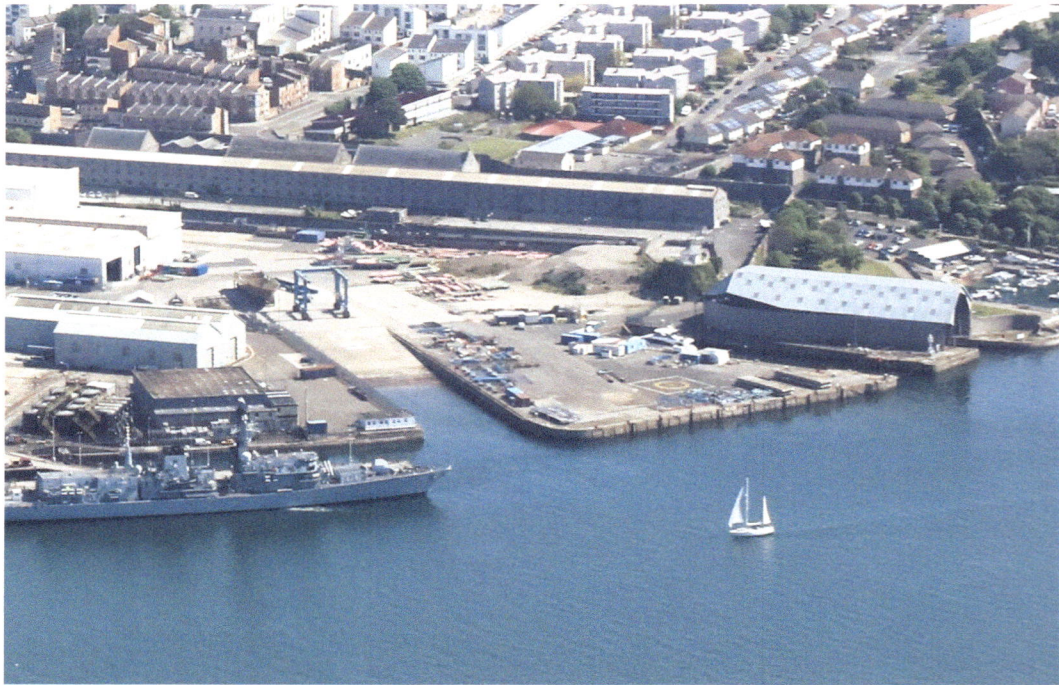

The extreme southern end showing No. 1 Slip and King's Hill behind.

At first the town was called Plymouth Dock, or simply Dock, and by the mid-eighteenth century it had a population of around 4,000. I have no idea how many were employed in the ropery but by 1808, according to Crispin Gill, there were 2,741 in total employed by the dockyard.

Crispin Gill also quotes figures for the population of the three towns in 1801 showing that Plymouth Dock, as it then was, had, in accordance with Daniel Defoe's prediction, easily outstripped Plymouth as the largest of the three towns with a population of 23,787 against Plymouth's 16,378. This in fact made it the most populous town in the south-west, which considering it had not existed 150 years previously is quite some feat. A vast proportion of the inhabitants worked in or depended upon the dockyard, and the dockyard itself continued to grow. By 1851 these figures had grown considerably, with Devonport, as it was called after becoming a separate borough in 1837, having 49,673 and Plymouth 37,499.

Between 1814 and 1821 wooden roofs were built to cover the dry docks and building slips.

The middle of the nineteenth century saw the dockyard's even larger expansion further north again, this time into North Yard, originally built as a steam yard to allow engineering and foundry workshops for the new steam propulsion and heavy engineering then coming into being, plus two large tidal basins. This took the dockyard as far north as the modern St Levan's Road gate and included the Quadrangle, which incorporated the various workshops required for heavy engineering, including a foundry. The new yard was joined to South Yard by a railway tunnel, which passed under Morice Yard. Powder mills, to supply the gunpowder for the fleet, were moved even further north from Morice Yard to Bull Point in St Budeaux.

A separate but closely linked development in the 1820s was Royal William Yard, half a mile downstream from the dockyard itself. Whereas the dockyard built and refitted ships and the ordnance yard supplied guns, gunpowder and cannon balls, Royal William, otherwise known

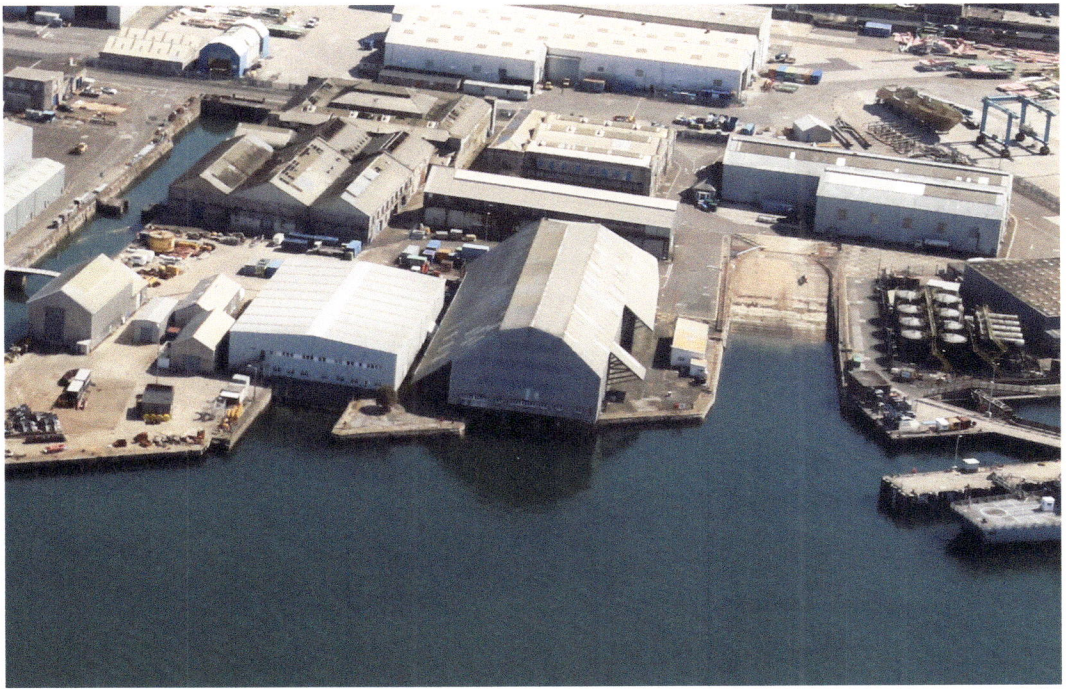

The Scrieve Board, originally a building slip that, like No. 1 Slip, was also covered with a wooden roof.

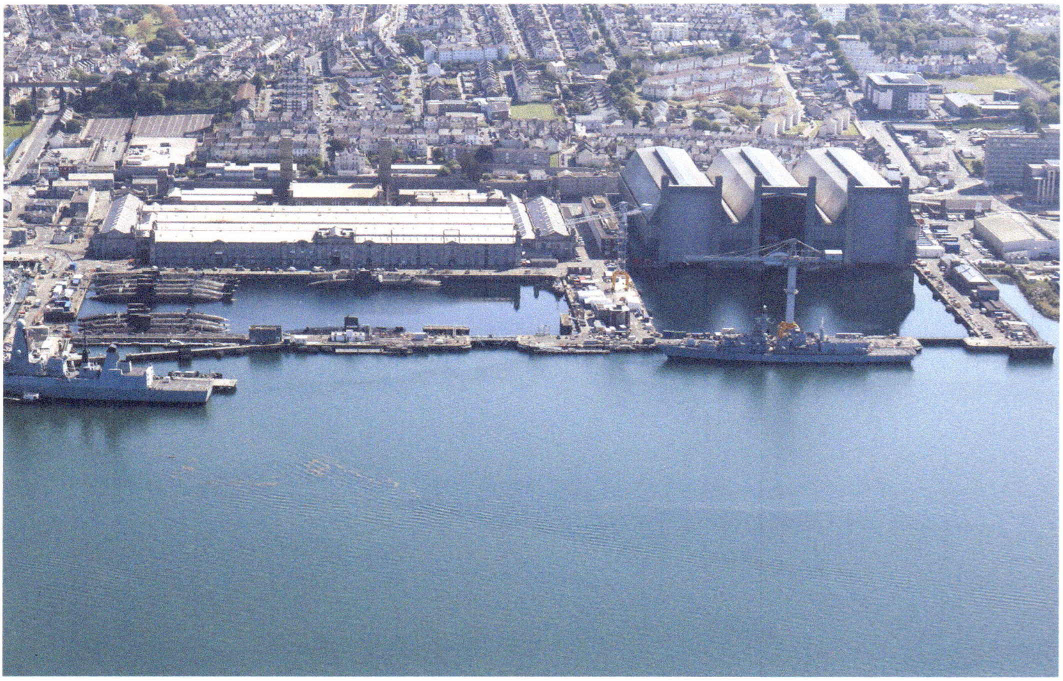

Above: The Steam Yard.

Below: The engineering factory or Quadrangle.

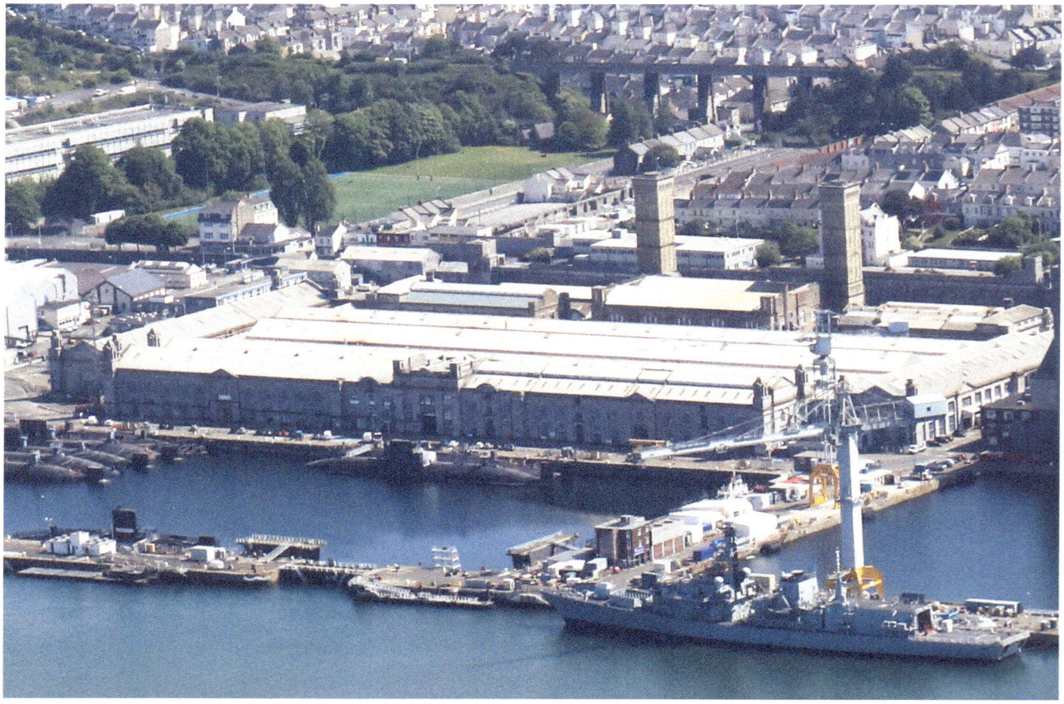

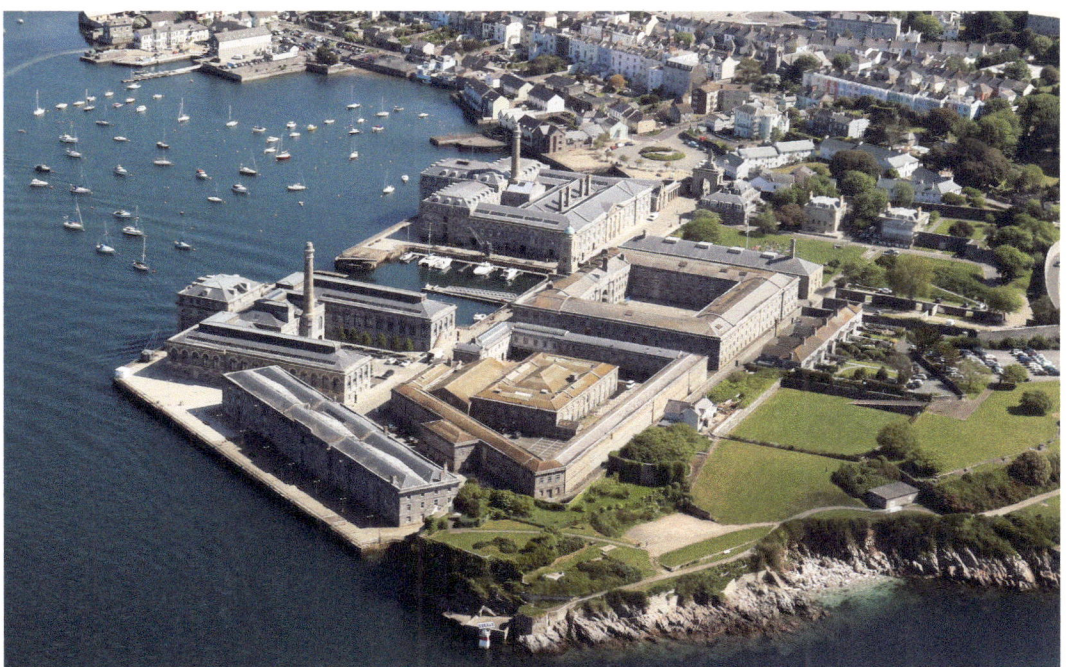

The Victualling Yard.

as the Victualling Yard, provided everything the sailors needed, i.e. food and drink. To avoid confusion, this yard was named after William IV, who was on the throne by the time it was completed in 1835, whereas the original dockyard had been started on the orders of William III.

There had been a victualling system locally even before the dockyard was built, but since 1729 there had been a brewery and cooperage at Southdown near Millbrook and bakeries and storehouses on Lambhay, beside Sutton Harbour. By the 1820s it was decided to centralise the victualling arrangements and so land was bought from the Earl of Mount Edgcumbe at Stonehouse, adjacent to Devil's Point, and John Rennie, who had taken charge of the construction of the Breakwater, was asked to oversee the design and construction. The Royal William Yard was operational by 1833 after only five years of building. Similarly to the work at South Yard, much of the stone needed to build Royal William Yard came from quarrying and flattening the hill which had previously occupied the site.

When completed the yard had a brewery (fresh water was unsafe to drink in those days, so everybody drank 'small' or weak beer! The brewing process and the alcohol would kill off any bacteria in the water), a flour mill, grain store, bakery, cattle yard and slaughterhouse and the vast Melville Square store block. The yard continued to be the fleet's victualling yard until it closed and was eventually sold off in 1992.

By its nature the dockyard increases its workforce during times of war and reduces it in peacetime. Following the defeat of Napoleon in 1815 men were laid off, but technical advances in the name of steam meant that the expansion into North Yard to provide engineering facilities for the steam engines now being fitted to a quarter of the Navy's ships provided a growth.

In 1841 in Henry Woolcombe's *Statistics of the Three Towns of Plymouth, Stonehouse and Devonport*, he quotes a total of 2,468 men (plus 510 convicts!) employed in the dockyard, Gun Wharf (Morice Yard) and in the gunpowder factories at Keyham Point and Bull Point.

By the 1850s further expansion of the dockyard was necessary, if only to keep pace with the larger ships by then needed. G. T. Green, in charge of construction for the yard at that time, said:

> There is at present but one dock in which first-rates can be docked in all, and in that at high water spring tides only, and when the ship has been lightened almost to her lightwaterdraught. Thus a first-rate coming into harbour with a 26 foot draught must be lightened to 20 feet ... She may have to wait ten days to obtain even that draught, and as high water spring tides occur at Devonport at 4 or 5am, the operation must, after all, be effected in the dark during the winter months, and at a very inconvenient hour at all times.

These comments led to the Keyham Extension of North Yard, which almost doubled the area of the then dockyard. This added the two huge tidal basins we still have today, plus dry docks described at the time as 'to accommodate ships larger than any war-vessel yet constructed' and a large section of wharf along its 4 miles of waterfront for tying ships alongside. The extension's construction work had employed 3,500 men according to Chris Robinson and it was opened in 1907 by the then Prince and Princess of Wales, the future George V and Queen Mary.

The first ship to use the new dry dock was the Devonport-built pre-dreadnought battleship HMS *Hibernia* (obviously this was before the latest aircraft carriers had been thought of!). During my apprenticeship in the dockyard I worked on HMS *Ark Royal* in this dock.

This extension made Devonport one of the biggest naval ports in the world and it ushered in a golden age as Great Britain started a huge rearmament programme to build the largest

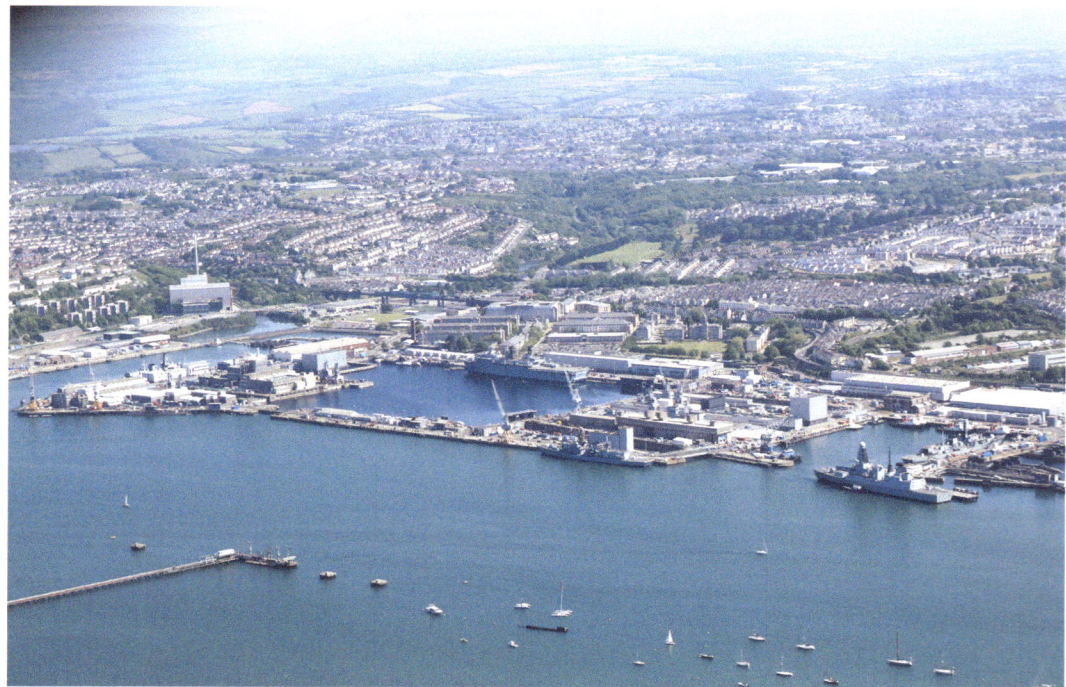

North Yard extension.

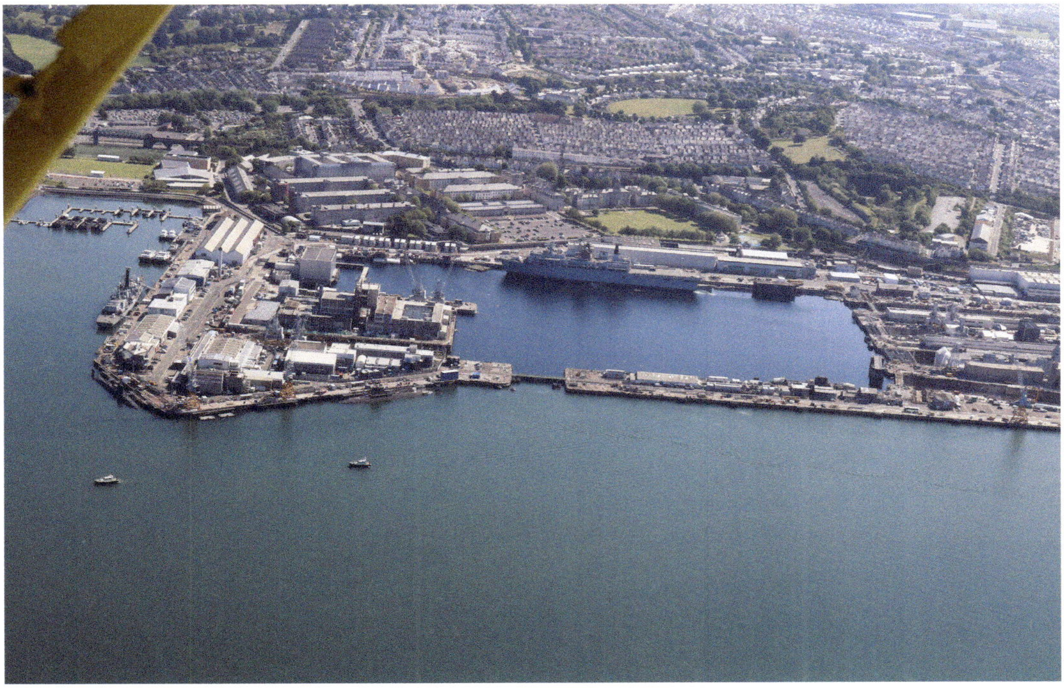

The Dockyard

Above: The huge No. 5 Basin, renamed Prince of Wales Basin.

Below: No. 5 Basin with RM Tamar in the background.

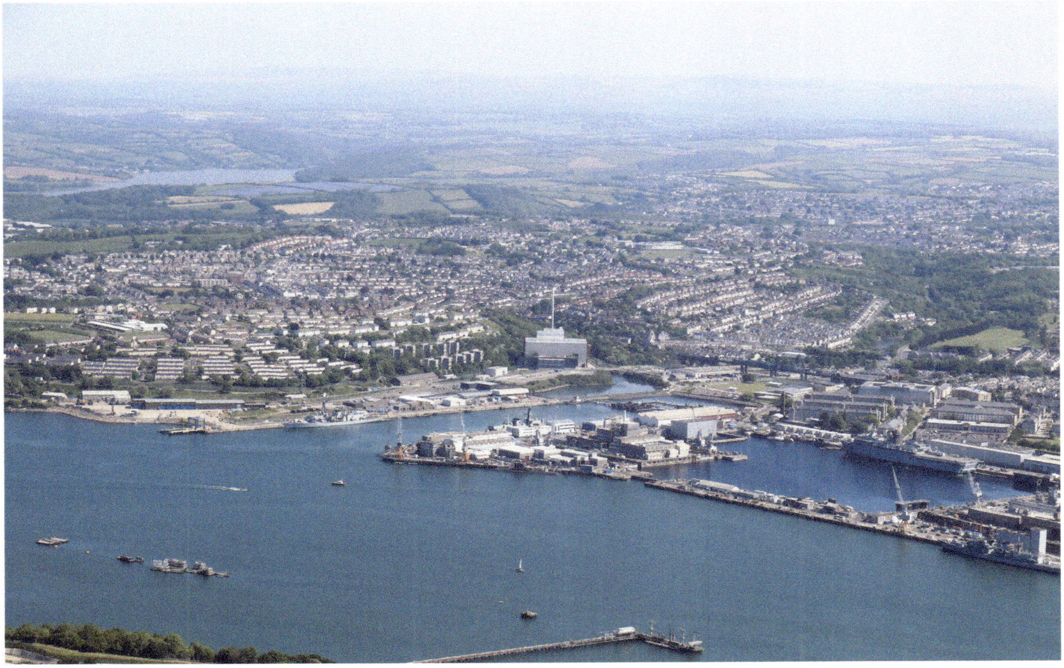

45

and most modern naval fleet in the world. At that time the Royal Navy tried to maintain what was called the 'two power standard', which meant it wanted to be at least as strong as the next two largest navies combined, and as Germany was building ships in an effort to become the strongest navy, the Royal Navy had to build more. They continued with their efforts until the Second World War when first Japan and then America overtook them.

The mid-nineteenth-century expansion of the yard also saw the Ordnance Depot moved – again! Having originally been at Mount Wise, then at Morice Yard, it was moved first to the now closed Bull Point north of North Yard and then to a larger underground site further up the Tamar at Ernesettle, where it still is to this day, although now known as Defence Munitions Plymouth.

The period from the expansion of the yard until the First World War coincided with the building of HMS *Dreadnought*, which made all pre-dreadnought battleships obsolete and started a massive building boom for everyone, Devonport included. During this period some huge ships were built there, including dreadnoughts HMS *Temeraire* (1907), HMS *Collingwood* (1908), HMS *Centurion* (1911), HMS *Marlborough* (1912), HMS *Warspite* (1913) and the famous HMS *Royal Oak* (1914), sunk at Scapa Flow in 1939. Also built at Devonport were battlecruisers HMS *Indefatigable* (1909, lost at Jutland in 1916) and HMS *Lion* (1910, damaged at Jutland). Having watched the frigate HMS *Scylla* being launched in 1968 it's difficult to imagine how such enormous ships could have fitted across the river!

The battle of Jutland resulted in the loss of fourteen ships: the battlecruisers *Queen Mary*, *Indefatigable* and *Invincible*; armoured cruisers *Defence*, *Black Prince* and *Warrior*; and *Destroyers Tipperary*, *Ardent*, *Fortune*, *Shark*, *Sparrowhawk*, *Nestor*, *Nomad* and *Turbulent*. Apart from those ships built in Devonport there were many for whom Devonport was their home base; of the thousands of men lost at Jutland many would have been Devonport men.

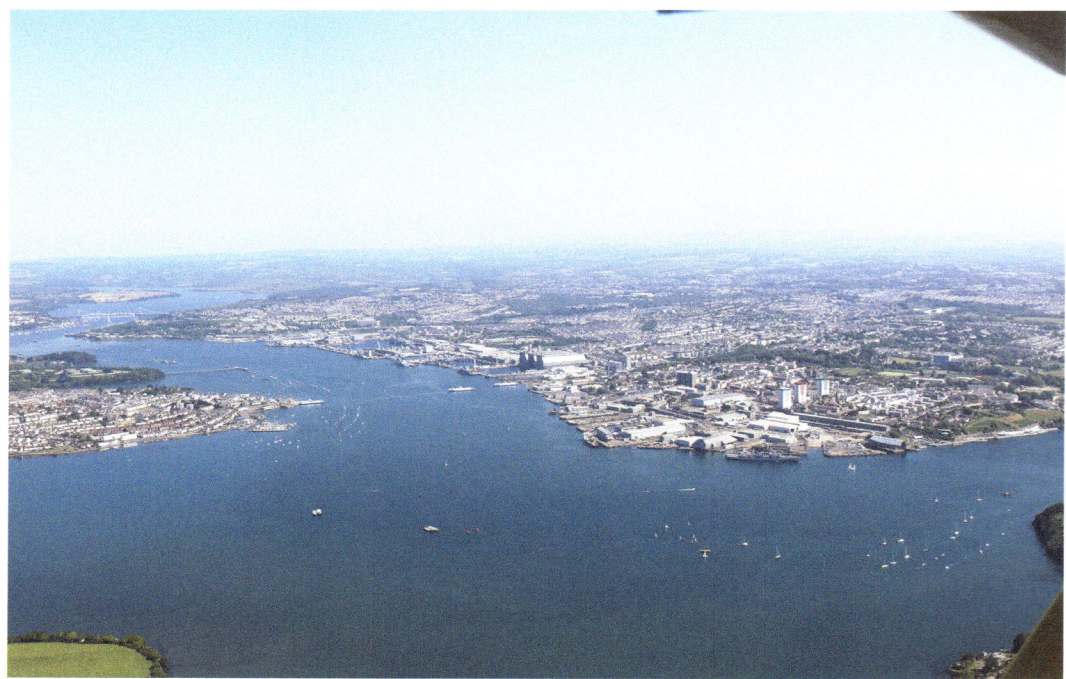

The extent of the dockyard along the Hamoaze, with Plymouth behind.

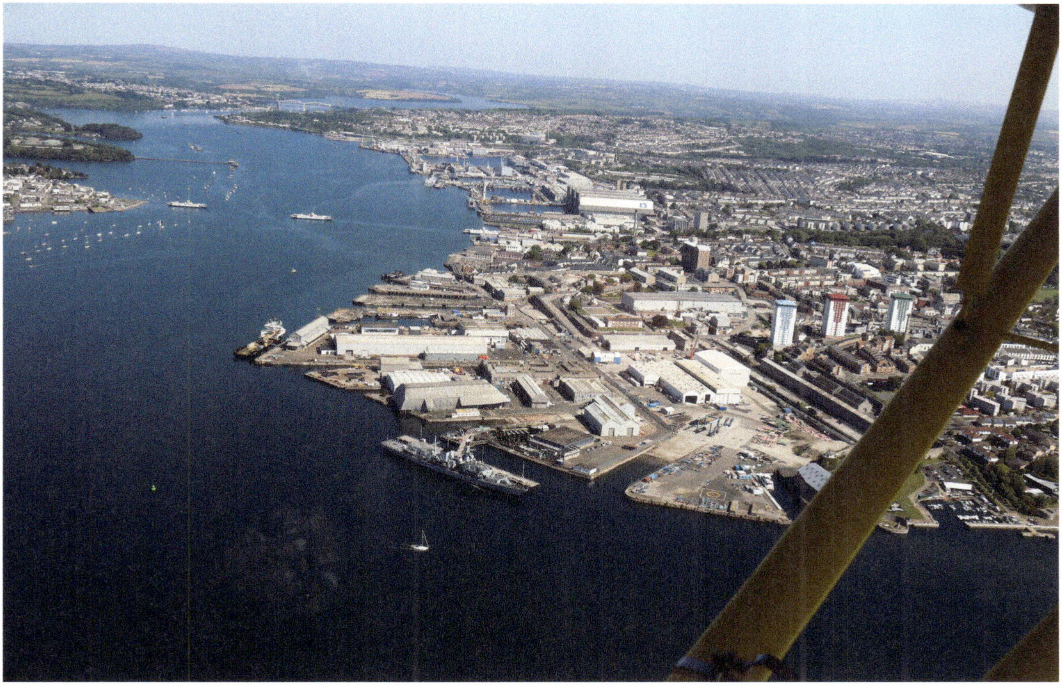

The Dockyard

Above: Looking north along the dockyard and Devonport.

Below: The Ernesettle area including DM Plymouth.

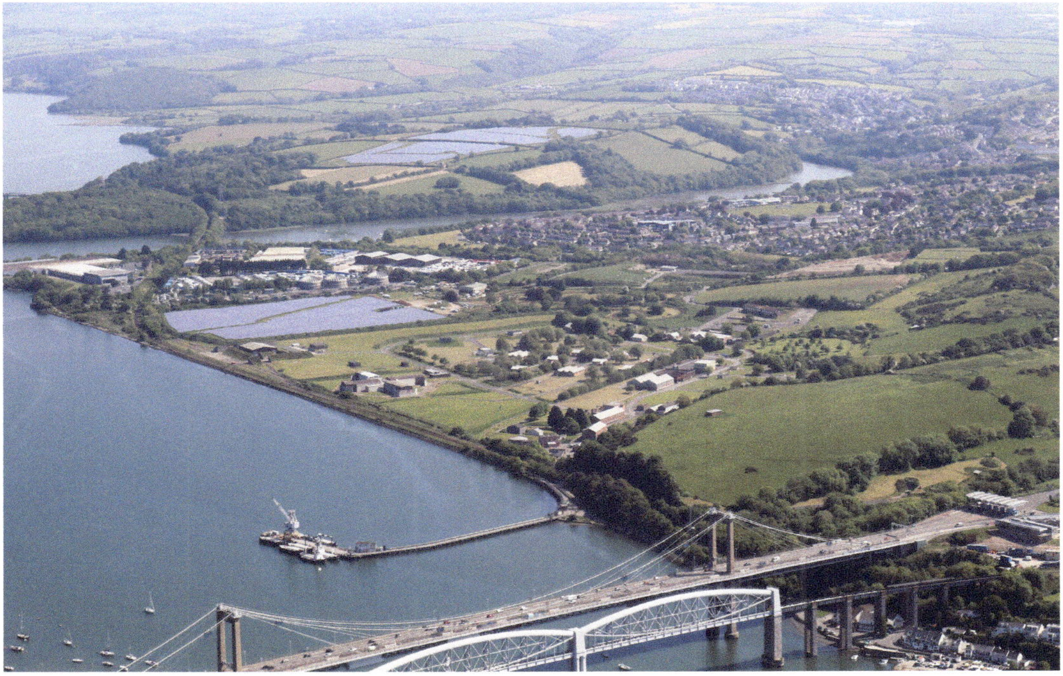

In an echo of G. T. Green's mid-nineteenth-century comments, which brought about the expansion into the North Yard Extension, in 1924 the then Chief Civil Engineer G. S. Jacobs quoted Earl Jellicoe's 1919 comment, 'August 1914 found us with a superiority in ships, but woefully lacking in dock accommodation.' As a result the entrance to No. 5 Basin was widened to 125 feet to allow the largest ships to enter.

With all this increased workload there was obviously also an increase in the workforce. At the turn of the century the dockyard employed 8,456 men, by the start of the First World War it had almost doubled to 15,803 and according to John van der Kiste in his *Plymouth: A City at War* by the end of the war it had reached 19,000.

During the Second World War the dockyard went into overdrive, with so many ships needing repair after action. Few ships were built then but the Admiralty policy was to use the facilities for repair, maintenance and modernisation of the existing fleet. Secrecy regulations meant that few people knew what was going on behind the walls but the dockyardees were working flat out, often around the clock, to keep as many ships as possible available for action. The Blitz, which flattened much of Plymouth, also caused a great deal of damage to the yard, but never enough to put it out of action.

Getting sufficient manpower was obviously a problem with so many men now in the services, but this problem was offset to a large extent by women who were trained to do what had previously been men's work and did it very well. According to Paul Bishop in his *Defence, the Dockyard and Diversification*, by 1947 the dockyard employed 21,000 people.

A copy of Plymouth Statistics available at the Plymouth and West Devon Record Office dated 1951 shows a total of 19,094 men and women employed in engineering and shipbuilding (most of whom would have worked in the dockyard), some 22.7 per cent of the working population. When I started my apprenticeship there in 1967 the dockyard

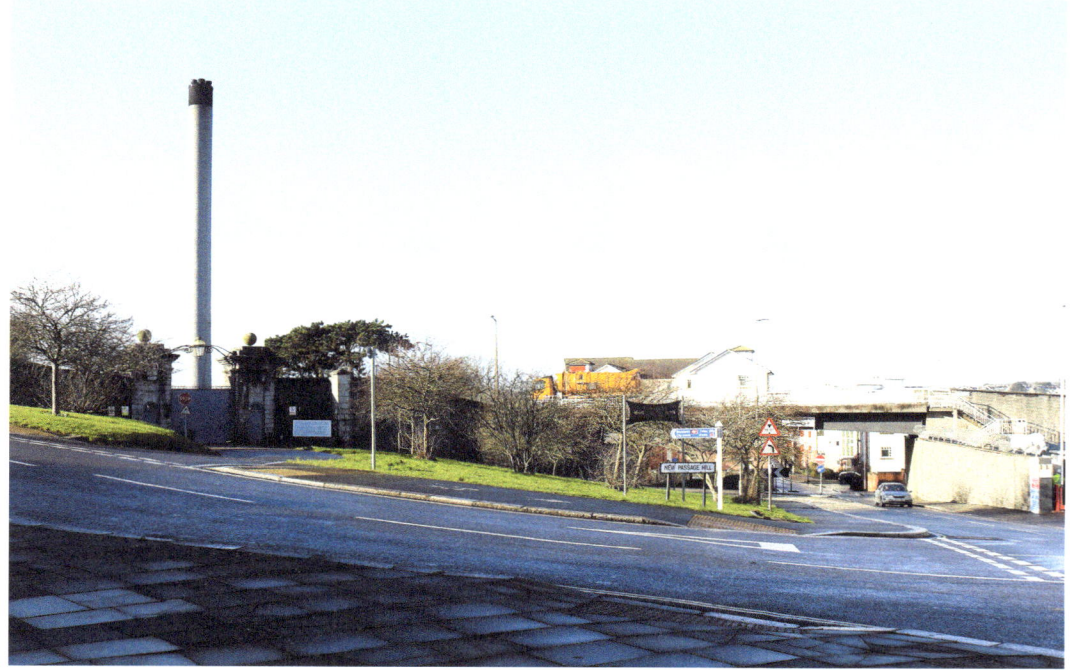

The flyover and Morice Yard gate.

employed approximately 14,000 with similar numbers employed in 1973. By this time as well as the railway tunnel there was a road flyover joining North Yard with Morice Yard and hence South Yard making movement of people and equipment throughout the yard very much easier.

The dockyard became a private company in 1987, by which time the workforce had fallen to around 12,000 when Devonport Management Ltd took on the contract to run the dockyard as a repair and maintenance yard for naval ships, with the freedom to take on private contracts as well. In 2007 DML was sold to Babcock International, who still run the yard at the time of writing. Today's employment figure is more like 5,000, many of whom are contract staff.

As well as fighting for contracts to repair and maintain naval ships, the dockyard went into the building of superyachts for billionaires working under the name Devonport Yachts, building the *Alamshar* for the Aga Khan and the *Vava II*, at the time described as the longest, largest and most sophisticated yacht built in Britain, for Ernesto Bertarelli and his wife Kirsty. Devonport Yachts has now been sold to Pendennis shipyard at Falmouth, which presumable means no more superyachts will be built at Devonport.

Given the reduction in defence spending by the government, who knows what the future holds? If we had a Labour government headed by its current (at time of writing) pacifist leader who has stated he would never push the nuclear button, will we still have a Navy worthy of the name? If we do will they need Devonport as a base? It is very difficult to think of Devonport without the naval connection but I suppose anything is possible.

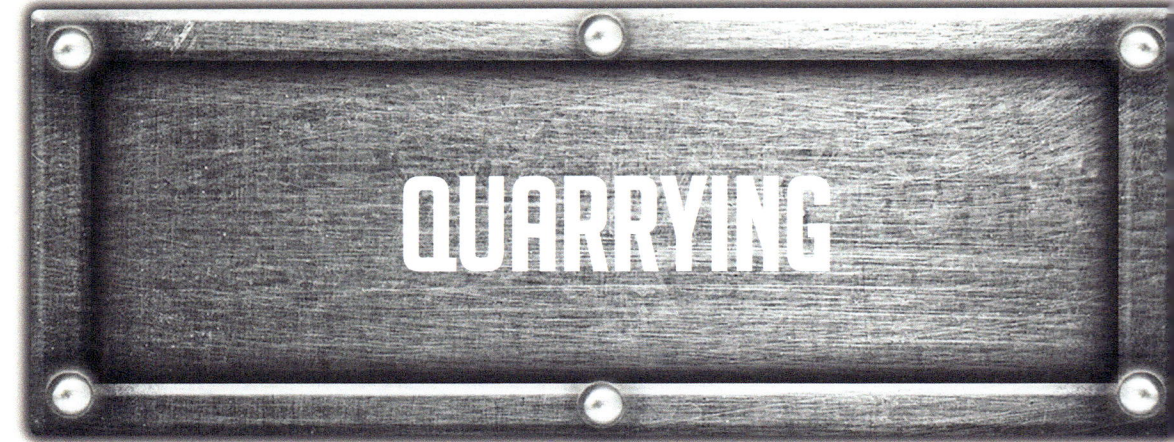

QUARRYING

Quarrying? In Plymouth? Really? Yes, and quarrying on a huge scale. Another asset that Plymouth had was its geology; the bedrock beneath much of the south of the city was limestone. It was described in the Local Development Framework published in 2007 as 'the farthest south western exposure of workable limestone in England'. It also says 'Limestone is a key feature of the city's physical geography. A band of Middle Devonian Limestone forming a long exposure up to a kilometre wide runs across the southern side of the city from The Hoe, through Cattedown to Sherford.' 'Limestone quarrying has been a significant feature of the city since its early development. The stone has been used for a variety of notable projects such as: the Plymouth Breakwater; the Eddystone lighthouses; Royal William Victualling Yard; Devonport Dockyard and many other important buildings throughout the 17th, 18th and 19th centuries.'

Having said all that, all the figures I've seen showing the breakdown of employment show those employed under the heading 'Mineral', the only heading that I assume covers limestone quarrying, account for only around 3 per cent of the working population and Crispin Gill quotes 'A writer "J.P."' saying that the Cattedown quarries on average employed 350 men. However, that 3 per cent/350 men have left a huge mark on the landscape of the city. Limestone was much in demand as a building material and also to be burned to produce quicklime, slaked lime and lime mortar or simply ground up and spread on the soil to reduce the acidity and make the soil more productive. For extremely acidic soils it was sometimes necessary to add quicklime to the soil but this is so corrosive and so inclined to spontaneous reaction with carbon dioxide, returning it to calcium carbonate, that it would have to be burned as near as possible to the farm.

In later times this gave rise to huge areas of the city being quarried away, notably Cattedown, West Hoe and the Stonehouse area. Even in the late nineteenth century R. N. Worth in his 1890 *History of Plymouth* said, 'The physical features of Plymouth ... have been greatly varied by the extensive quarrying operations ... in the Devonian Limestone. For centuries this limestone has been the chief source of lime for the country around; and of late years it has been worked for building and ornamental purposes.'

Much of the Cattedown area, south of the modern Clovelly Road and between Victoria Wharf and Laira Bridge, was quarried at various times over the centuries. Many of the early quarries were owned and operated by small firms, families even, although over the years many of them merged or were bought out to form ever bigger operations. During

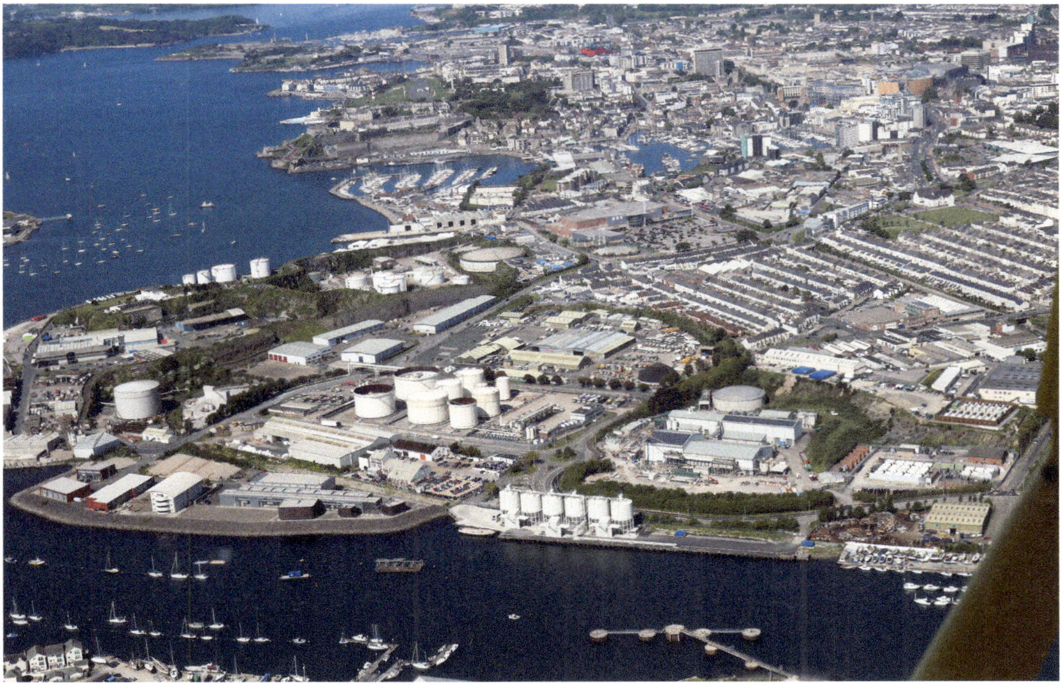

Above: Cattedown quarries area today.

Below: The quarried area of Cattedown including the Prince Rock Quarry.

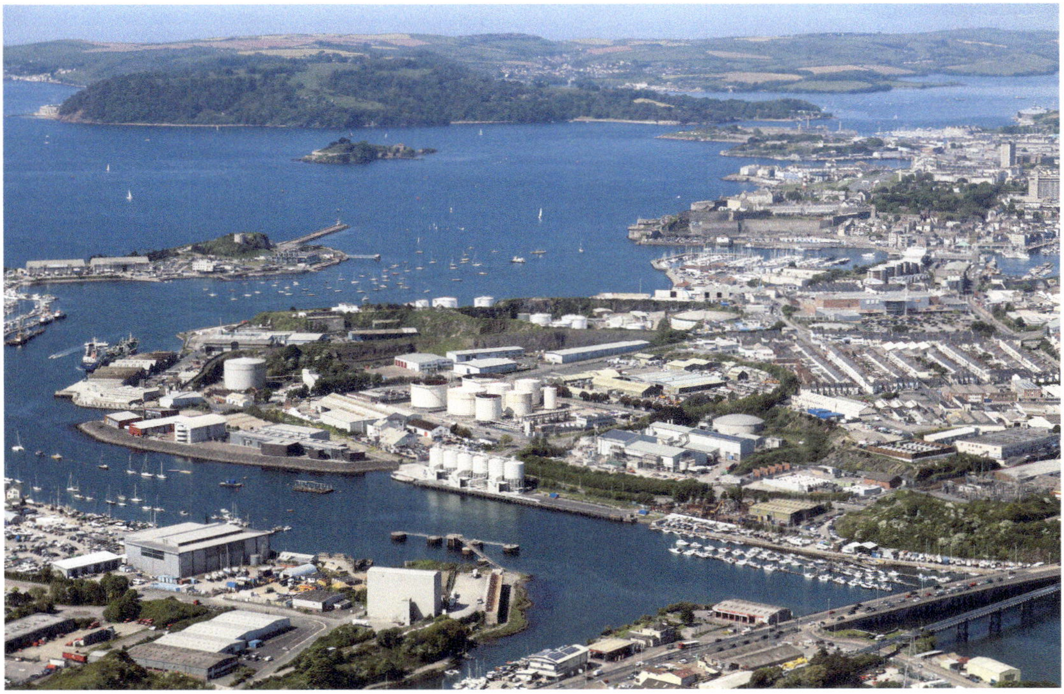

the nineteenth century a vast area was quarried in four separate sections by Benjamin Sparrow and/or one of the companies he was involved with, including Sparrow & Sons, Sparrow, Symons & Co and Sparrow Bros. These companies also owned and operated the wharves at Cattedown from 1836 onwards along with Richard Hill and his family, who were shipbuilders. Obviously having wharfside access meant the limestone and its products could be shipped easily and quickly to where they were needed, and indeed the company also owned a fleet of sailing barges to carry the rock.

The largest part of the area was owned by Lord William Thomas Graves, 3rd Baron Graves of Gravesend, who lived at Thankes Park, Torpoint, with some smaller sections owned by Benjamin Sparrow or Symonds and Sparrow. By 1866 when the first edition Ordnance Survey maps were published many of the quarries were named and it is those names I will use throughout, with explanations to clarify where they are. Over the years different historians have given them different names, and these are mine.

The largest quarry I will call the Cattedown Quarry, which extended over the area now covered by the Plymouth City Council Depot, the adjacent fuel and oil depot, the industrial estate west of Macadam Road and Shapter's Way. It originally stretched all the way along the shore from the eastern end of Cattedown Wharf as far as Laira Bridge, then gradually it

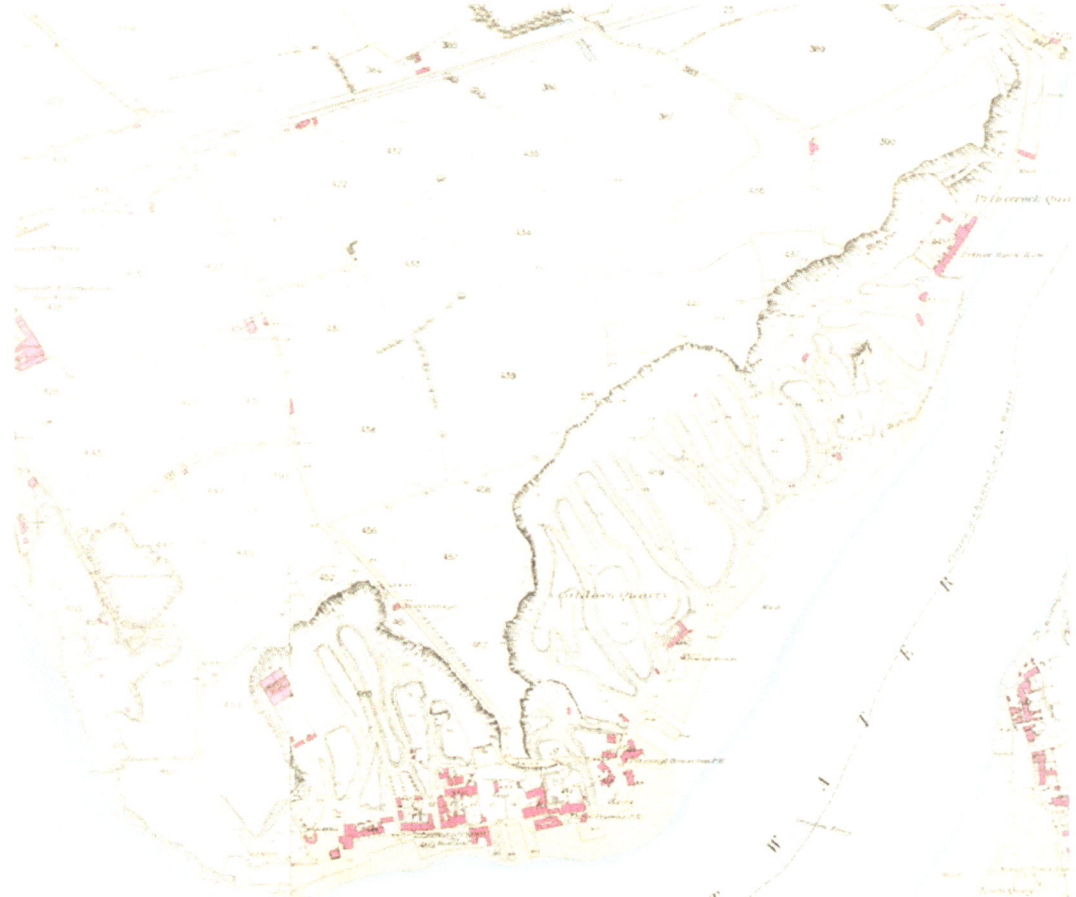

Cattedown quarries from an 1866 OS map. (Courtesy of the National Library for Scotland)

ate away at the rock until in the centre it reached as far as the modern South Milton Street over a quarter of a mile north. The tithe map of 1840 shows Lord Graves owning most of that area, although at that time it was listed as pasture. The north-eastern end of this huge quarry, nearest Laira Bridge, was called Prince Rock Quarry and that was owned by George Soltau and also listed as pasture.

To the west of Cattedown Quarry was Deadman's Quarry. This smaller quarry just south of the modern Clovelly Road was accessible from the road we now call Breakwater Hill off Clovelly Road and now houses Greenergy Plymouth. This area was owned by Sparrow and

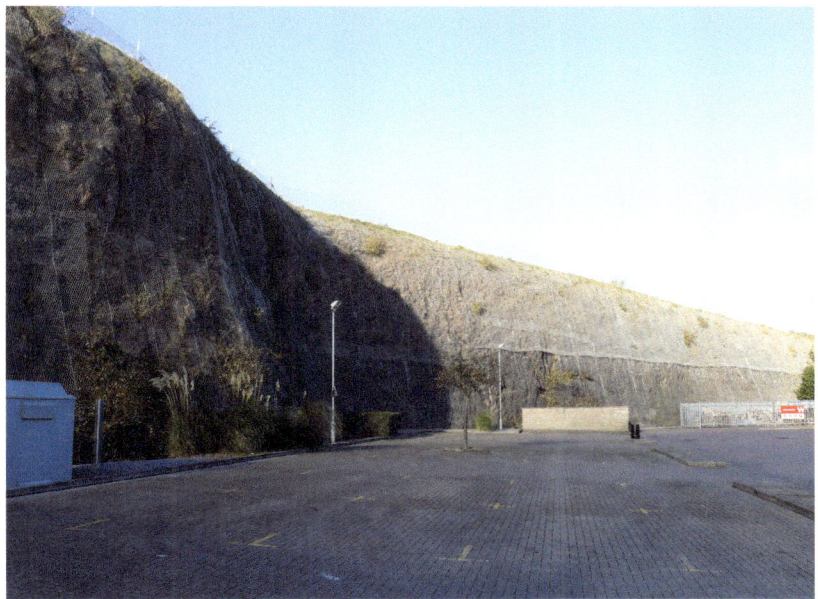

The parking area at Macadam Road showing the old quarry walls.

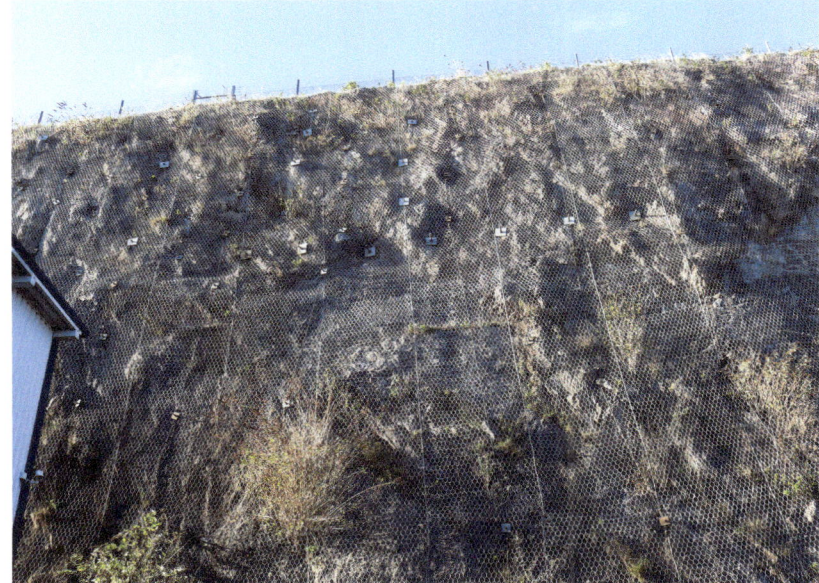

Close-up of the quarry walls at Macadam Road.

Symons in 1841 and grew from a much smaller quarry in the south-west of its area to fill all the space between what was then called Cattedown Road, now the South West Coast Path joining Cattedown Wharves to what we now call Clovelly Road, and what was then called Cattedown Lane, now a truncated and closed off lane that ran from the cul-de-sac end of Cattedown Road after it crosses South Milton Street down to the old Passage House Inn, now Pressure Lines on Cattedown Road.

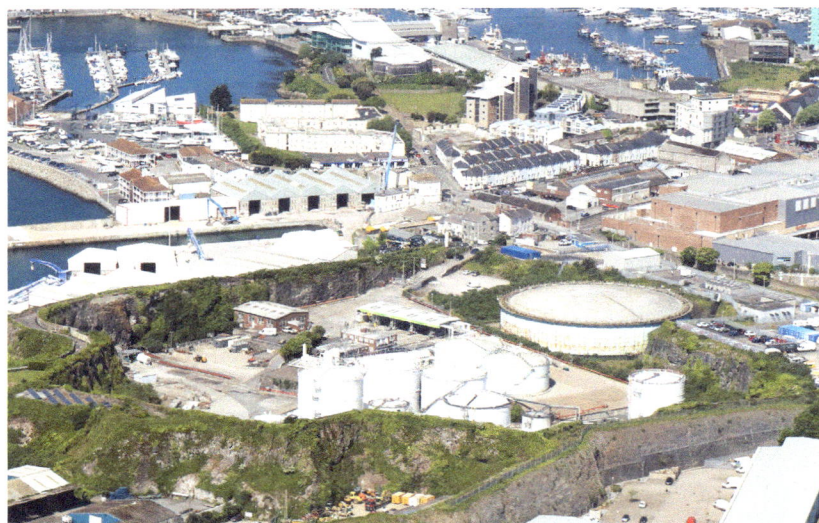

Deadman's Quarry with Victoria Wharf behind.

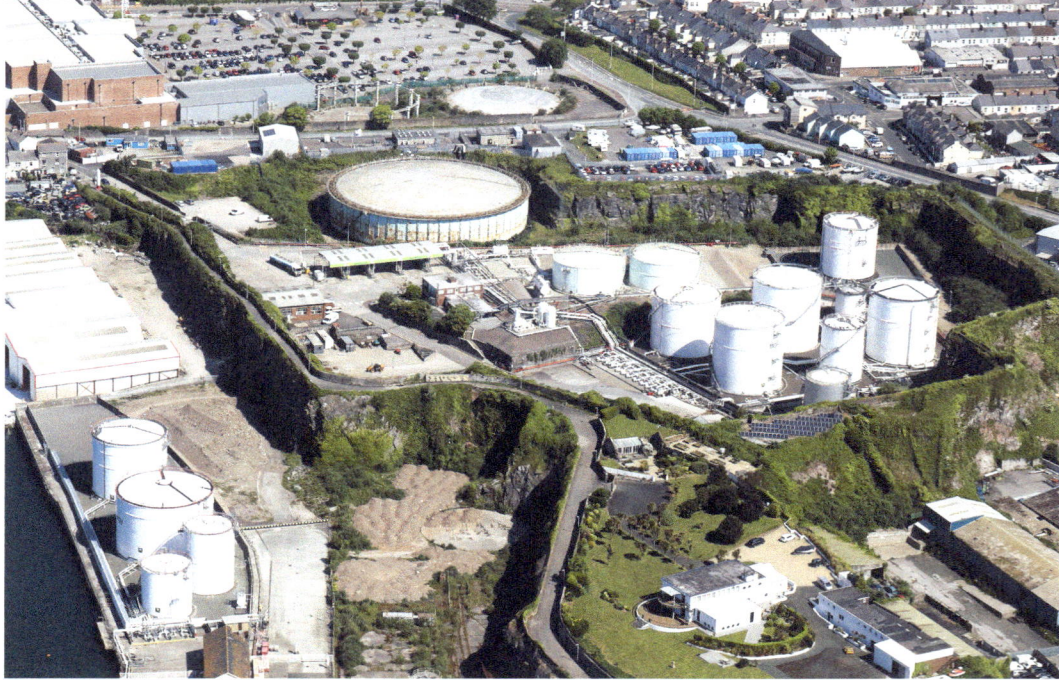

Deadman's Quarry close-up.

South of Deadman's Quarry is the Middle Quarry, which was also partly owned by Sparrow and Symons, the rest leased from Lord Graves. This is similarly bounded by the lower end of the old Cattedown Road and Cattedown Lane and runs from its junction with Deadman's Quarry to Cattedown Wharf. It is now also an industrial estate housing Interfish and RPB vehicle breakers among many others. This contained the site of the cave, known as Worth's Cattedown Bone Cave, where bone fragments, both animal and human, plus evidence of flint implements, were found in the autumn of 1886.

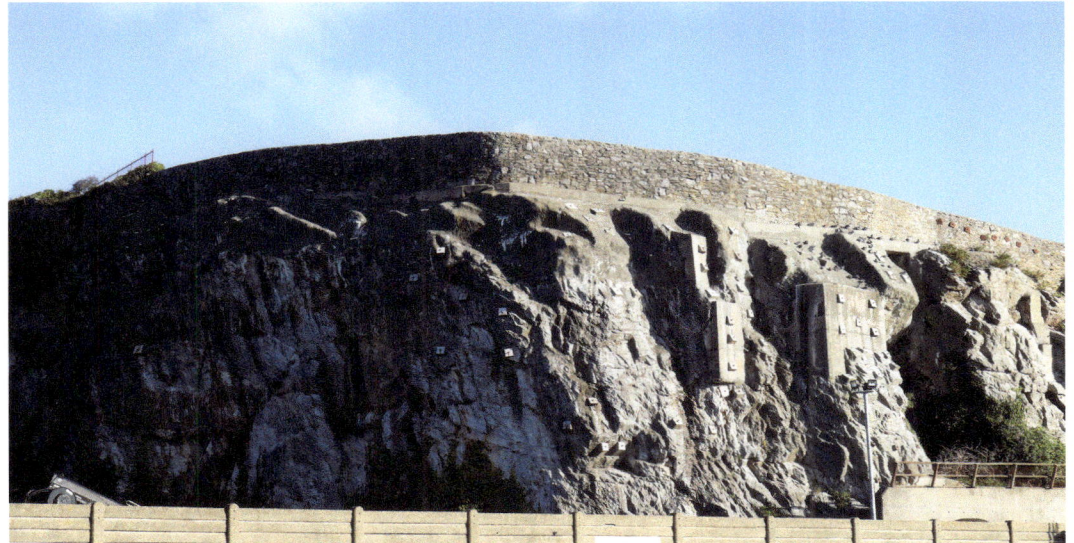

Above: Middle Quarry wall with Cattedown Lane above.

Below: The Middle Quarry, now home to MAN Trucks.

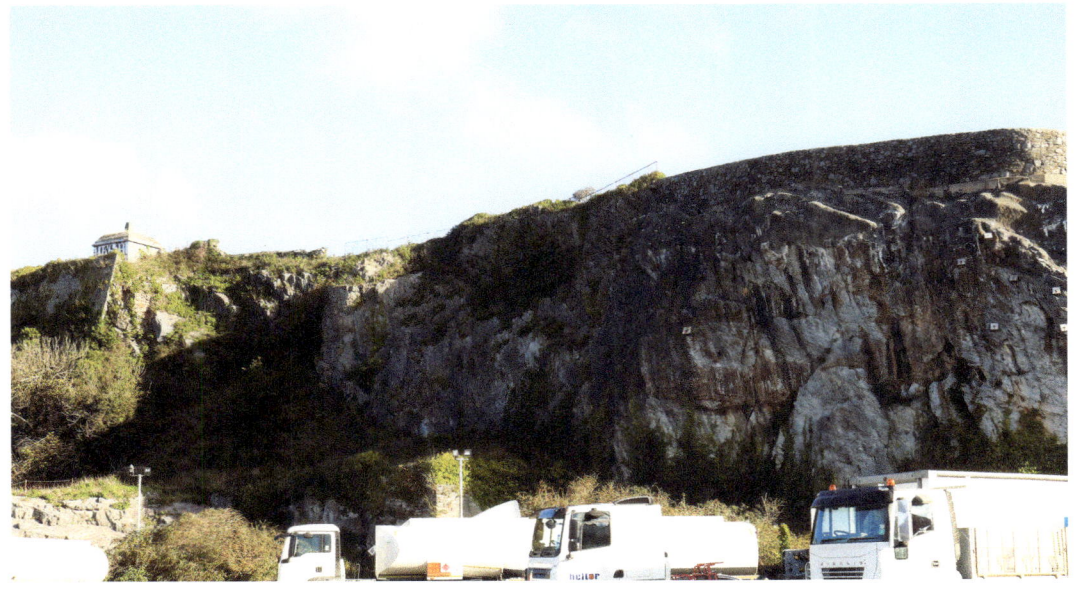

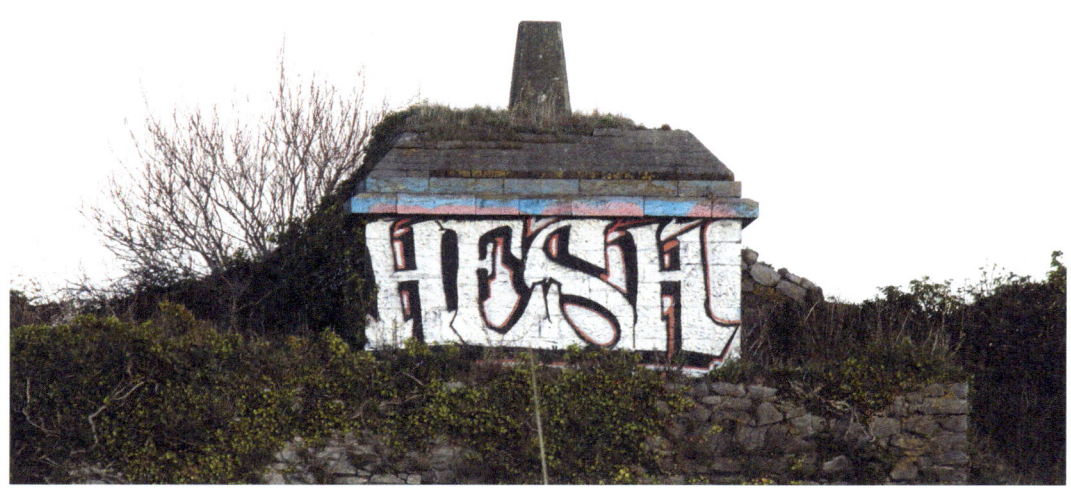

Above: Close-up of the Middle Quarry chimney base, now topped by an OS trig point.

Below: 1888 view of the Middle Quarry and the chimney taken from Turnchapel. (Courtesy of Devon Karst Research Society)

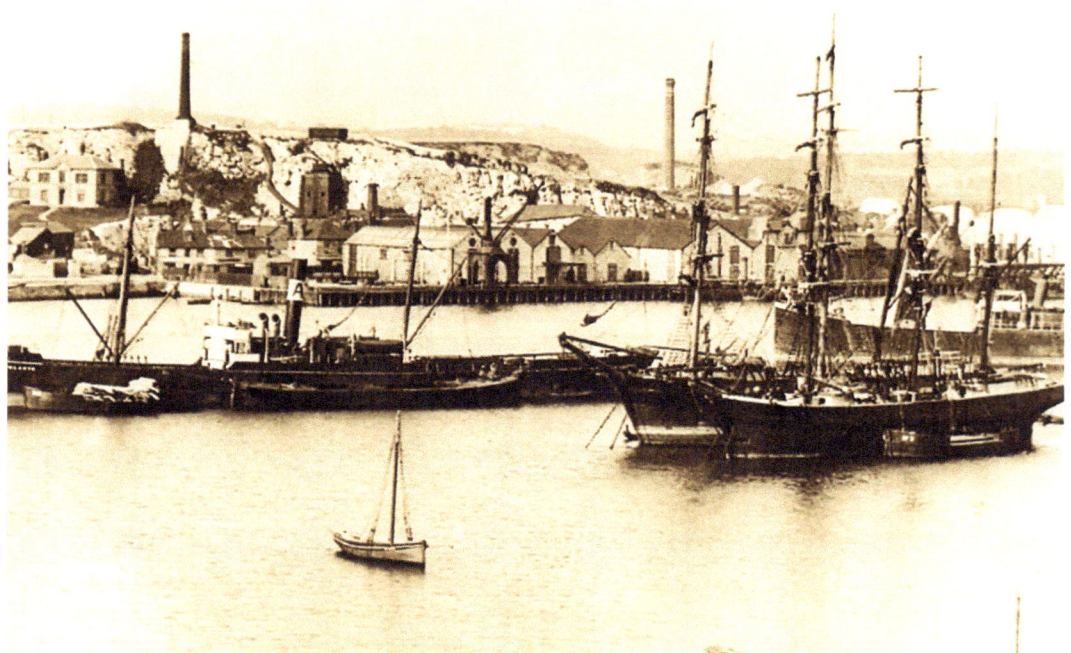

Further west again, beside Victoria Wharf and between the South West Coast Path and the river, was yet another quarry, known as Carpenter's Rock Quarry after a rock formation at the southern end. The tithe map gives Symons and Sparrow as major owners, with a small field near Victoria Wharf owned by John Bayly. This now houses more oil tanks belonging to Greenergy Plymouth. It was in this quarry that a cave was discovered, during blasting operations in 1889, known as Burnard's Bone Cave, which contained prehistoric animal bones including those of woolly rhinoceros and cave hyena.

Looking from above it is obvious that the divisions between these quarries were comparatively thin sections of limestone. The obvious question to me is as Sparrow and Symons ended up owning and operating all these quarries, why did they never knock down the valuable limestone in between them? Originally it might have been because of the different ownership of the neighbouring quarries but also I suppose because at the time they carried the only public roads giving access into the area. Until Clovelly Road, Macadam Road and Oakfield Terrace Road were built in the twentieth century there would have been no other access to the wharf. Oakfield Terrace Road was the first road to appear, on the 1907 6-inch OS map, then ending at the top of the quarry face south of South Milton Street, although the L&SWR rail tracks did connect the area by rail at that time. Clovelly Road did not appear until the 1957-surveyed 1-inch OS map and Macadam Road is an even more modern one.

Benjamin Sparrow also owned two houses in Lipson Terrace, still existing at the top of Lipson Road. According to the 1852 street directory he later moved to

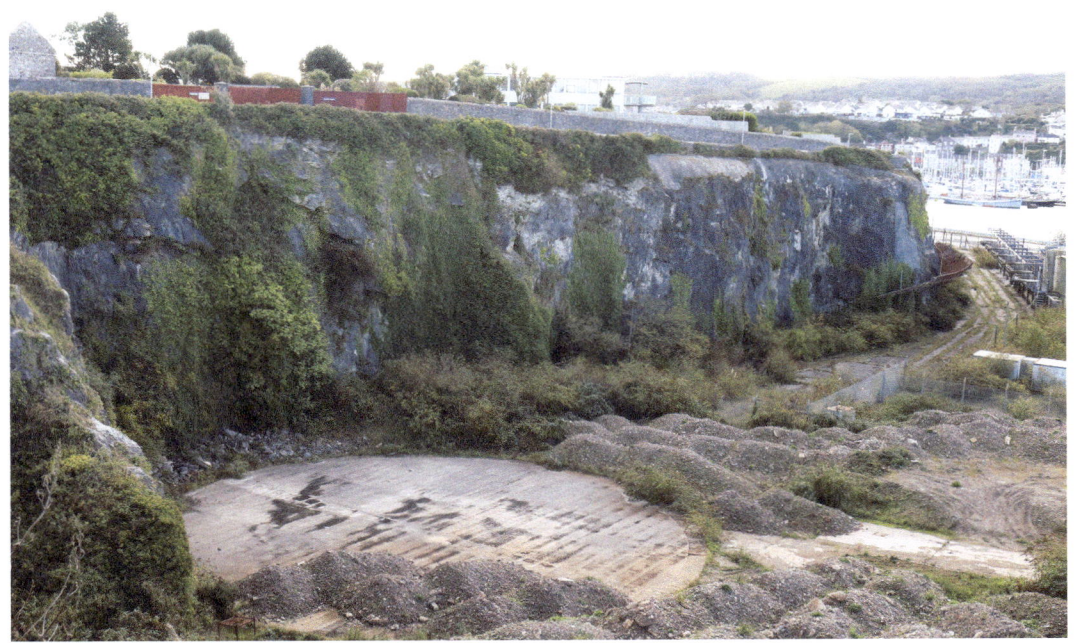

Carpenter's Rock Quarry from the South West Coast Path.

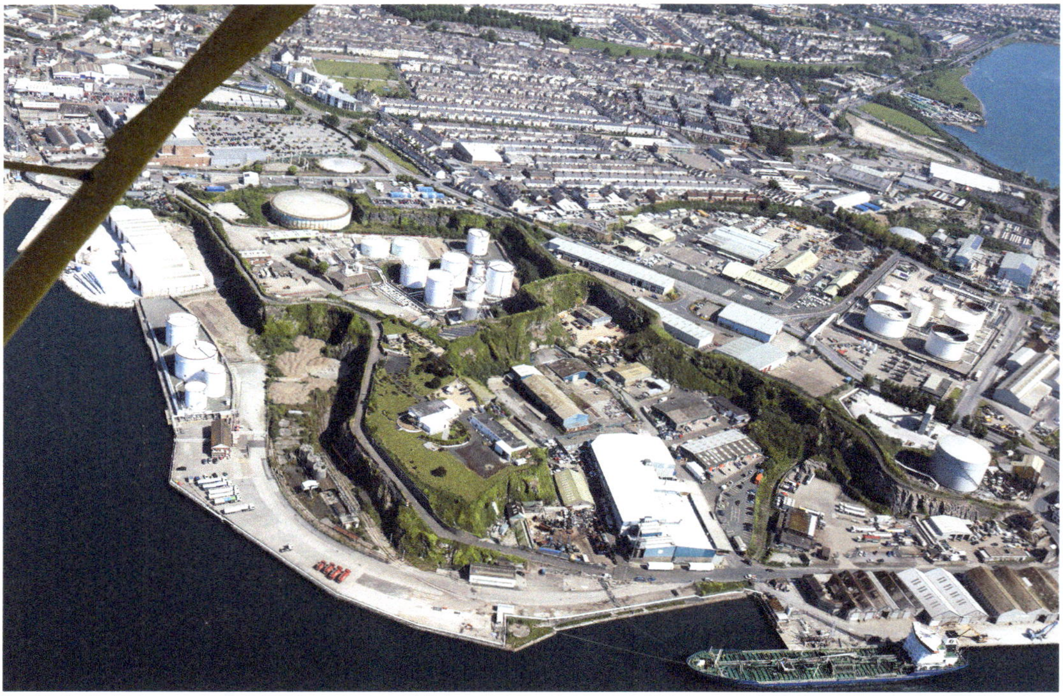

Above: Aerial view of Carpenter's Rock Quarry.

Below: Close-up showing the thin divisions between the quarries.

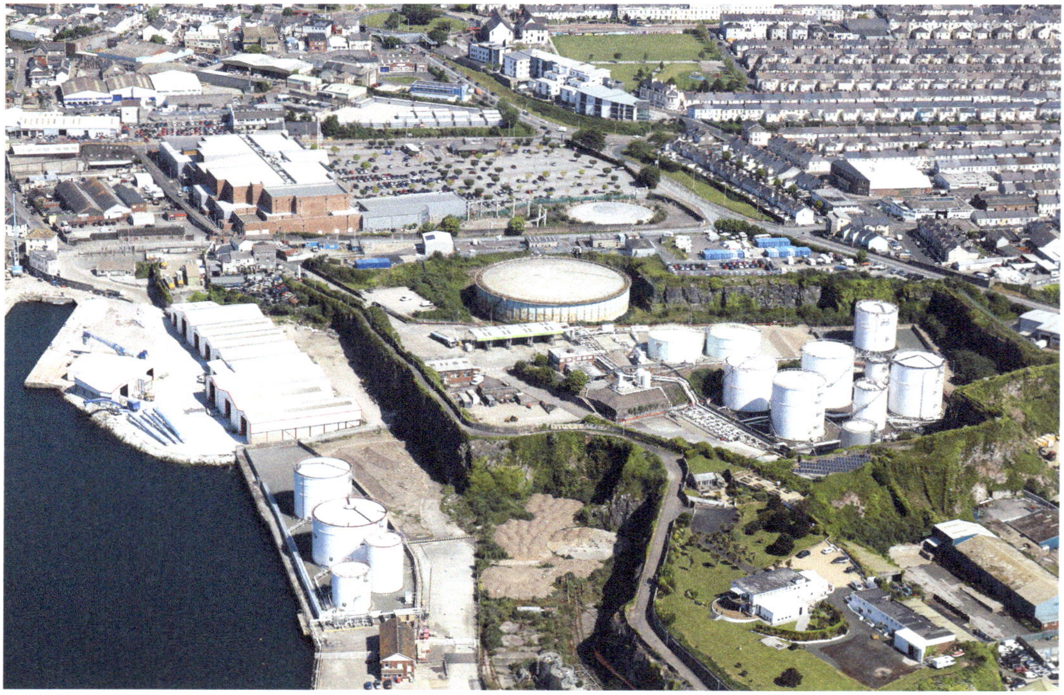

No. 6 Brunswick Terrace beside what was then called Jubilee Street, now Exeter Street, more or less where Screwfix is today. That same directory lists Sparrow & Sons as limestone merchants and shipowners and, separately, their partner Richard Hill of Catdown [sic] as a shipbuilder. His shipwrights' yard was the area now occupied by MAN Truck and Bus Plymouth.

The Sparrows and Hills continued to be involved with the quarries and wharves until the end of the century, with Burnard, Lack and Alger taking over much of the by then worked out Middle Quarry as a chemical and fertilizer company (the Plymouth Chemical Works from 1882). By the turn of the century Burnard and Alger were apparently running the whole business, with F. J. Moore & Sons Lime and Stone Works, taking on the quarries (along with five others including Hooe and Plymstock) by around 1910, although Moore had been listed as leasing Prince Rock Quarry and then owning it by 1900. By 1923 Shell Mex & BP were listed as partners, becoming owners by 1939. The current owners are Cattedown Wharves Ltd, a company first incorporated on 19 March 1920.

The quarry owners and operators, firstly Sparrow and Symons and then F. J. Moore & Co., also owned coastal sailing vessels, including the Phoenix, which delivered lime to farmers around the coast and also stone to be burnt in local limekilns. Alan Kitteridge in his book *Sail and Steam* has several photos showing the sailing smack *Phoenix*, owned first by Lewis Sparrow and then sold to F. J. Moore, beached at Thurlestone, tied up at Salcombe, anchored near Noss Mayo and another showing it at Bantham Quay to unload limestone. When Benjamin Sparrow Jr died in 1877 he and his brother owned thirty vessels, seventeen of which were listed by name in the appraisal of his estate.

Thomas Gill quarried West Hoe and also owned a soap works near Millbay. He had bought all of West Hoe right up to the eastern side of Millbay according to the tithe map, then simply an unused hill mainly listed on the map as pasture or fields, and ending in a cliff overlooking Millbay Docks, and quarried it away leaving us with the low-lying flat area we now call West Hoe. Having levelled the area he then started building roads and houses, including West Hoe Road, Great Western Road, Grand Parade and Radford Road, all of which are still with us today. He also built Millbay Pier in 1844 and a canal leading from Millbay, then little more than a natural inlet, to a private dock in the floor of his quarry in order to move stone more easily. The canal passed under the large white block of flats between Custom House Lane and Great Western Road and the dock ran under the houses on the east side of Great Western Road as far as Radford Road, beneath the tennis courts. Much of the stone was used by his soap factory in Millbay.

Mr Gill was also a director of the South Devon Railway Company, which brought the railway from Exeter into Plymouth and became a director of the docks company, which took over his pier in 1846 and went on to construct the Great Western Docks, now called Millbay Docks. The arrival of a train station within half a mile of his quarry, plus the burgeoning dock right beside it, obviously made exporting limestone from his quarry very much easier, quite apart from the amount of limestone needed in the building of the inner dock, which he presumably supplied.

The evidence of all Mr Gill's work can be seen today in the sheer rock faces beside West Hoe Park and the streets and houses of West Hoe itself.

Quarrying was carried on to a much lesser extent in Stonehouse on land owned by the Earl of Mount Edgcumbe. North of Millbay Docks, between the modern Millbay Road and East Street and between the section of Stonehouse Street that joins Millbay Road, where the old St George's Hall/Stonehouse Town Hall used to be, and Hobart Street there used to be a hill, commonly known as Stonehouse Hill or Battery Hill after the defensive battery

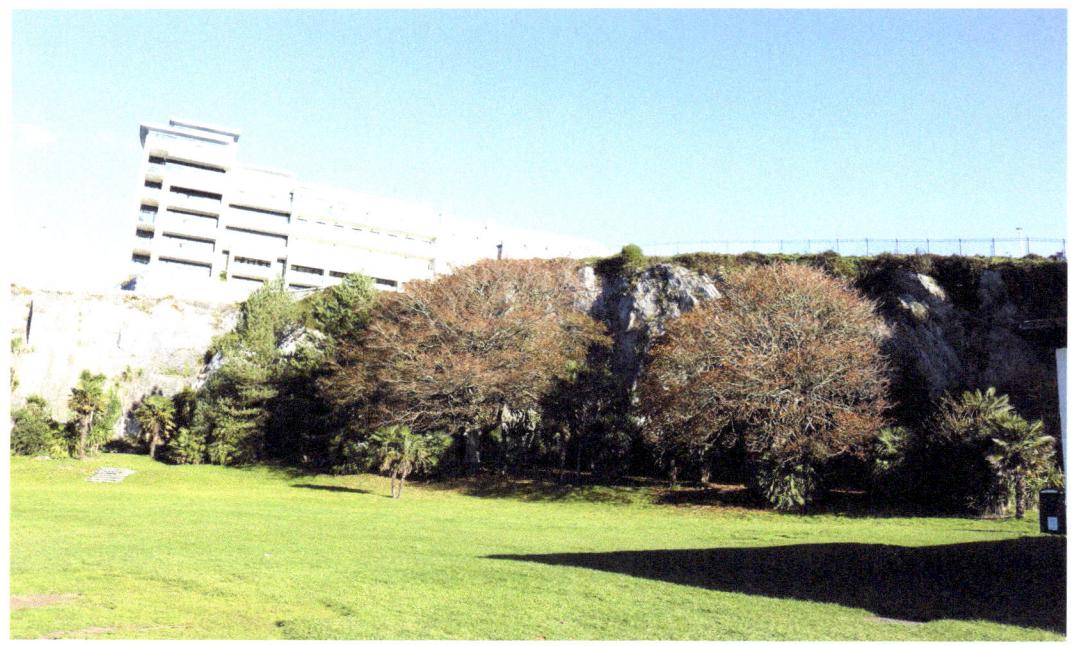

Above: West Hoe Quarry today is much overgrown.

Below: West Hoe Quarry and Millbay Pier from the air.

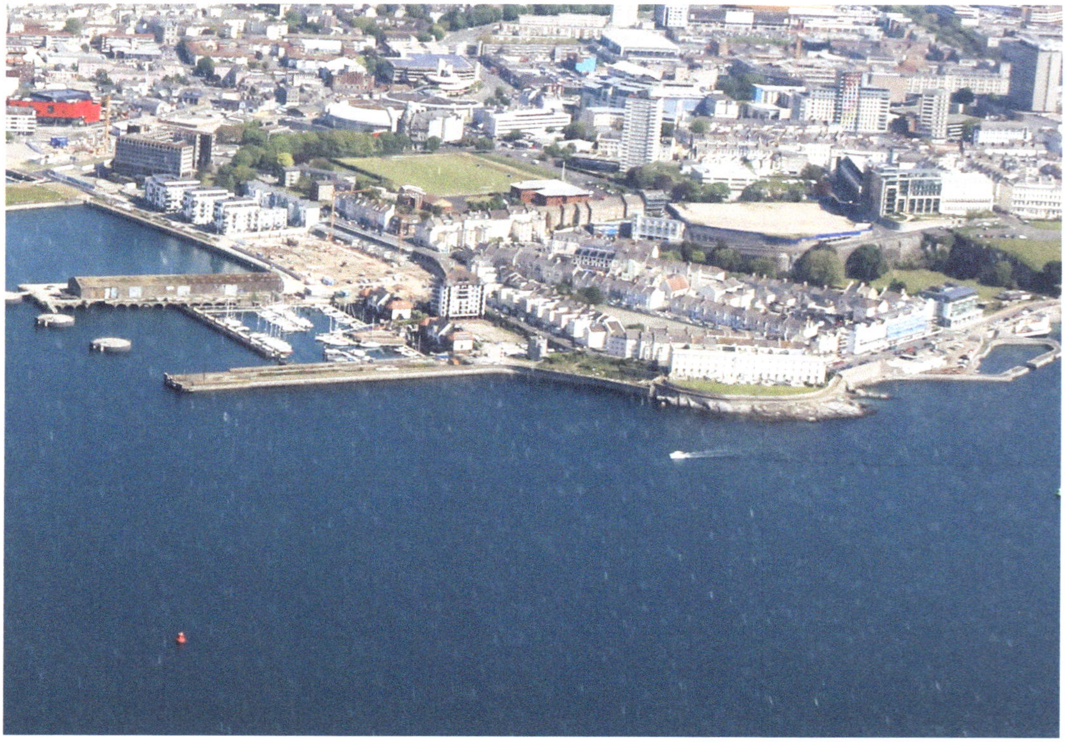

that was once built on top of it. The 1866 OS 25 inch map shows this hill, by then with no battery on it, and at both western and eastern ends it shows quarries, the western end being under what is now called Emma Place (which explains why the houses there have such deep basements!) The quarry had access to Millbay Docks via a gap between the warehouses on North Quay. Crispin Gill tells us that the person who leased the quarry from the Earl of Mount Edgcumbe in 1885 was none other than F. J. Moore.

As nothing remains today of Stonehouse Hill – in fact the area now slopes gently down from Stonehouse Street towards Martin Street – we have to assume that between them these quarries removed all the stone from the hill. They also removed all trace of yet another bone cave (or series of caves) that had first been discovered during quarrying operations in 1776 but was explored by Mr C. Spence Bate FRS in 1865 and found to contain remains of rhinoceros, horse, ox and deer.

In his article for the Plymouth Institution and Devon and Cornwall Natural History Society, dated 1881, named 'On an ossiferous fissure in the Battery Hill, Stonehouse', R. N. Worth described a 'huge fissure extending from the surface of the hill-top to the bottom of the workings – a depth of some sixty feet' varying in width 'from two feet to ten or twelve' plus various side chambers, in which were found fragments of bone and teeth from various

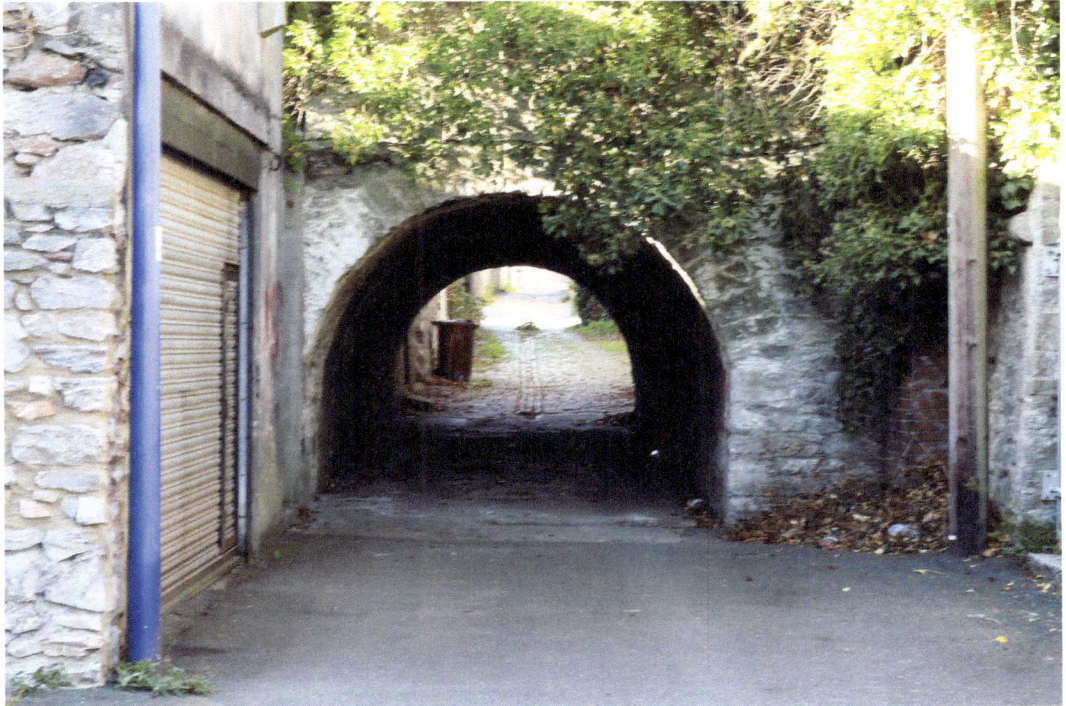

Tunnel from Stonehouse Quarry to Slate Lane, rear of Emma Place.

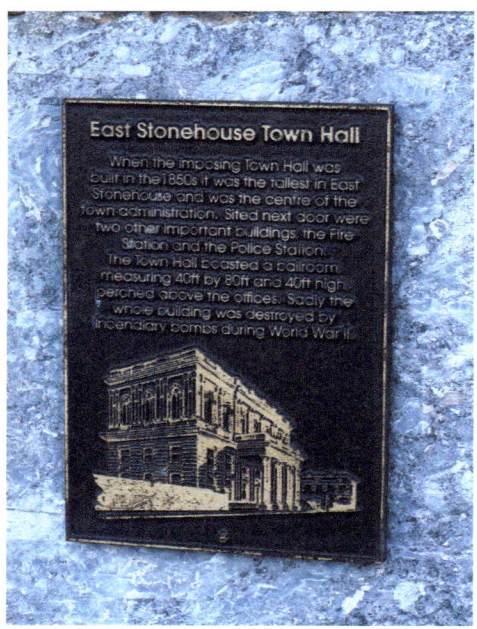

Site of Stonehouse Town Hall in Stonehouse Street.

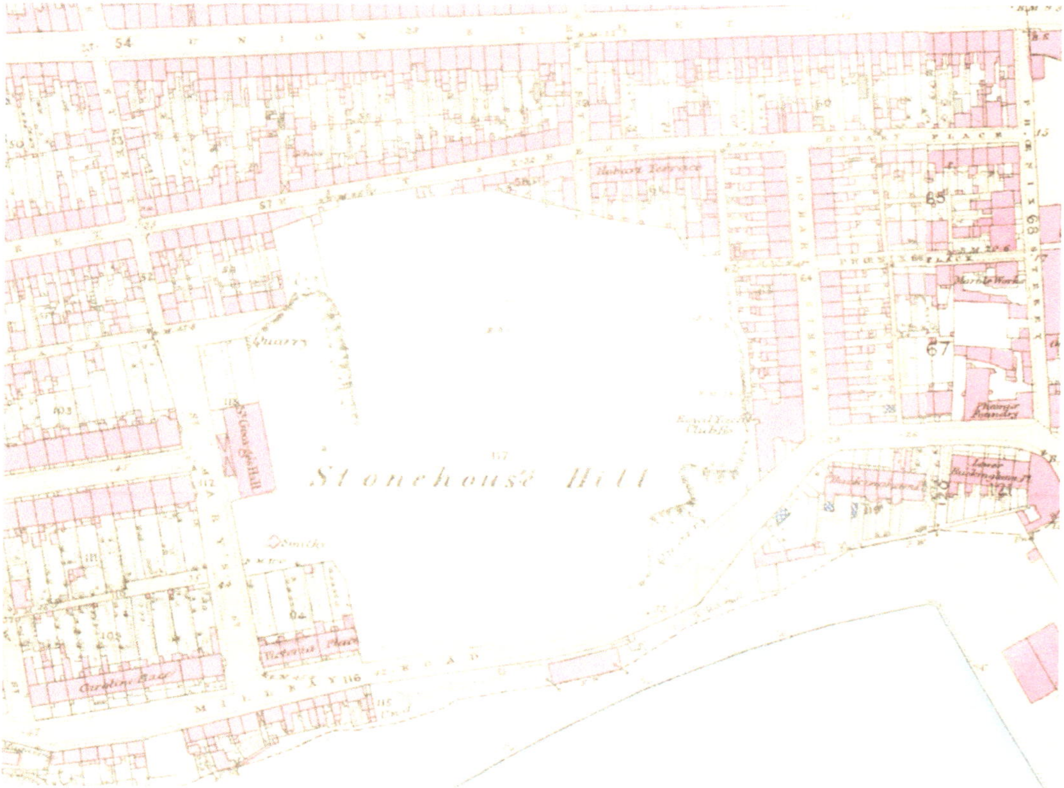

Stonehouse Hill quarries from an 1866 OS map. (Courtesy of the National Library for Scotland)

Quarrying

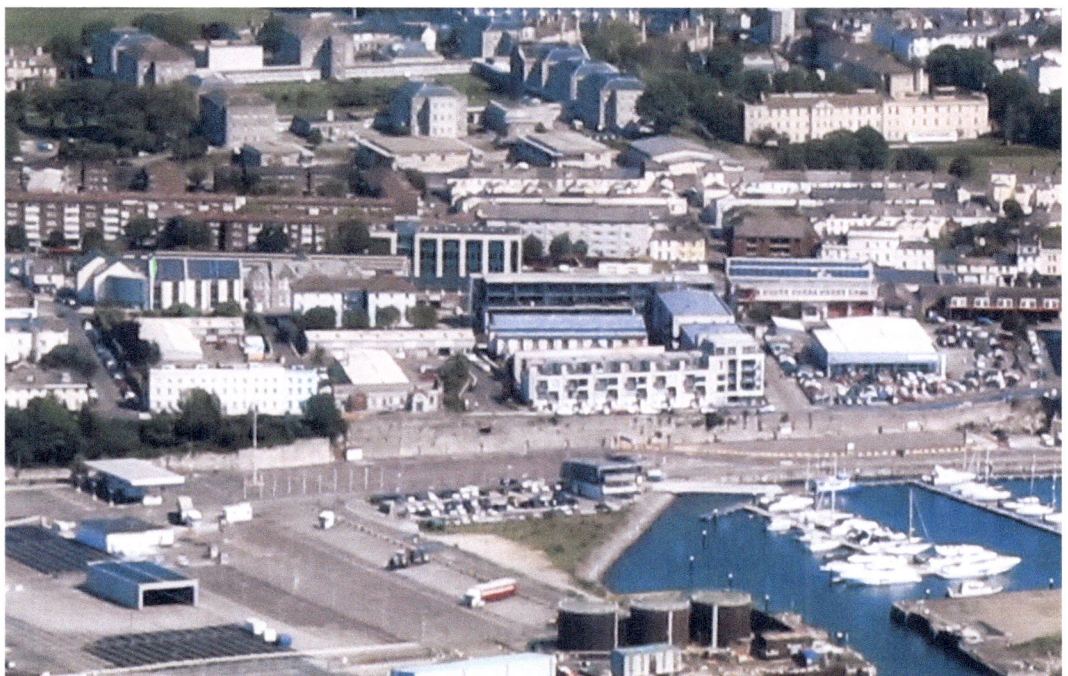

Aerial view of the Stonehouse Quarry area today beyond Millbay Docks.

extinct and surviving animals from extinct rhinos to cats, dogs, wolves and foxes. All traces of this fissure were removed or buried.

The old battery is commemmorated by the name Battery Street and the quarry used to be remembered by the pre-war Quarry Lane, which ran parallel to Emma Place and ended opposite where the modern George Place joins Stonehouse Street. The quarry site itself is now mainly the Miller Court industrial estate, with the eastern end being the site of Murray's VW car dealership.

Further west again is Richmond Walk and in the area between Stonehouse Bridge and Mount Wise the huge white cliffs show just how much stone must have been taken from them in the past. As with much in this area, the quarries were under government control. In 1843 an account of the building of St Michael's Chapel in what was then Navy Row but is now known as Albert Road, just up the hill from Exmouth Road, concludes by saying that 'the stones used in the erection are obtained gratuitous from the government quarries at Richmond Walk'.

The Devonport Characterisation Study of 2006 includes:

After the purchase by the Board of Ordnance of land at Mount Wise in 1759, the local inhabitants found that they no longer had unhindered access to the sea. As a consequence, the Duke of Richmond arranged in 1790 for the path to be built which became known as Richmond Walk along the length of the waterfront from Mutton Cove to Stonehouse Bridge.

The first quay on the eastern part of Richmond Walk was built in 1784–89, and by 1834 the existing quays in that area were complete. A later railway link reinforced the largely industrial use, though for a period of time the railway was used to bring

Above: Aerial view of Richmond Walk with quarry faces visible.

Below: Quarry faces in LTC's yard at Richmond Walk.

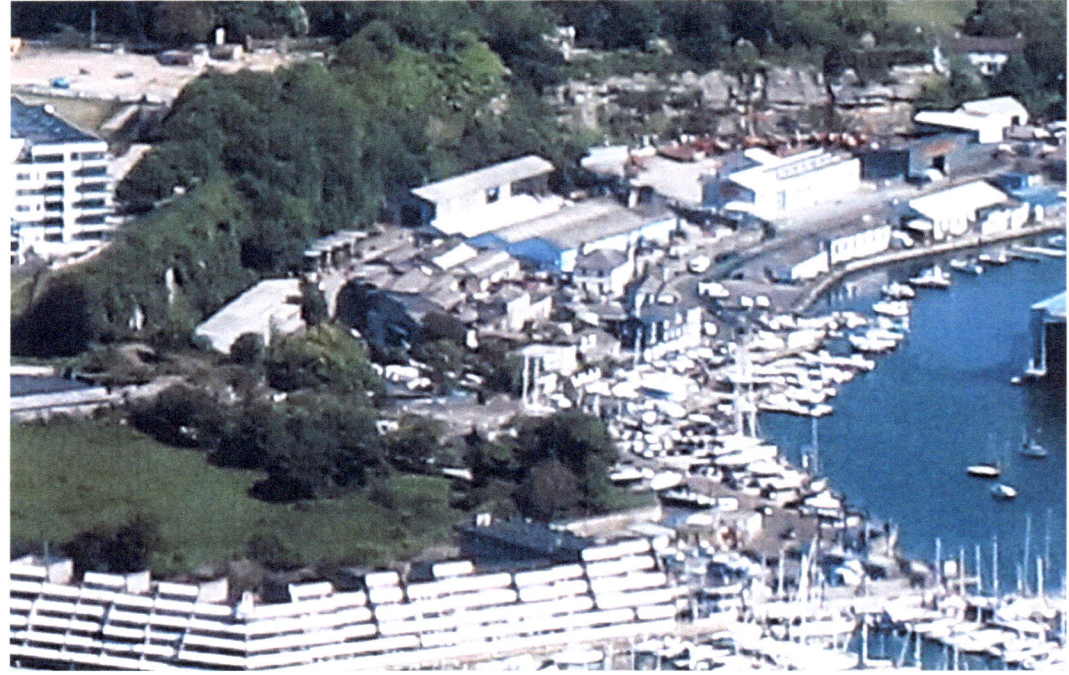

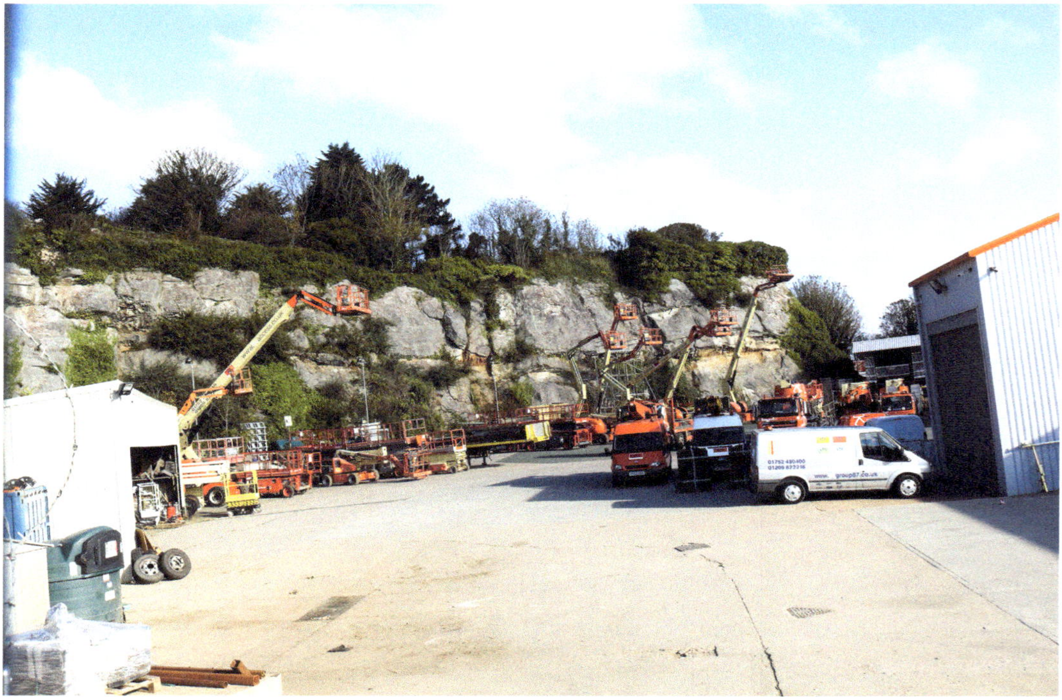

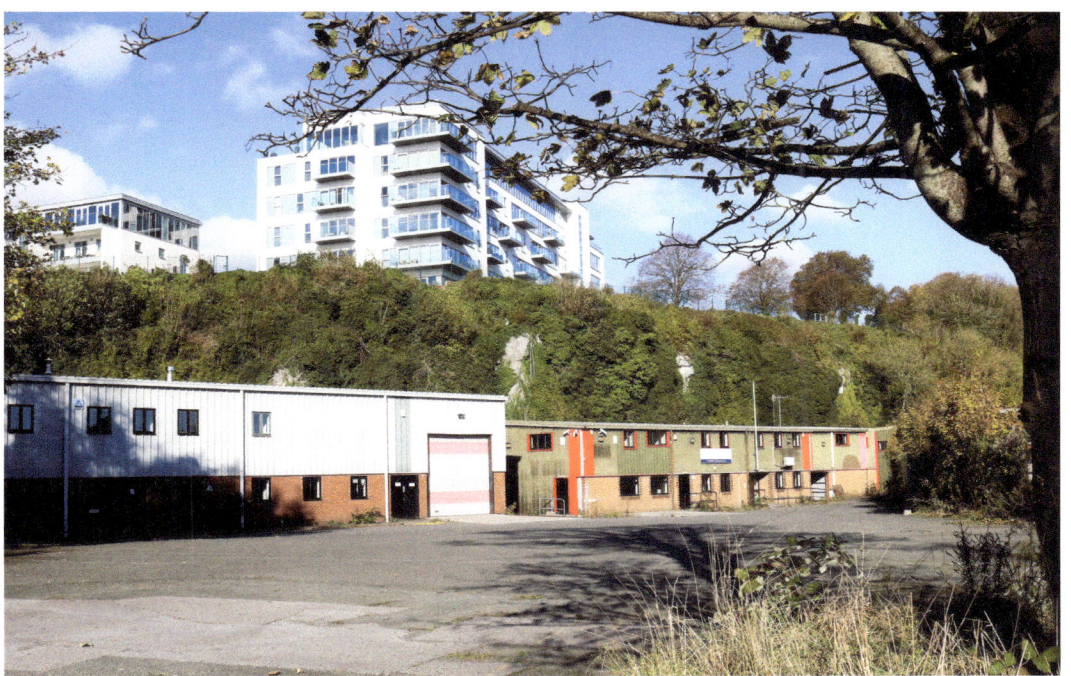

The quarry face in Richmond Walk with industrial units below and modern flats above.

passengers to the Ocean Quay terminal (site of the Mayflower Marina) to meet the tenders of the LSW Railway.

However, despite the mix, the area is characterised by the use of grey Plymouth limestone, for example along the Dock Line walls to Mount Wise, and in the boundary walls along Richmond Walk. Quay walls and buildings such as the ruined boathouse and outbuildings to the terrace are built of dressed limestone. The quarry face and the stone have an important texture, which creates interest in the townscape.

Most of Richmond Walk is still mainly for industrial or commercial use, many of the businesses having connections to the sea and boating including, of course, the Mayflower Marina, with just a few houses and a large block of flats on the old Ocean Quay transatlantic liner terminus site.

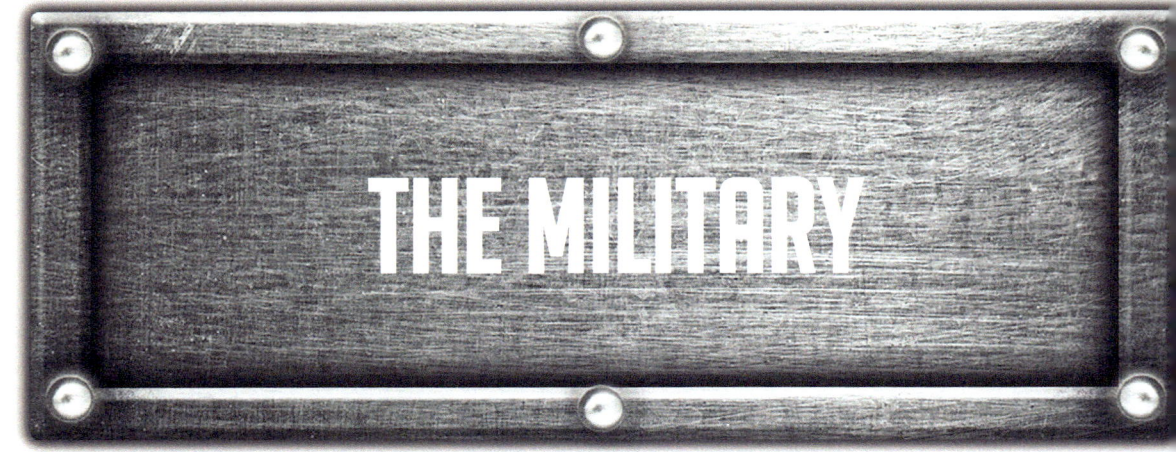

THE MILITARY

Although today Plymouth is less dependent on the military, in previous centuries we were hugely dependent with military bases scattered around the area, many of which no longer exist. Below I will attempt to give an idea of how the numbers and bases changed over years.

I have previously mentioned the fact that Plymouth was considered 'England's premier western port' and by the sixteenth century Francis Drake Francis Drake had petitioned the Elizabeth I to build a fort on the Hoe to defend the town. At this time a series of defensive blockhouses were constructed along the waterfront, stretching from the one at Fisher's Nose, now occupied by the Royal Plymouth Corinthian Yacht Club, two at Millbay, which no longer exist, one at Firestone Bay, which is now the Artillery Tower restaurant, one at Devil's Point and the matching one across the river in Mount Edgcumbe. A fort was also built on Drake's Island at around the same time.

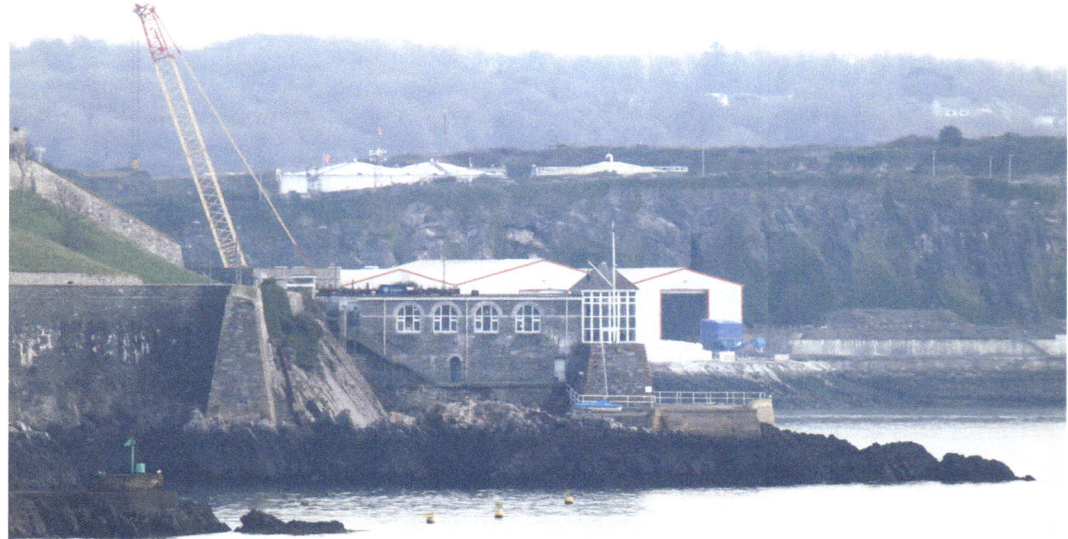

Fisher's Nose blockhouse.

Above: Fisher's Nose blockhouse from the air.

Below: Devil's Point blockhouse.

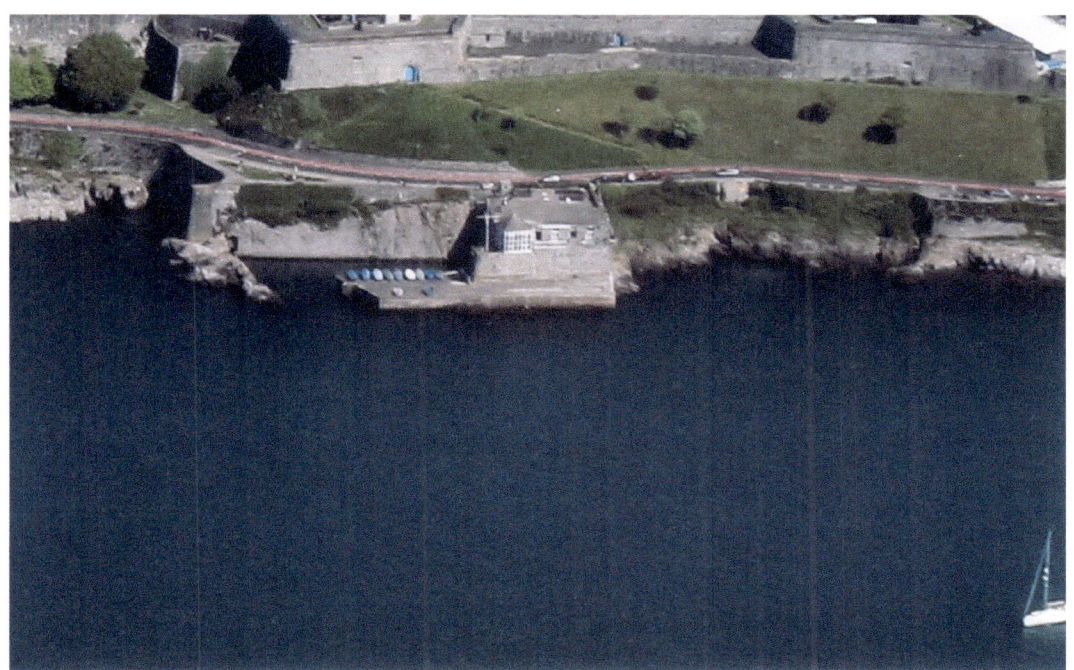

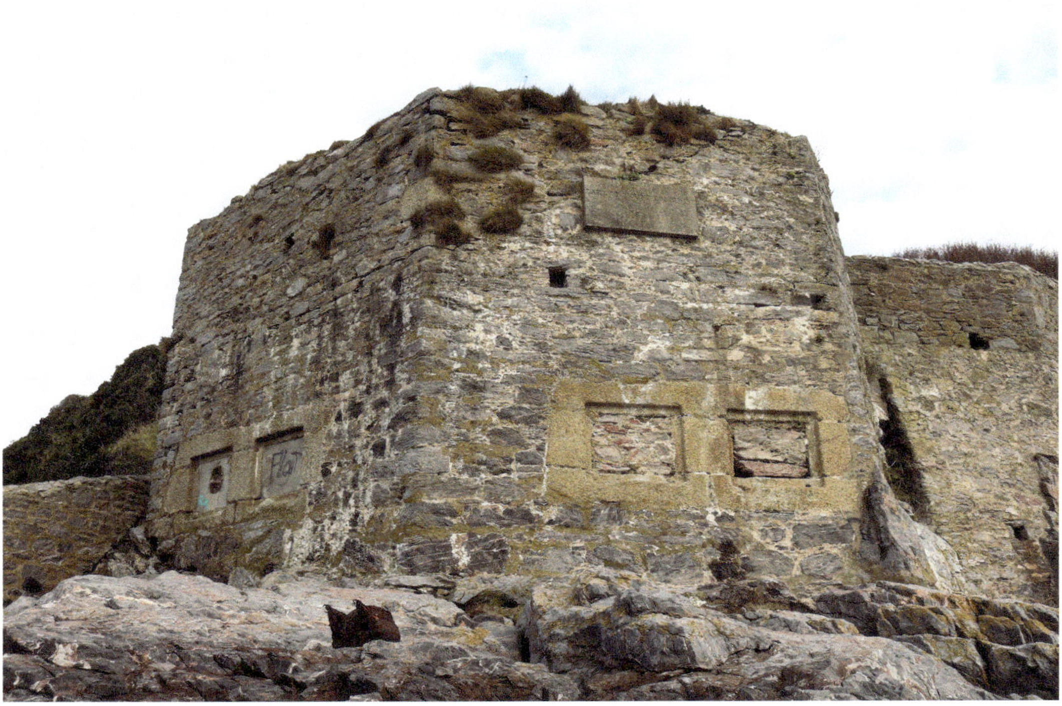

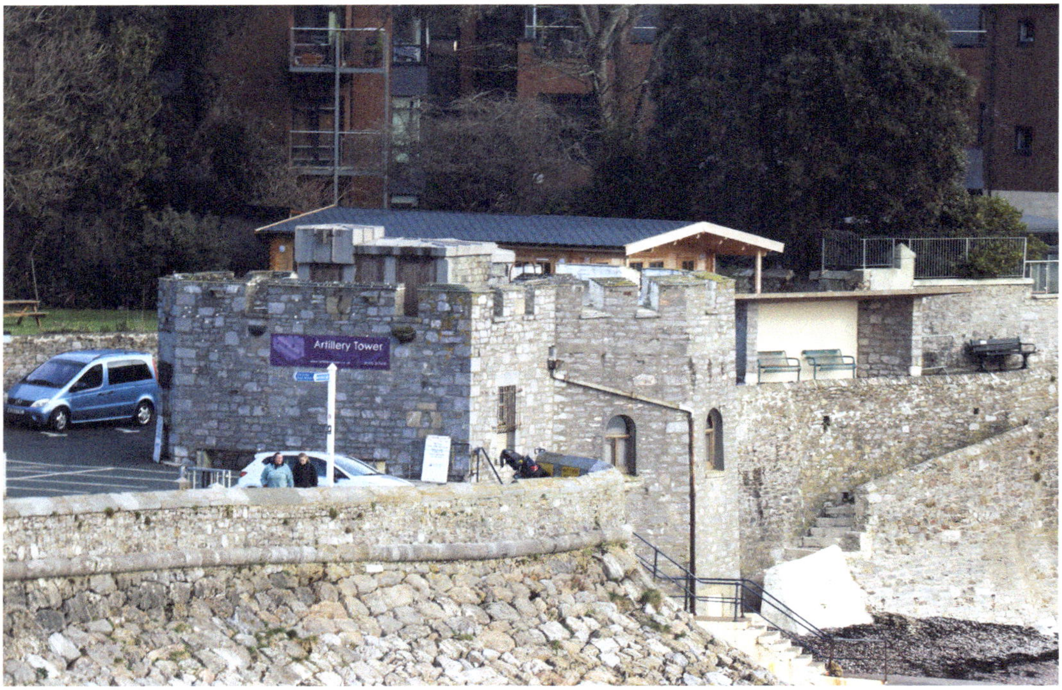

Above: The Artillery Tower, now a restaurant.

Below: Drake's Island.

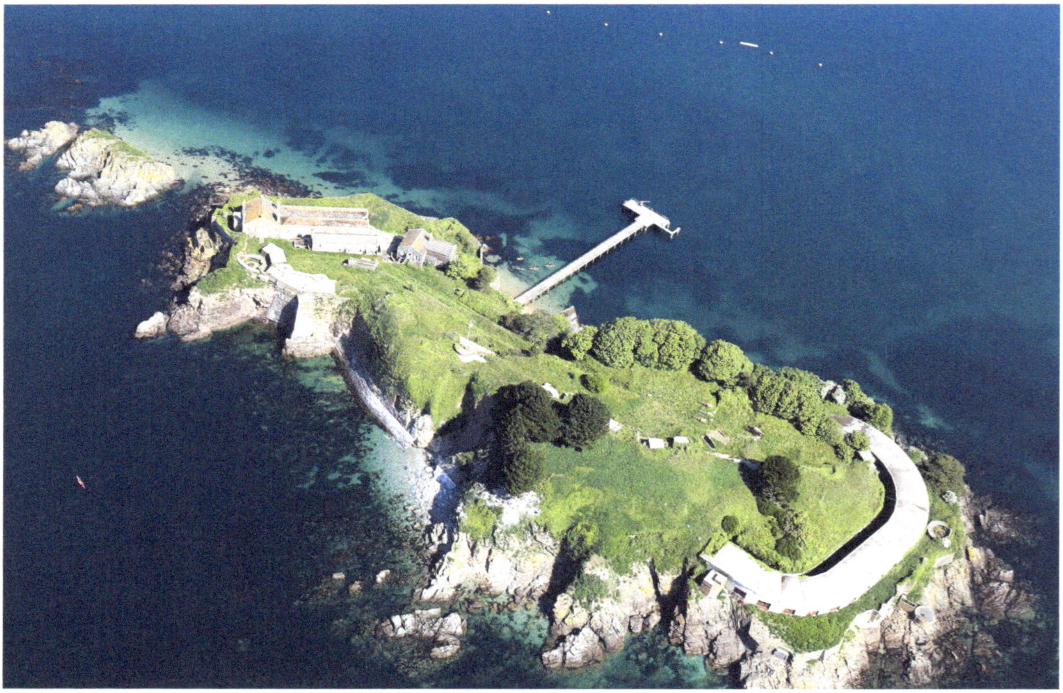

In the seventeenth century Charles II decided to build a much larger fort on the Hoe, which would surround and incorporate Drake's original fort, and work commenced in 1665. This was named the Royal Citadel and is still with us, and still in use by the army to the present day. Built around the same time, completed in 1667, was an artillery battery on the other side of Sutton Harbour, later named Queen Anne's Battery. As far as I can tell from the census reports none of the above-mentioned blockhouses, nor this battery, were manned by the nineteenth century.

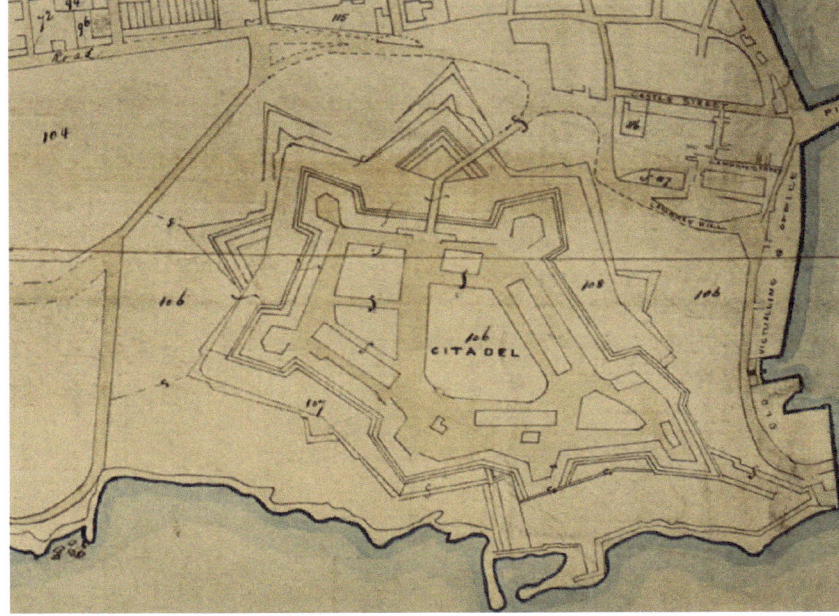

Citadel map from an 1840 tithe map. (Courtesy of Devon Archives & Local Studies Service)

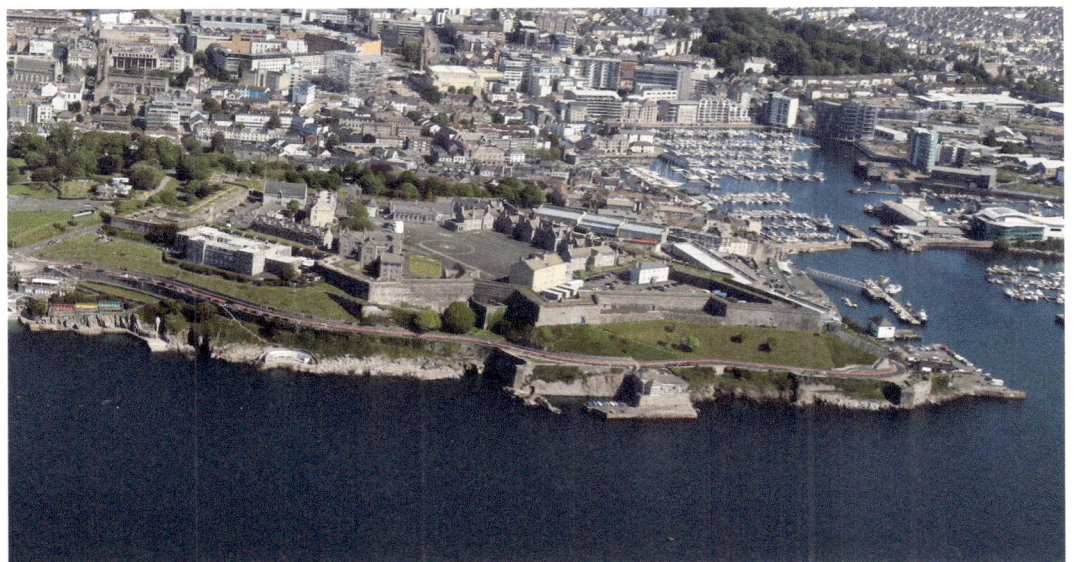

Royal Citadel with Fisher's Nose blockhouse in front.

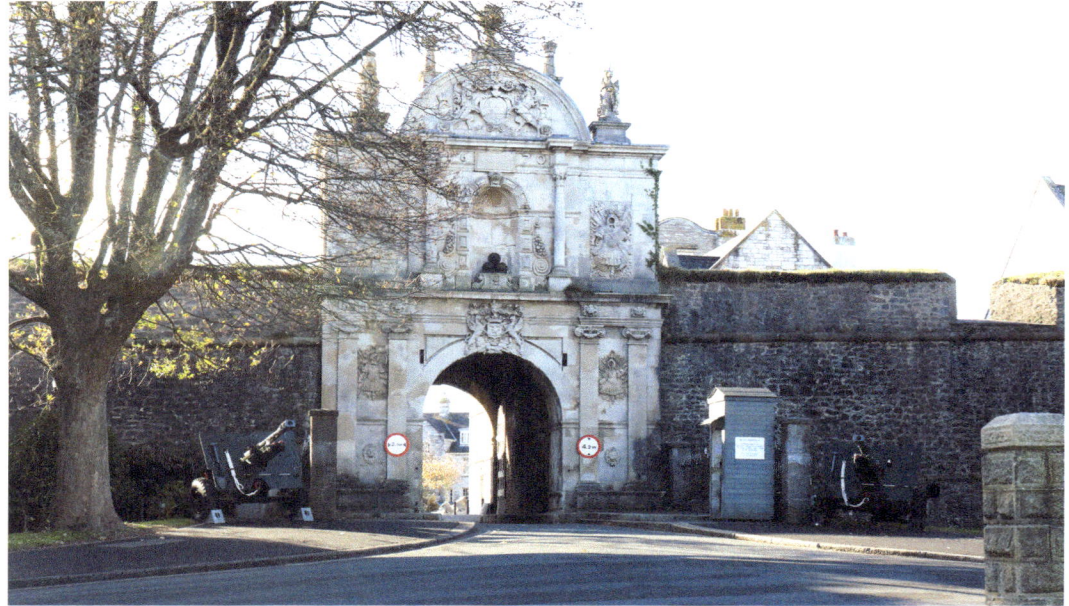

Royal Citadel gatehouse.

As mentioned elsewhere the dockyard opened by 1700, giving the Royal Navy a home in Plymouth for the repair and building of ships, although at that time there was no shore base. Sailors waiting for postings lived on hulks – old ships anchored in the Hamoaze.

Between 1756 and 1785 Plymouth completed the hat-trick by building Stonehouse Barracks as a home for the more recently formed (1664) Royal Marines, then known as the Duke of York and Albany's Maritime Regiment of Foot. The barracks as built then was much smaller than the modern one, consisting of little more than the modern parade ground with the original entrance being on the long-gone northern part of Barrack Lane. There was at that time a row of houses lining the eastern side of Durnford Street where the impressive modern entrance, built in 1867, now stands. The southern end of Barrack Lane is the modern Admiralty Street. The modern barracks have also extended east to include the old Stonehouse Prison and part of Millbay Docks adjacent to the ferry terminal and car park.

By the mid-eighteenth century it was realised that the dockyard was vulnerable to attack by both seaborne raiders coming into the Sound, which the existing defences could counter, and from land by forces landing elsewhere, which they could not, so a defensive ditch was dug around the outside of the town of Dock (as it was then called), enclosing and protecting the dockyard. This was known as 'The Dock Lines' and it stretched from the River Tamar north of the Gun Wharf in Morice Yard around to the Tamar again below Mount Wise, effectively putting the whole town of Dock under military control. In 1787 this was further fortified by the addition of six barracks, known as squares, and a wall, known as the King's Interior Boundary Wall. It's amazing to think now that anyone entering or leaving Devonport from Plymouth had to do so via a defended arch at Stonehouse Hill; those entering via Fore Street or what we now call Marlborough Street had to do so via what the tithe map of 1841 called 'Barrier Gate with drawbridge'! The seaborne defences were further strengthened by the addition of various fortifications along the shore, including the redoubt at Western King, to protect the dockyard from seaborne attack.

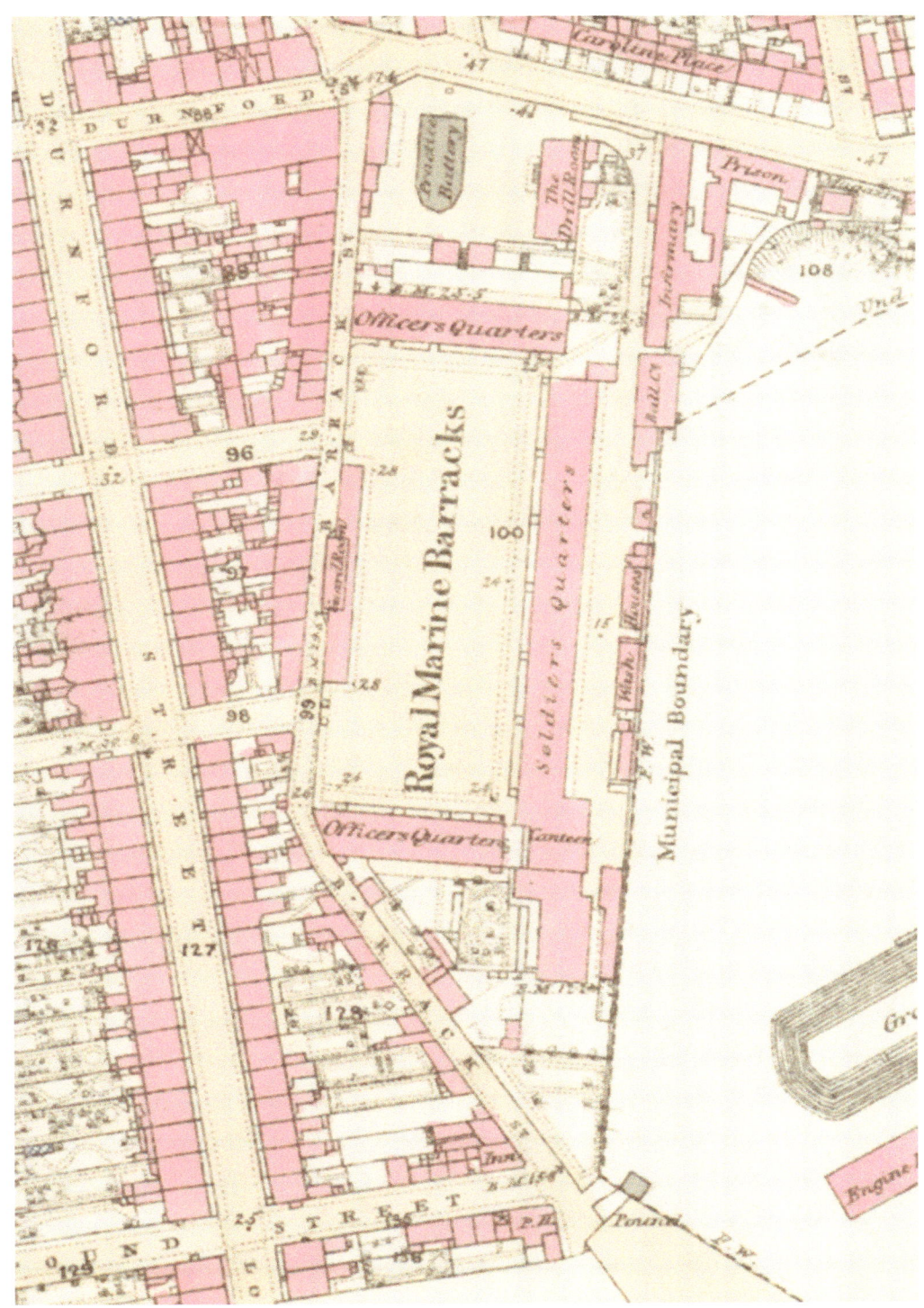

Stonehouse Barracks from an 1866 OS map. (Courtesy of the National Library for Scotland)

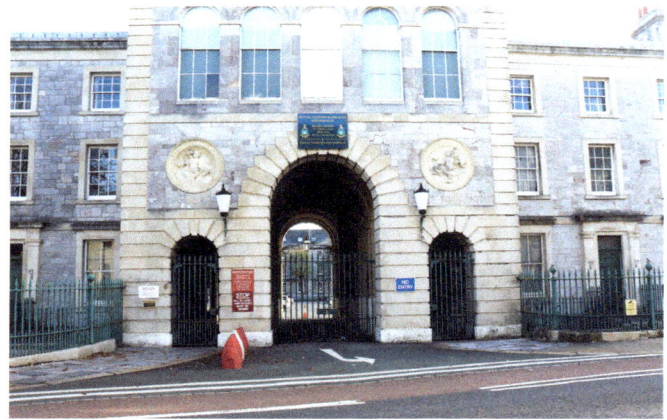

Left: Stonehouse Barracks gatehouse.

Below: Devonport lines from an 1840 tithe map. (Courtesy of Devon Archives & Local Studies Service)

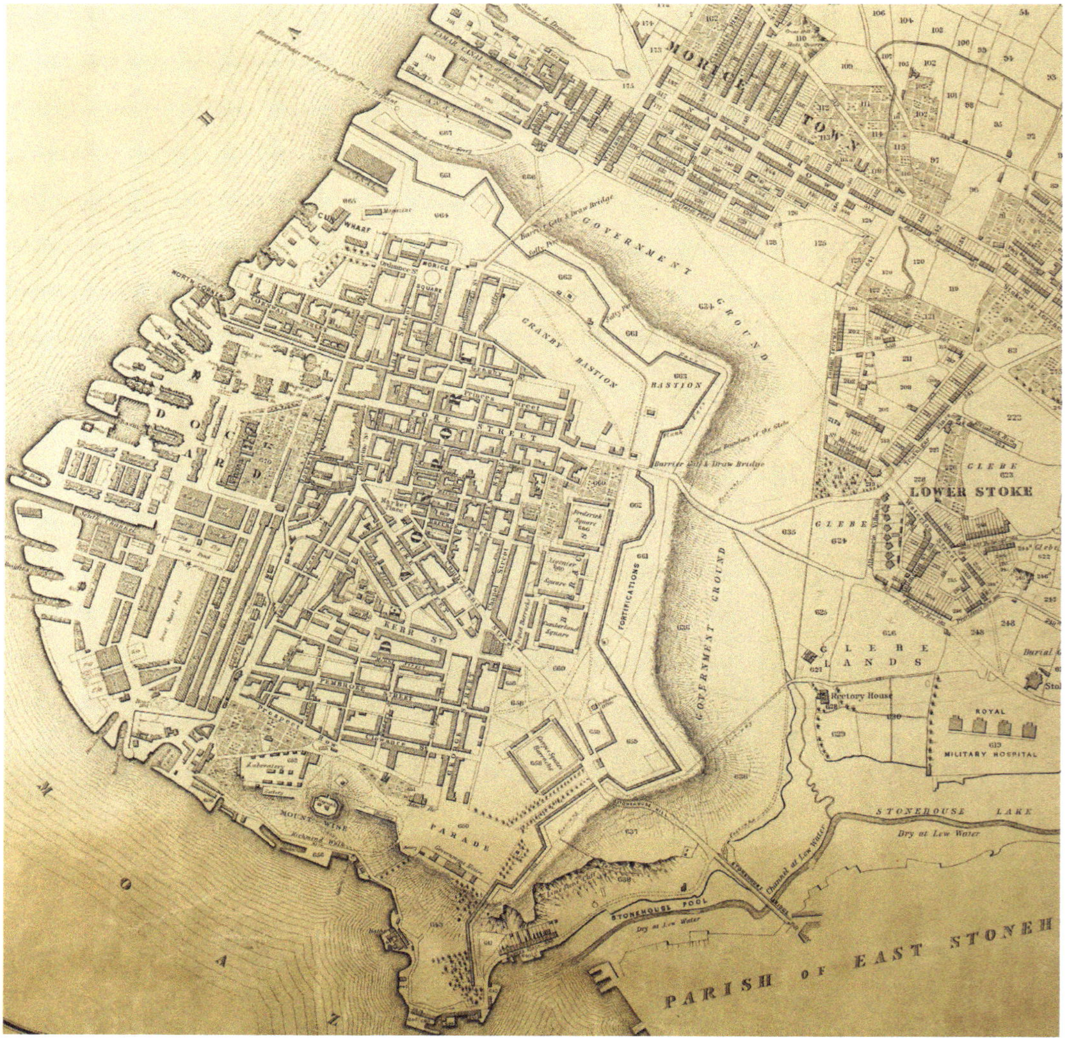

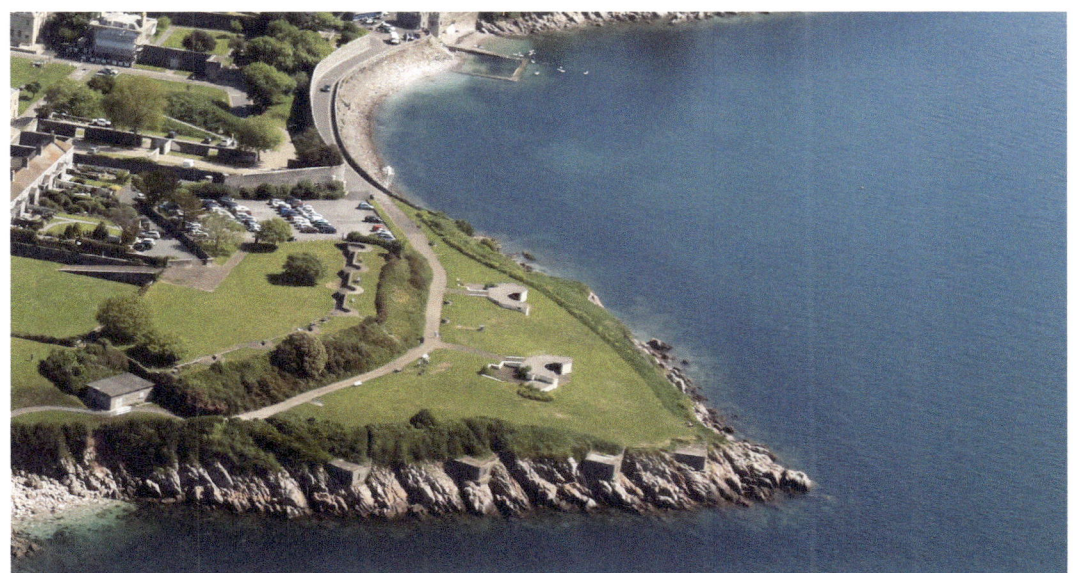

Above: Western King Battery from the air.

Below: Western King ground view.

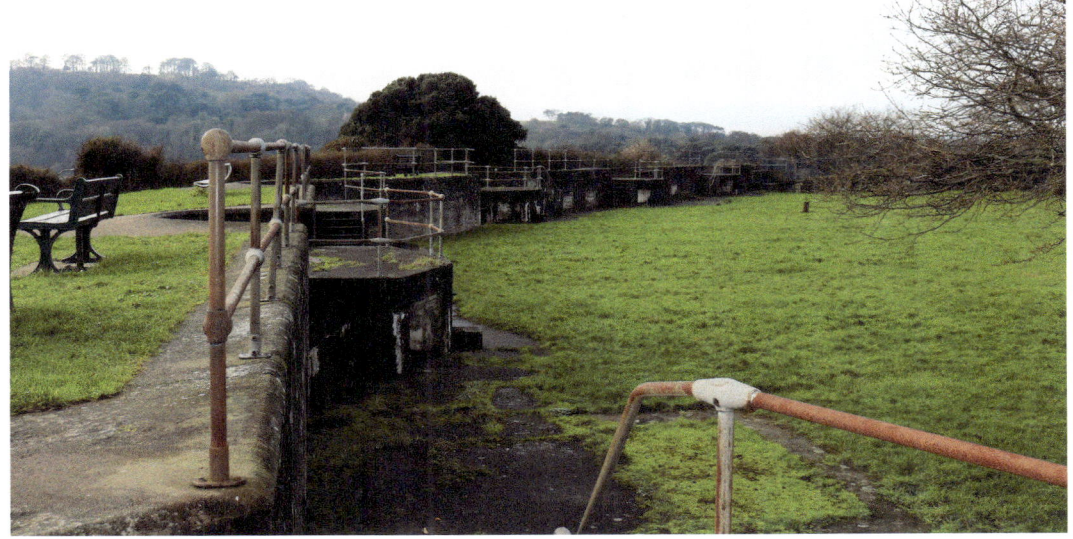

From the 1850s onwards the old squares were demolished and replaced by Raglan Barracks; the drawbridges were demolished in the 1860s. Amazingly, however, there are still a few traces of the lines in existence. Bluff Battery (overlooking Richmond Walk and Stonehouse Hill) was built to defend the lines and is still there, plus a few parts of the old wall at the top of Devonport Hill. There is also what looks very much like a defensive ditch behind Bluff Battery but this does not appear on any map before the 1880s so was probably cut to allow the access between Richmond Walk and Devonport Hill.

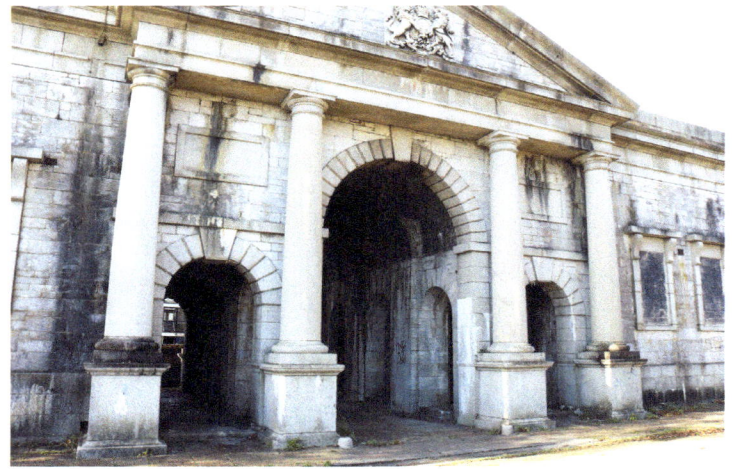

Raglan Barracks entrance.

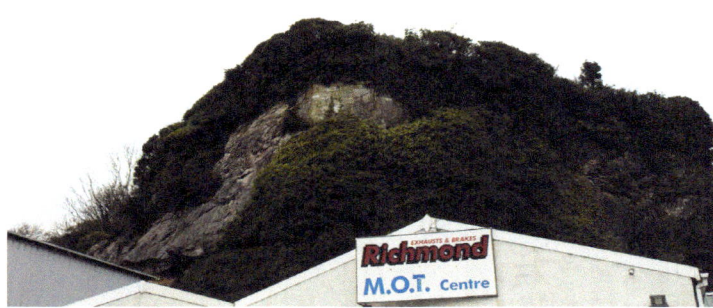

Left: The much-overgrown Bluff Battery.

Below: Traces of the Devonport Lines still existing.

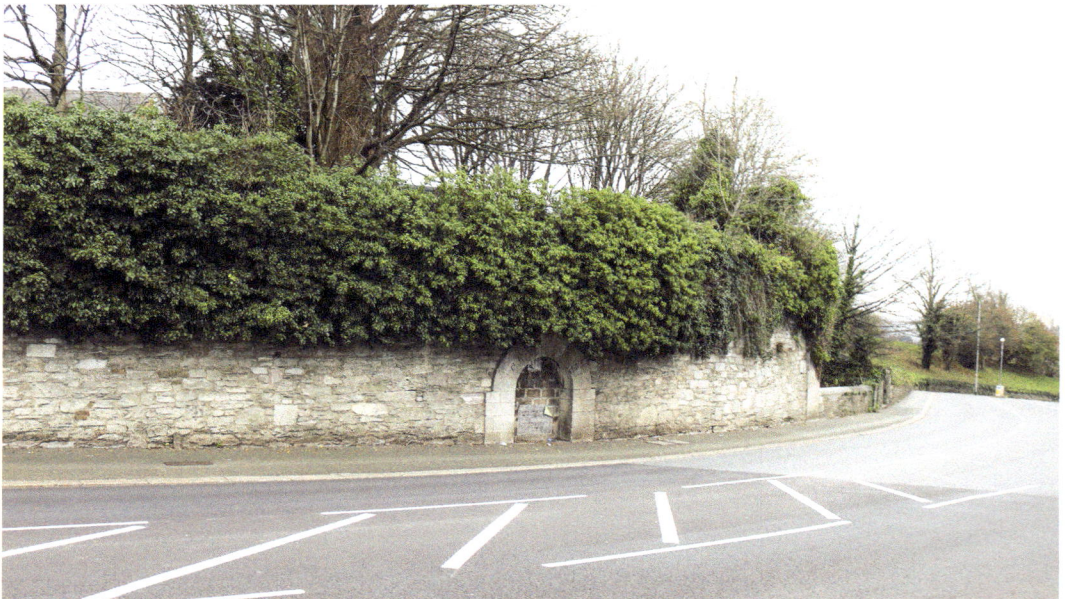

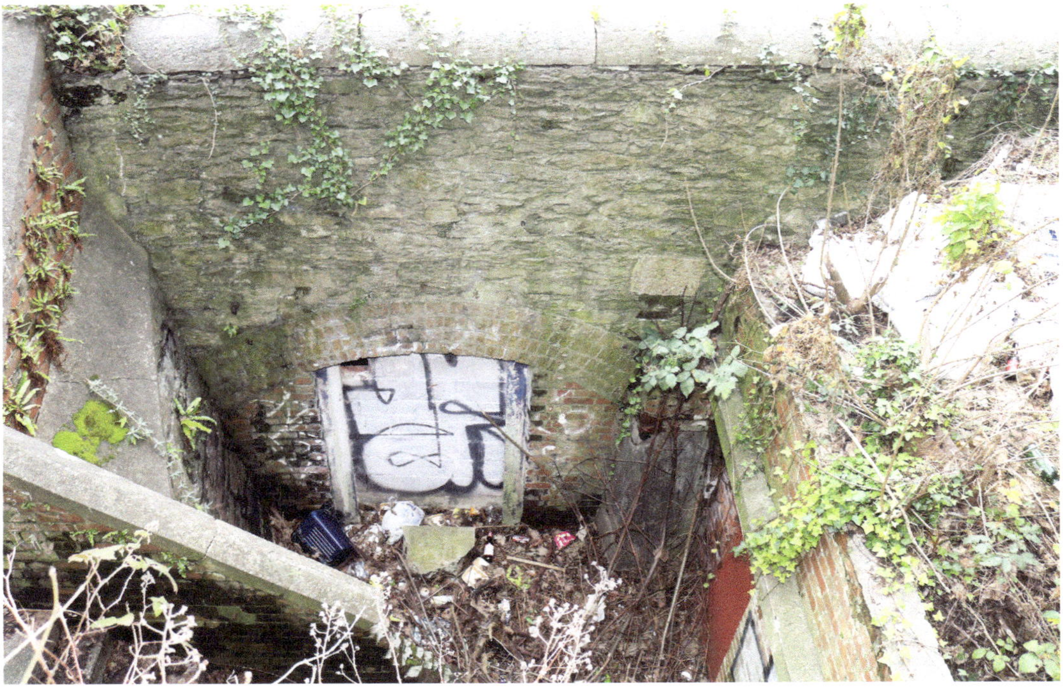

Above: Steps leading down to remains of the lines.

Below: Cavernous tunnel under Devonport Hill.

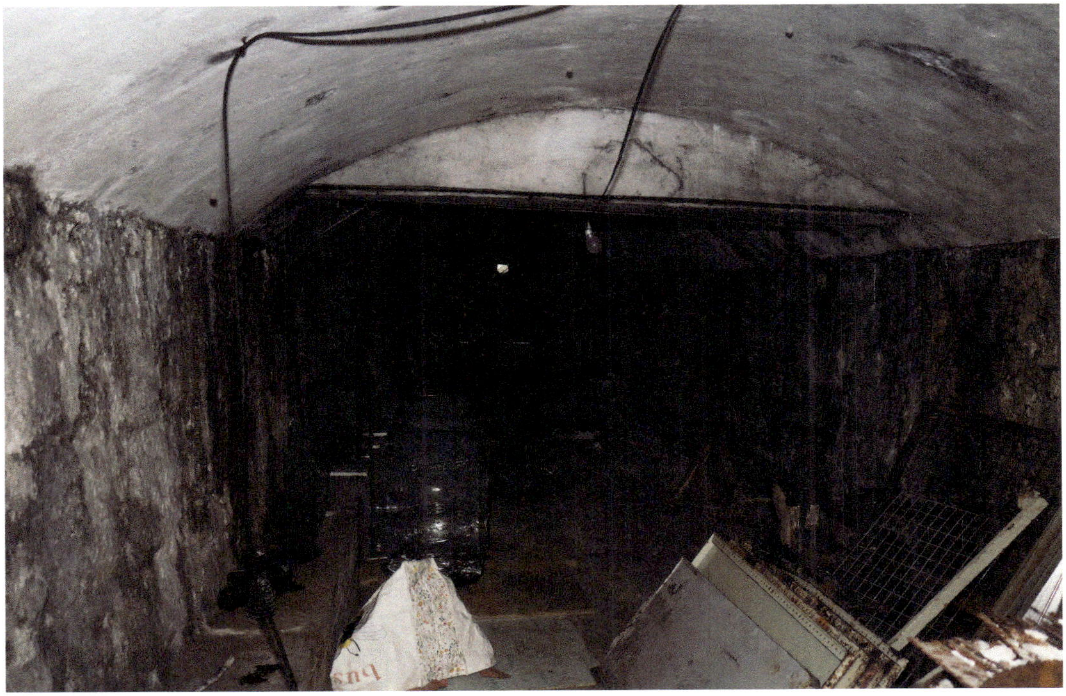

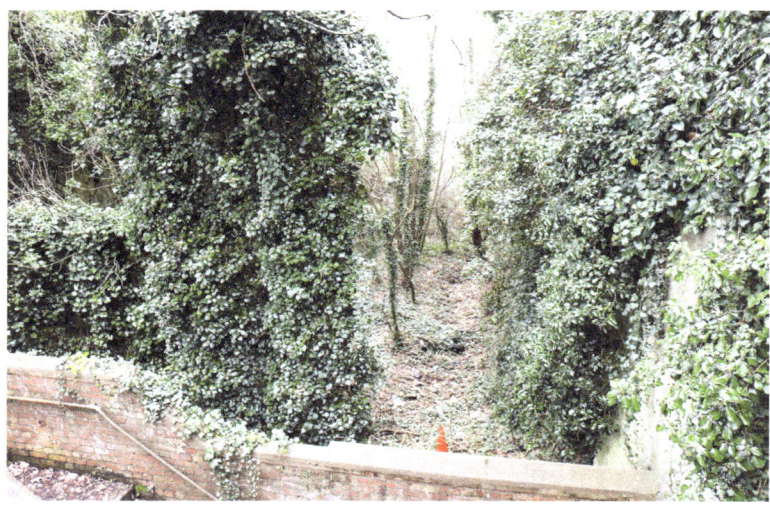

Ditch behind Bluff Battery.

Near to Raglan Barracks was Mount Wise, and a plan of 1811 shows the Royal Laboratory, built for the Board of Ordnance. It comprised a collection of widely spaced buildings for the manufacture of musket cartridges and other ammunition and explosive devices such as rockets, used by the Royal Navy. The complex was converted to barracks by 1834, and remained in military use well into the twentieth century.

Yet more military connections exist such as that in Millbay, where the early eighteenth-century prison, used at different times to house prisoners from wars with France and America, became Millbay Barracks in the early nineteenth century.

After the defeat of Napoleon Bonaparte in 1815 there was something of a hiatus as far as the military were concerned. After 1815 there were minor wars going on somewhere, but our next major war was in the Crimea from 1853 to 1856, so the 1840s were likely to have been relatively quiet. Despite that the 1841 census shows many hundreds of people from a wide variety of regiments living in the already existing fortifications and barracks around the Three Towns.

In 1841 Bull Point Barracks, then recently built to defend Bull Point Ordnance Yard, was home to the Sherwood Foresters under Captain Pearse. With their families the number totalled ninety-one.

In the Citadel was the 53rd (Shropshire) Regiment of Foot with a major as Commanding Officer (CO), total 746.

In Devonport lines:

Cumberland Square barracks had a major from the 85th, the King's Regiment of Light Infantry (Bucks Volunteers) as Officer Commanding (OC). Total 195.
Frederick Square had as OC a lieutenant from the Royal Artillery (RA). Total 92.
George Square had a lieutenant-colonel of 11th (North Devonshire) Regiment of Foot as OC. Total 235.
Granby Barracks had as OC an assistant surgeon (although with no sign of which regiment he was from). Total 79.
Ligonier Barracks had as OC a lieutenant-colonel of the 11th Regiment. 186 Total
Picquet Barracks were almost empty. A garrison sergeant major from the 85th Regiment plus various people the 11th Regiment. Including families this totalled 78.

Drakes Island was almost a married quarter. The 53rd Regiment were there under a lieutenant. Including various family members this totalled 56.
Millbay Barracks also had the 53rd Regiment under a lieutenant. Total 219
Mount Wise Barracks was also home to the 11th Regiment, with a major as OC. Total 273.
Stonehouse Barracks had two colonels RM, presumably one of them was OC. Total 437.

This means that in 1841 there were a total of 2,687 people living in the barracks mentioned above, the vast majority serving in the military and all relying on it. As the naval personnel were living on the hulks and many more soldiers were living with their families in rented houses throughout the area I have not included them in the calculation, so the final total would be many more. (Just as an aside, two of the regiments named above who had been garrisoned in Plymouth in 1841, the 53rd and the 85th, were amalgamated in 1881 to become the King's Shropshire Light Infantry.)

Bull Point Barracks was built as a defensible barrack to house the soldiers who guarded the Ordnance Depot at Bull Point. This still stands in more or less original condition and is described by Historic England as 'the only barracks (defensible) built around Devonport for the defence of the Dockyard which still remains'.

By the late nineteenth century the military landscape of Plymouth had changed radically. During the 1860s tensions grew between Britain and France, so by 1872 a ring of forts, including a larger one on Drake's Island to replace the pre-existing Tudor one, plus a tower inside the Breakwater, had been built to protect the city from the expected French invasion.

The so-called Palmerston forts started to be built in 1863 and were finished between 1868 and 1871 so none were likely to have been manned by the 1871 census, although according to *Plymouth:*

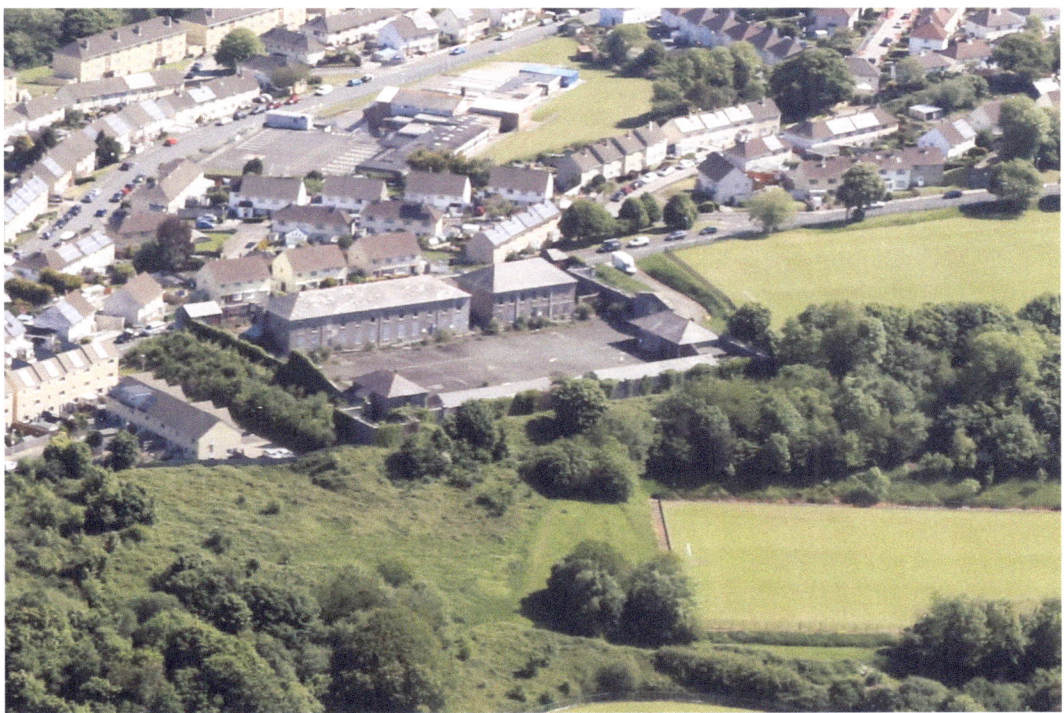

Bull Point from the air.

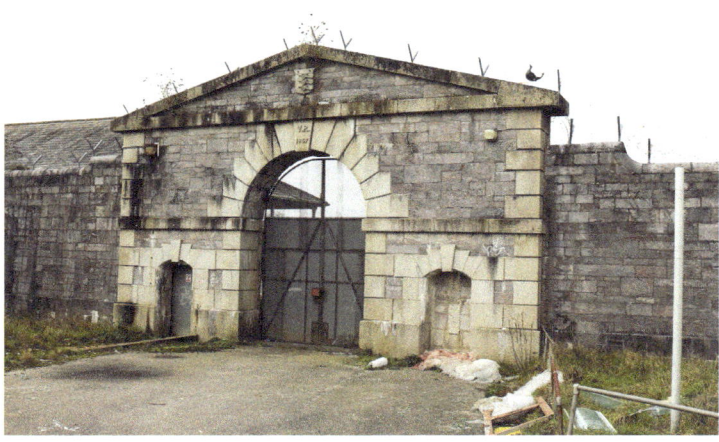
Bull Point gatehouse.

A Maritime City in Transition by Brian Chalkley, David Dunkerley and Peter Gripaios, that year's census showed a total of 2,982 soldiers and marines billeted in the three towns with a further 6,370 sailors on board the ships in the port.

Lord Palmerston died in 1865 before any of the forts had been completed. Their use seems patchy, with some used rarely, others as far as I can tell never having been manned at census time, if at all. The Palmerston forts formed a ring around Plymouth, stretching from Tregantle in the west to Bovisand in the east, but as with everything else in this book I am restricting my interest to the ones in the Plymouth area. These are Agaton

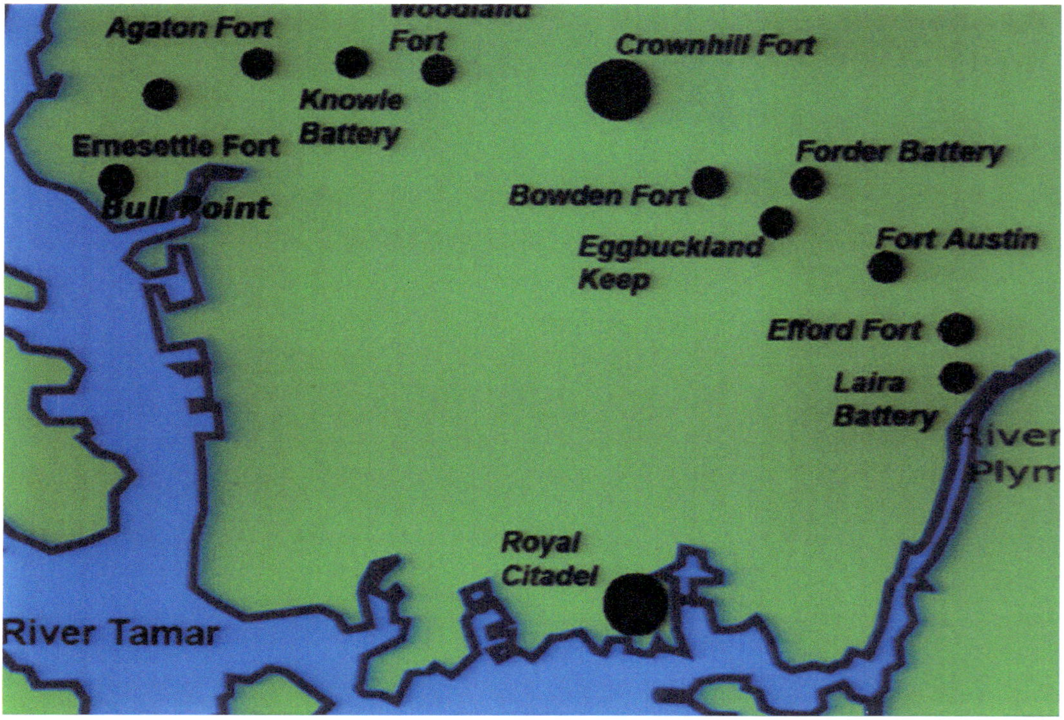

The Victorian-era forts.

Fort, Bowden Battery, Crownhill Fort, Efford Fort, Eggbuckland Keep, Ernesettle Fort, Forder Battery, Fort Austin, Knowle Battery, Laira Battery and Woodland Fort. If manned as planned they alone would have needed 931 soldiers, manning a total of 174 guns, but few if any seem to have ever had their full complement of either.

By 1901 the military landscape had changed significantly, with many more places needing personnel. The 1901 census tells a completely different story from that of sixty years previously. The Palmerston forts were complete but by then obsolete. When built they were impregnable, with solid walls and with cannon in casemates or behind thick walls to protect them against anything an enemy could throw at them. Any infantry attempting to storm the forts would have to climb down into and run across the defensive ditch, allowing troops inside the caponiers, bastions on each corner of the fort with musket slots and cannon casemates, to mow them down in a murderous crossfire.

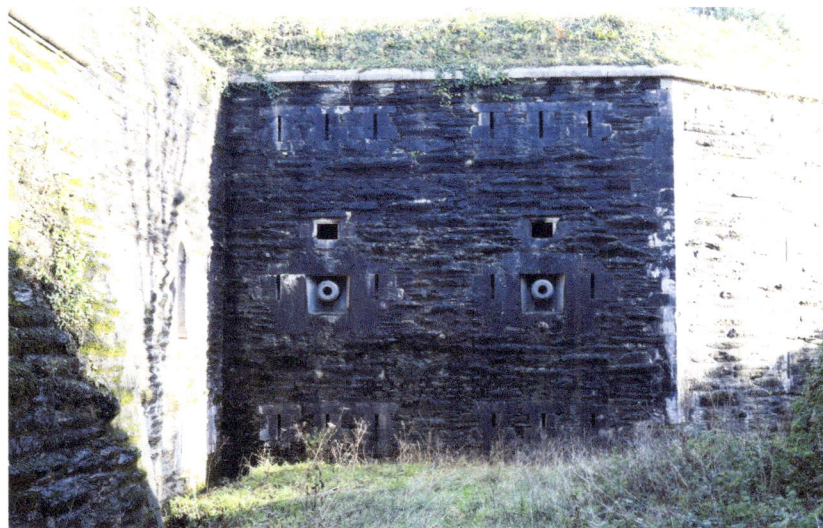

A view along Crownhill Fort's defensive ditch towards a caponier.

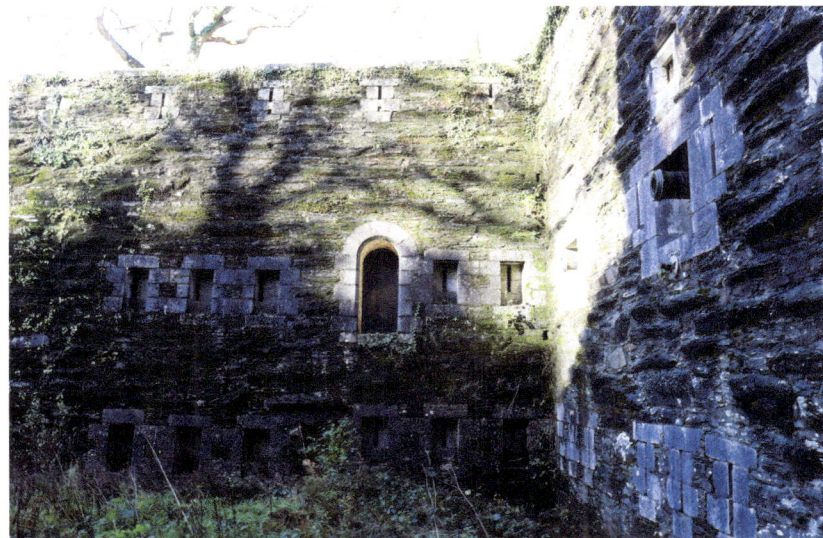

Close-up of the caponier showing the mouths of the cannon plus lots of rifle slits.

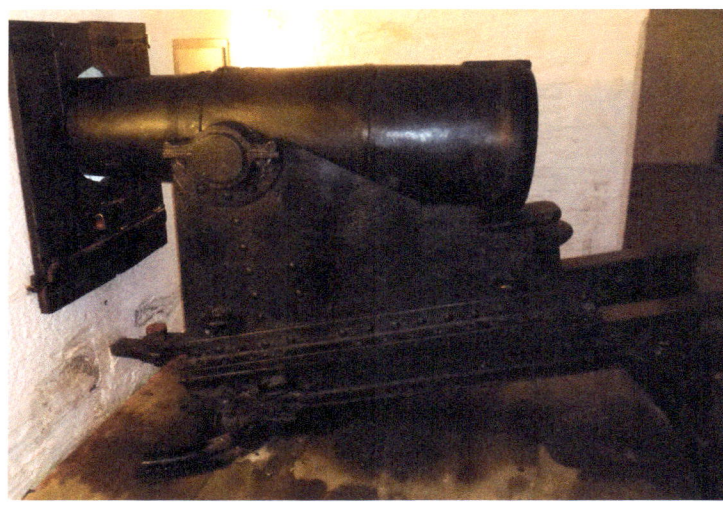

32-pounder cannon inside the east caponier. (Care of Landmark Trust)

Heavy siege howitzers first came into use in 1880s. These immediately rendered all the Palmerston forts obsolete because instead of any attacker having to try to batter down the impregnable walls they allowed him to lob shells over those walls and assail the defenders inside. There would no longer be any need to attempt to storm the forts, as the enemy could sit outside and lob shells in until the defenders surrendered.

As an aside much later during the Second World War, Fort Eben-Emael was a supposedly impregnable Belgian fort, designed and built in the mid-1930s to protect Belgium from German attack and thought to be the strongest fortress in the world. Although built much later, it was constructed along similar lines to the Palmerston forts. Nazi paratroops and gliders simply came from above and took the place by surprise, defeating the Belgian forces.

After this enormous expense the forts were never needed. By 1871 Napoleon III had been defeated in the Franco-Prussian war (fleeing to exile in England!) and the forts became known as Palmerston's Follies, after the prime minister who had ordered their construction. Despite being obsolete the forts were generally used in some way, as can be seen from the census results below.

Also new were the RN barracks to the north of the dockyard, which were completed by 1889 to replace most of the hulks that had previously housed sailors whose ships were under repair or refit, and those awaiting posting.

The old Emigration Depot below the Citadel, which had been built in 1847 to facilitate people who wanted to emigrate to America, Canada or Australia, became redundant when those countries stopped their assisted passages in 1897. The building was taken over by the Torpedo Depot of the Royal Engineers and renamed Elphinstone Barracks.

So, in the 1901 census we find:

Agaton Fort had a bombardier from the Royal Artillery and two gunners. Total 3.
Bull Point Barracks was commanded by a lieutenant from the Tipperary Artillery Militia. Total 43 people.
The Royal Citadel was commanded by a major from the Royal Artillery. Total 333 people.
Crownhill was very complicated by this time because now there was a barracks, a married quarters, the fort and Crownhill huts. As far as I can make out the barracks and married

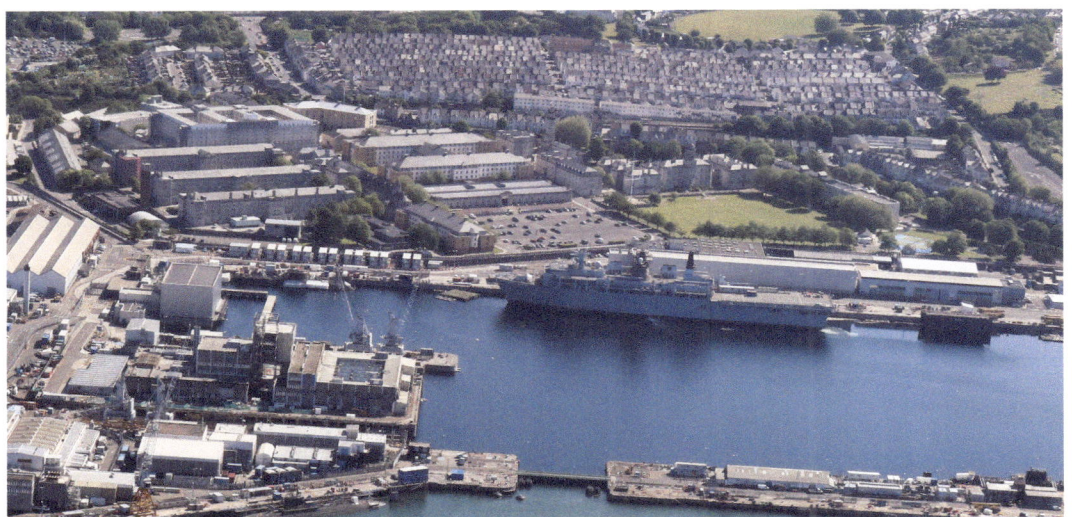

HMS Drake top right beside the dockyard's No. 5 basin.

quarters were what became Plumer Barracks, the huts became Seaton Barracks and the fort was separate.

First the barracks, which at that time housed the Royal Welch Fusiliers (RWF) and was commanded by two majors RWF. Total 307.

The married quarters had a total of 120 people living there.

The fort itself housed the RA under the command of a lieutenant from the Durham Artillery. Total 37.

The huts were commanded by a lieutenant from the Royal Engineers (RE). Total 33.

Drake's Island was commanded by a corporal from the Royal Garrison Artillery (RGA) with a bombardier and four gunners plus two civilians, one with his wife. Total 9.

Efford Fort had a corporal RGA with three gunners, plus eighteen family members in the married quarters. Total 22.

Elphinstone Barracks housed the Royal Engineers under a quarter master sergeant (QMS). Total 156.

Ernesettle Fort is mentioned for the only time but with nobody there! It is listed on the census form as unoccupied.

Knowle Battery also has its only appearance, manned by a gunner RA, his wife and two children. Total 4.

Millbay Barracks was commanded by two 2nd lieutenants RGA. Total 234.

Mount Wise barracks had a captain RE. Total 50.

Now we come to Raglan Barracks where every regiment seems to have had very mixed-up personnel. Firstly Granby Barracks, which seems to have had a huge mix of mainly married personnel living there. I will list the census return in full to give an idea how complex it was.

The most senior officer was a lieutenant/riding master from the Army Service Corps (ASC) with his wife, family and servants. From the same regiment there were two company sergeant majors (CSM) and two staff sergeant majors, two staff sergeants saddlers, two staff sergeants wheelers all with families, a company QMS, seven sergeants, eight corporals, 5 lance corporals (L/Cpl), 203 drivers and fourteen privates.

There was also a warrant officer (WO) on the garrison staff and there were from the Royal Artillery a regimental sergeant major (RSM), a WO, two CSMs, a sergeant and two gunners with families.

From the Royal Engineers there were two staff sergeants with family, two QMS, a sergeant, a corporal, two lance corporals (L/Cpl), a sapper, an electrician with family and fifteen drivers.

From the Royal Garrison Artillery there was a sergeant, a bombardier, nineteen gunners and four trumpeters.

From the Army Ordnance Corp there were a CSM and a sergeant, a staff armourer and six privates.

Now for the odds and ends! There was a QMS Prison Dept, a sergeant infantry, a sergeant from the Duke of Cornwall's Light Infantry with family, a sergeant from the Military Fort Police with family, a sergeant military police, a sergeant musketry instructor with family, a sergeant from the Army Gymnastic staff, four corporals from the Army Pay Corps, several soldiers from unnamed regiments with families, a soldier, Somerset Light Infantry, three soldiers from the Military Police, several families of absent soldiers, fourteen privates, infantry, a driver, Royal Field Artillery, a private, Army Pay Corps, a private, Royal Welch Regiment, two privates from the Royal Marine Light Infantry (RMLI) and twenty-three civilians. Total 675 people.

The Raglan Married Quarters had four barrack wardens with a total of 270 people.

Raglan Barracks North had as CO a lieutenant-colonel from the 5th Provisional Battalion. Total 409.

Raglan Barracks South had as CO a major from the Gloucester Regiment. Total 281.

RN Barracks (known as HMS Vivid) Officers' Quarters had a commander RN. Total 17.

The main barracks had a Boatswain and his wife as the only family, plus 879 other ranks including a couple of sergeants RM, a petty officer RN, but mainly seamen, stokers and marines. Total 883.

Stonehouse Barracks had as OC a colonel commandant with his wife and servants. Total 906 people.

Woodland Fort had thirty members of the RGA, all teenage boys plus just a bombardier and three gunners. Possibly a training establishment? Total 34 people.

Who knew there were so many ranks and regiments? This means that in 1901, despite the forts being so sparsely populated, a total of 4,826 people entirely dependent on the military were living in barracks around Plymouth, with hundreds more service personnel living in private houses around the city. Despite the opening of HMS Vivid barracks there were still several groups of training ships anchored in the Hamoaze, including HMS *Indus* (artificers), HMS *Cambridge* (gunnery), HMS *Defiance* off Weard Quay on the Lynher (torpedos and mines) and the long established HMS *Impregnable* moored off Cremyll (boys training). Many of these survived after the First World War with HMS *Defiance*, in its third guise (the renamed HMS *Vulcan*), lasting until the 1950s and HMS *Cambridge* becoming a shore station at Wembury Point until 2001. It is perhaps surprising that Raglan Barracks remained in use until after the Second World War and it was demolished in 1969, leaving just the gatehouse to remind us of its existence.

Despite never being used in anger against their original threat and having been rendered obsolete by modern munitions the Palmerston forts were very solid structures that still belonged to the military and many were used during the Second World War as garrisons, storage areas and bases for anti-aircraft batteries. Many of them had to be manned for many years and some, including Crownhill Fort, were still owned and operated by the army until the 1980s. They have now been taken over for various uses as detailed below.

Agaton Fort now has the local VOSA Test station built on its old parade ground and despite the original buildings being blocked up and not used they are kept in good order.

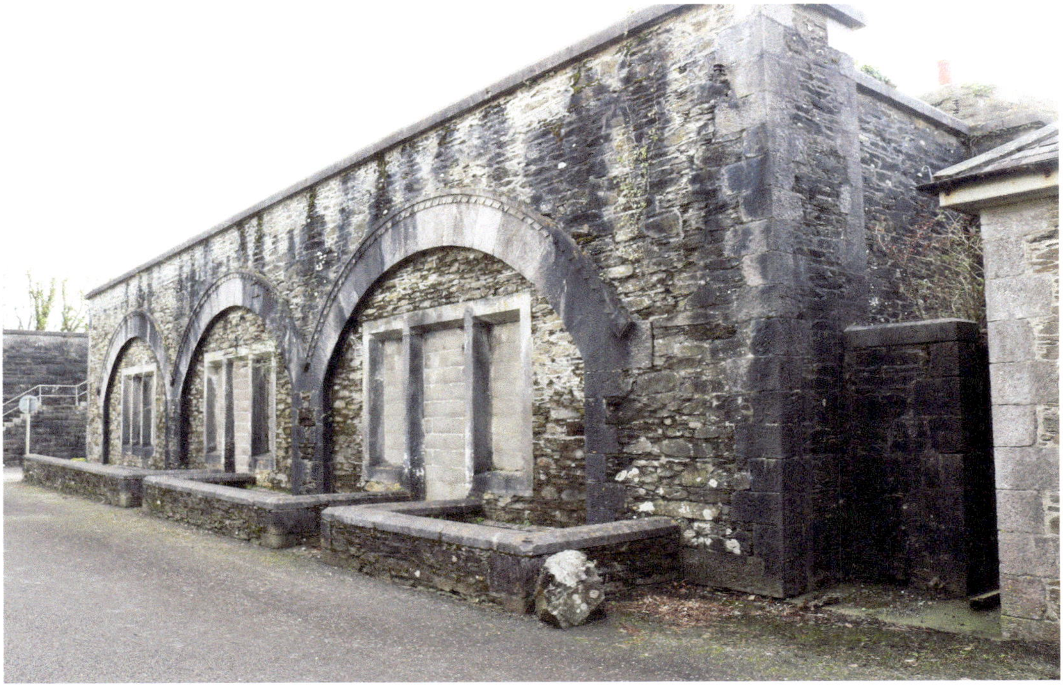

The Military

Above: Agaton Fort's accommodation.

Below: Access steps inside Agaton Fort's main gate.

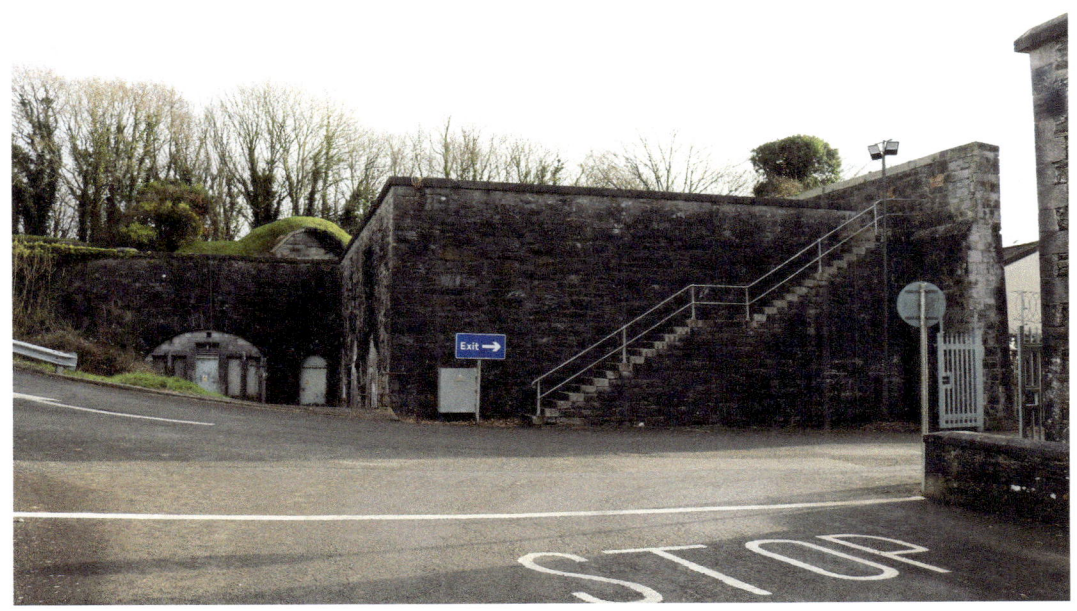

Fort Austin was used for many years by Plymouth City Council as a depot. The gatehouse was Plymouth's Emergency Centre until 1992, where presumably our lords and masters on the council would go in the event of nuclear war, leaving the rest of us to die of radiation sickness. The council moved out some time ago and for a while the fort was home to several businesses. It is currently empty.

As with most of these forts it had a defensive ditch, but this was down the hillside to the north. It had a caponier located on the outside of the ditch, known as the counterscarp, reached by tunnels from the fort, which went via a mortar pit part way down.

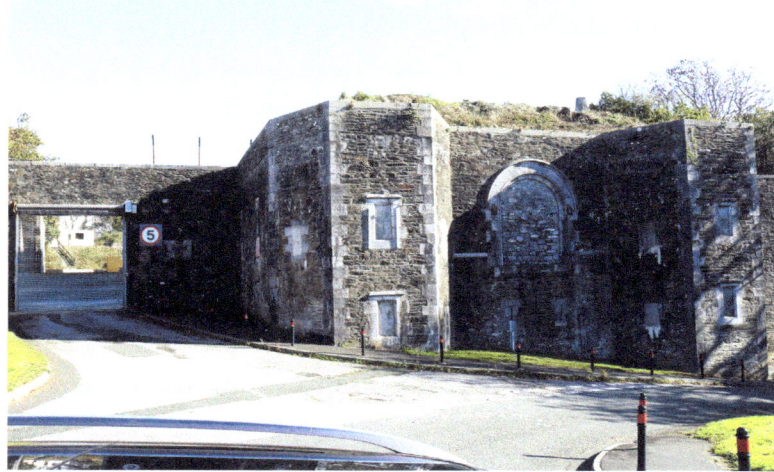

Left: Fort Austin.

Below: Counterscarp caponier.

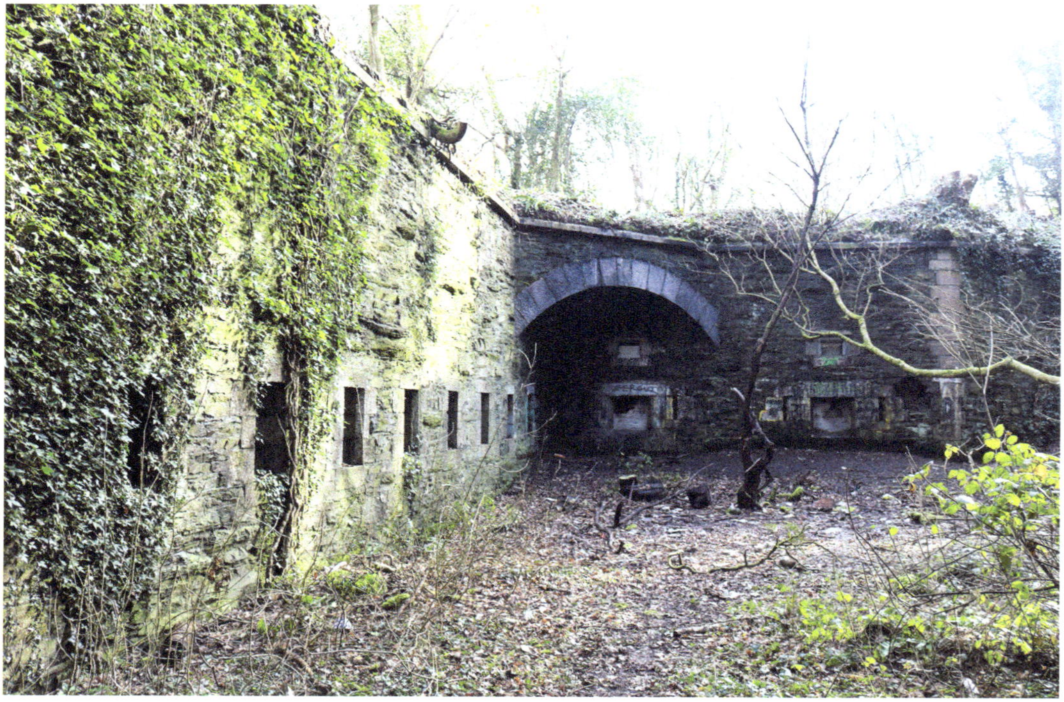

The Military

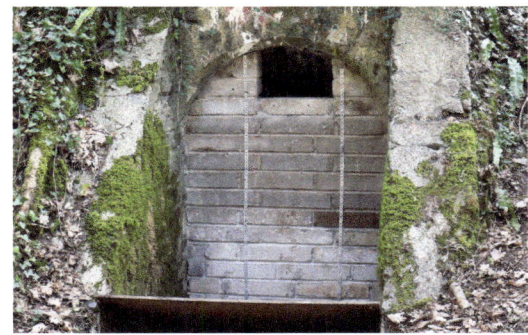 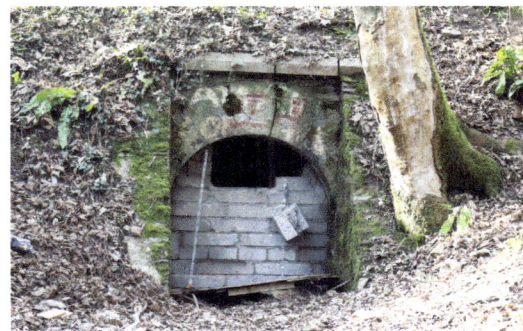

Above left: Blocked tunnel access to the caponier.

Above right: Blocked tunnel from Fort Austin to the mortar pit.

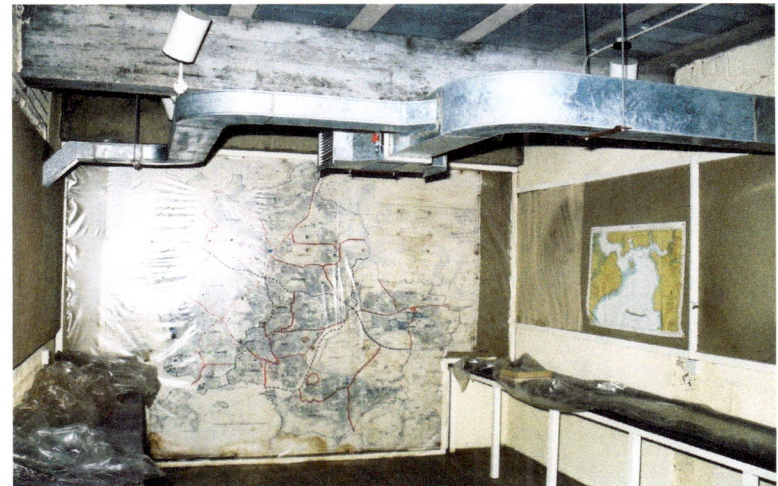

The interior of the bunker at Fort Austin. (Courtesy of Steve Johnson, Cyberheritage)

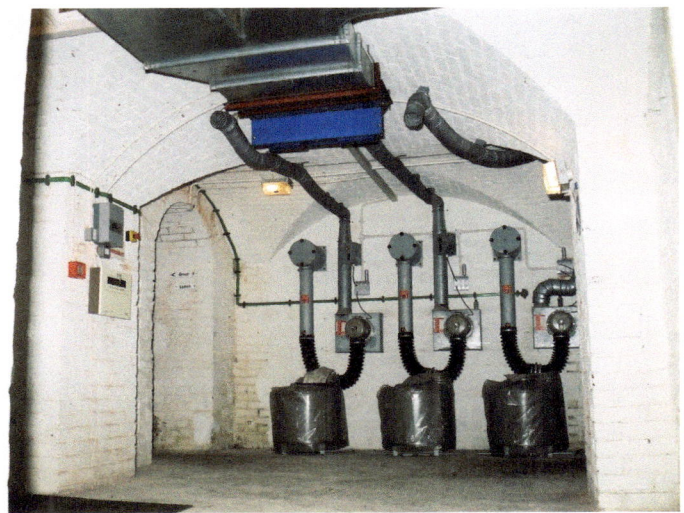

Austin's bunker ventilation system. (Courtesy of Steve Johnson, Cyberheritage)

Bowden Fort is a very successful and long-standing garden centre, although its entrance gate has been demolished.

Efford is used as winter storage showmans' caravans.

Eggbuckland Keep was at one time a DIY store and has recently been sold.

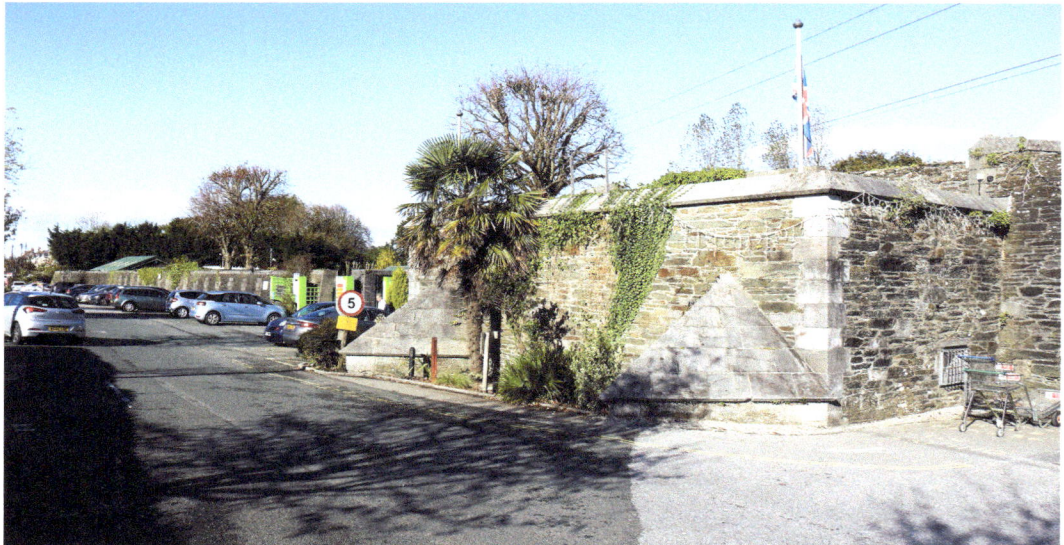

Above: Bowden Fort.

Below: Efford Fort gatehouse.

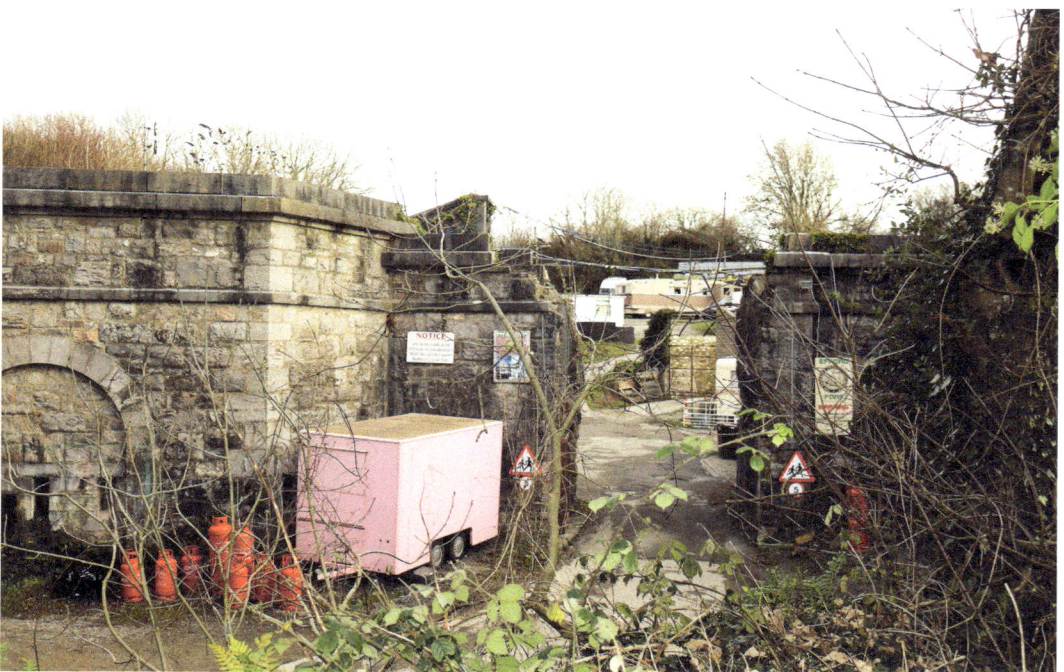

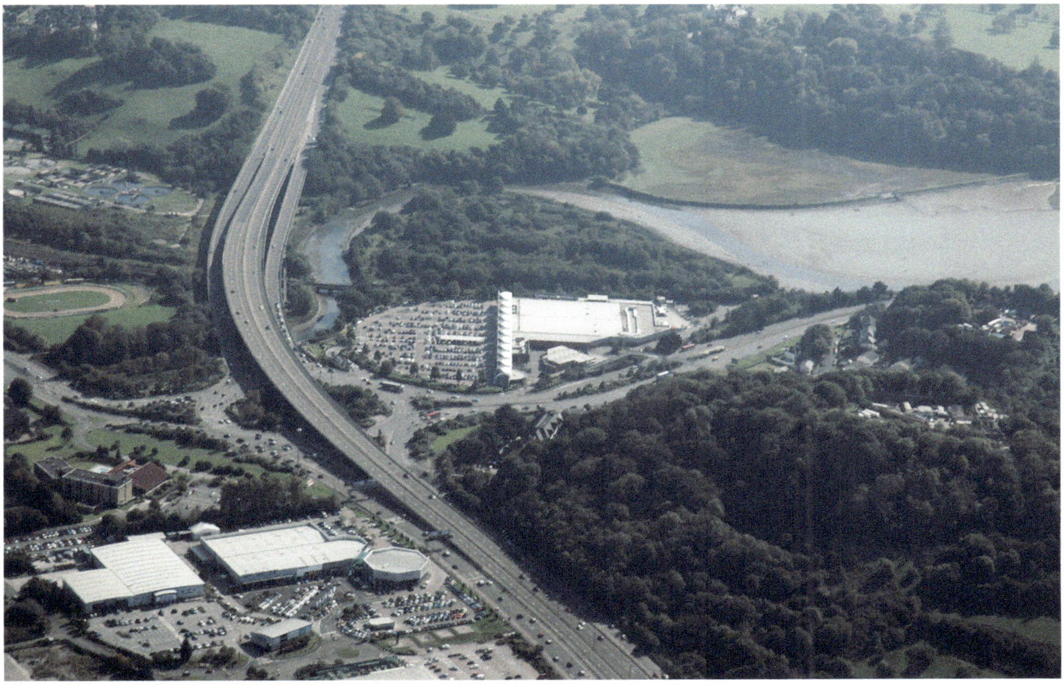

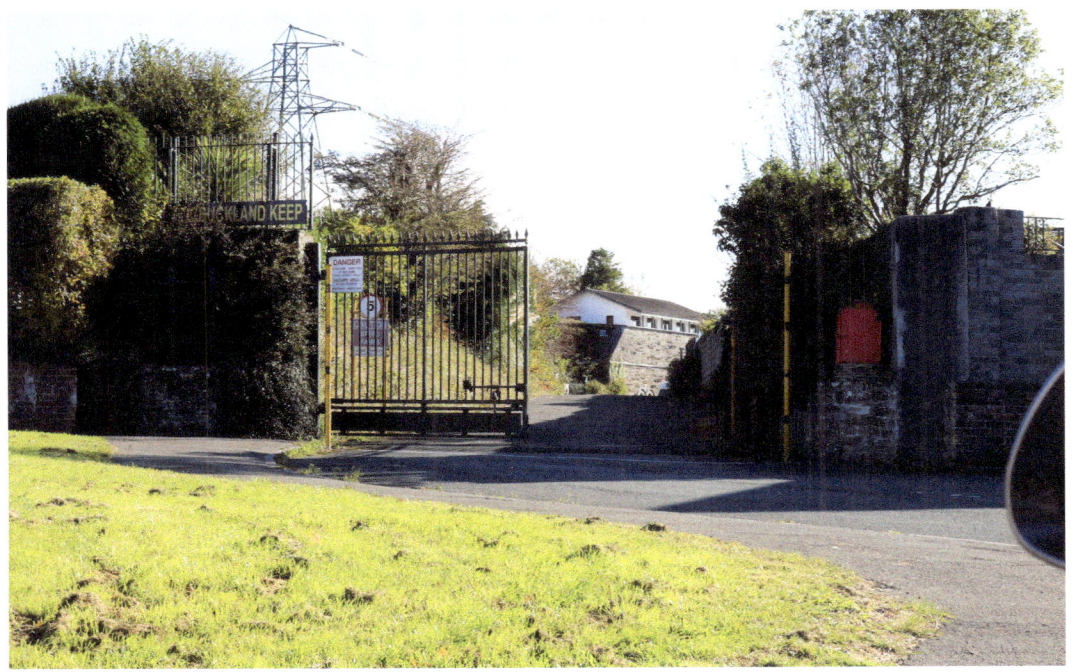

Above: Efford Fort from the air, centre right, with Sainsbury's below. (Courtesy of Steve Johnson, Cyberheritage)

Below: The entrance to Eggbuckland Keep.

Ernesettle Fort is still on the MOD land surrounding Defence Munitions Plymouth, the old Ernesettle Armaments Depot, which it was built to defend. Access to it is thus very difficult but my friend Steve Johnson was given access in the 1990s. It is now totally lost in overgrown woodland.

Forder Battery now houses a huge antenna, although the battery is partly demolished and completely overgrown by bushes with housing all around it.

Knowle Battery has been partly demolished and a primary school has been built on the grounds.

Laira Battery houses various successful businesses. I was allowed access by one of the business owners and parts of it are in surprisingly good condition.

Woodland is now a community centre.

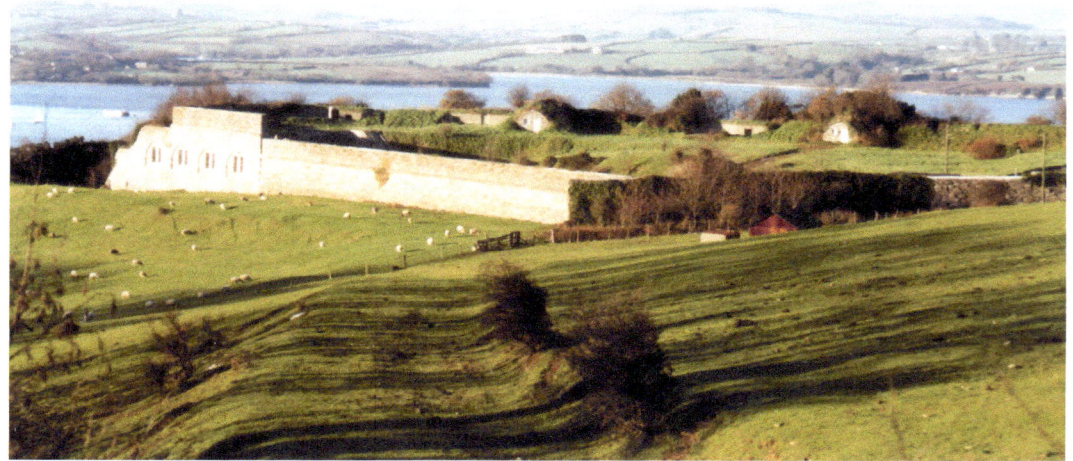

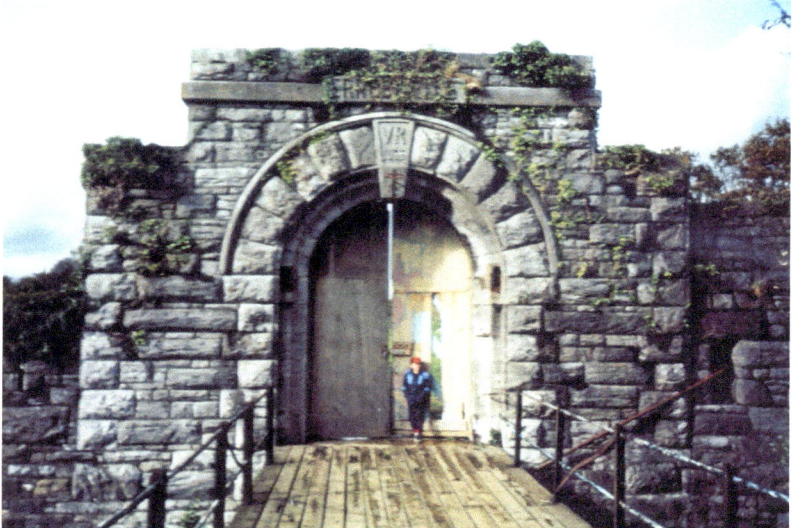

Above: Ernesettle Fort from the south in the 1990s. (Courtesy of Steve Johnson, Cyberheritage)

Left: Ernesettle Fort gatehouse in the 1990s. (Courtesy of Steve Johnson, Cyberheritage)

The Military

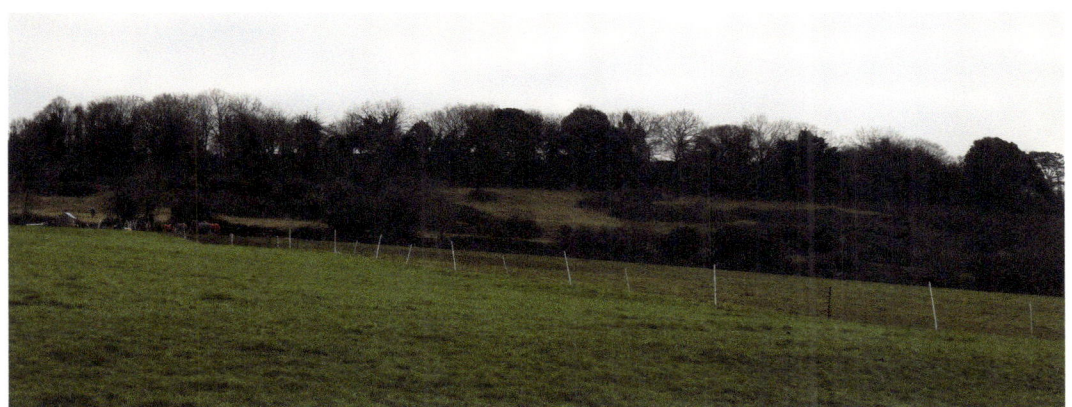

Above: Ernesettle Fort today.

Right: Forder battery, totally overgrown and housing a huge antenna.

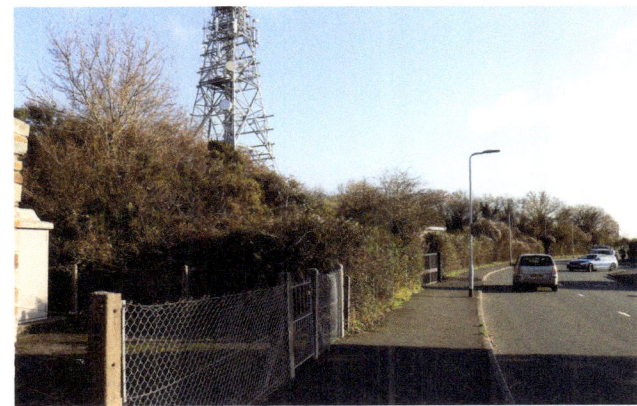

Below: Forder Battery somewhere in the midst of those trees.

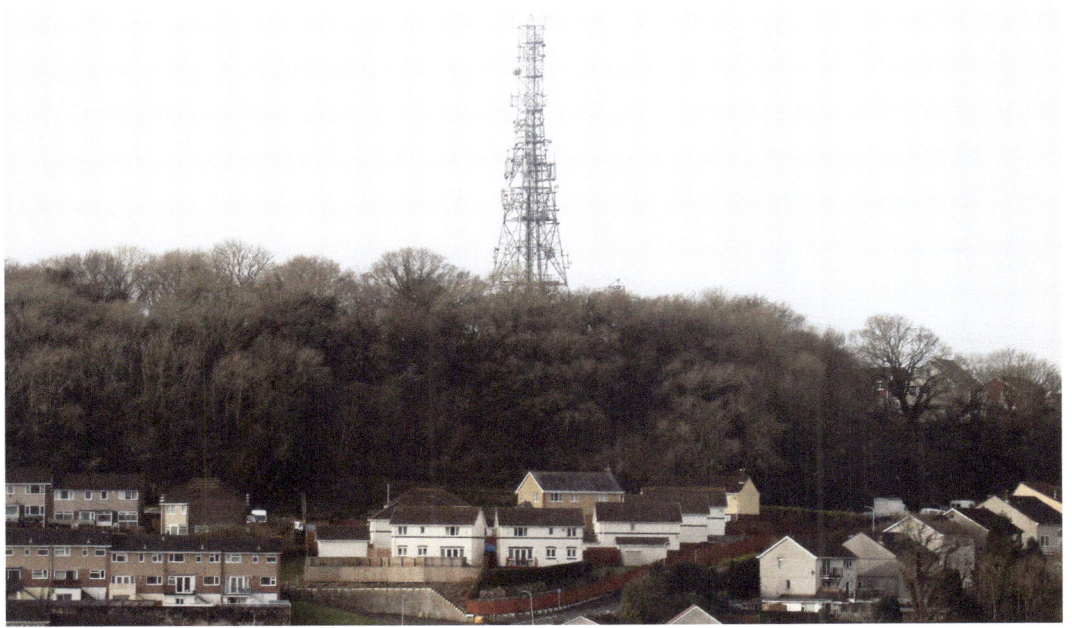

89

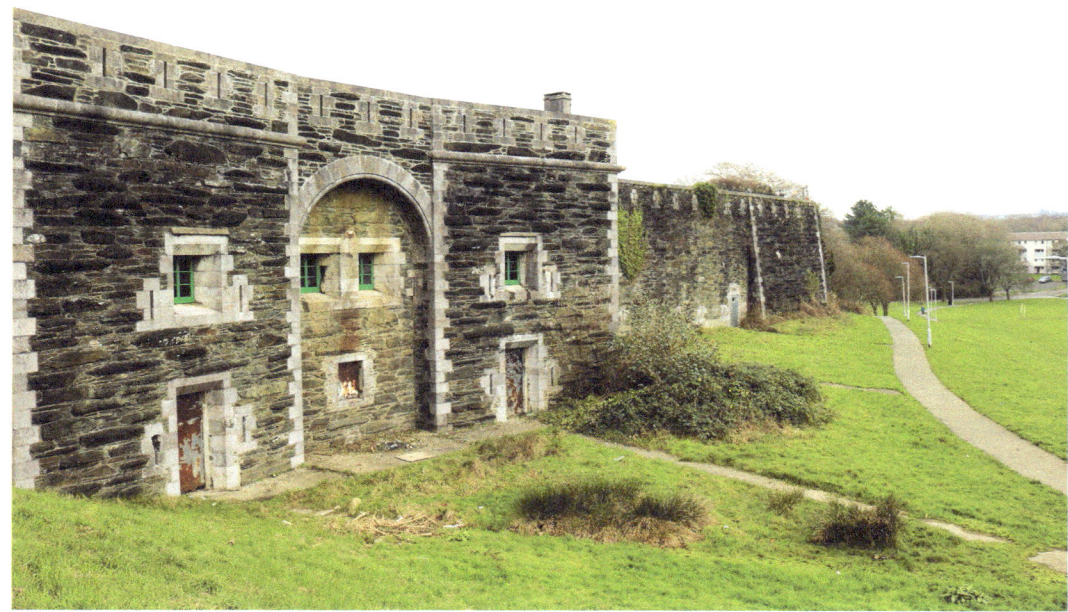

Above: The only old part of the exterior of Knowle Battery still existing.

Below: Laira Battery's gatehouse has been demolished. Many businesses are now based there.

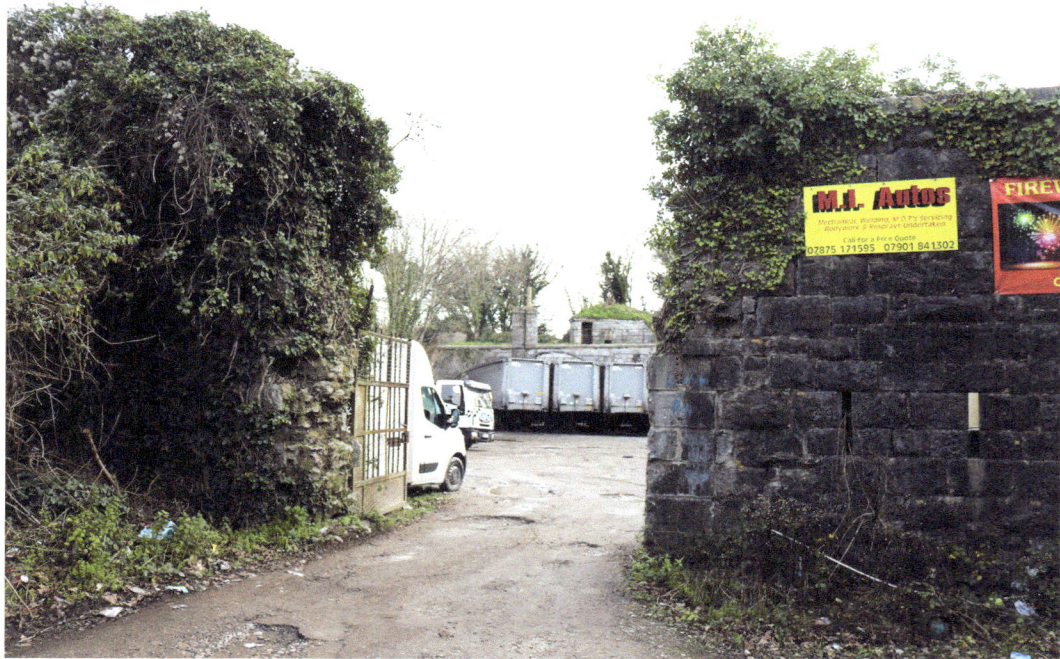

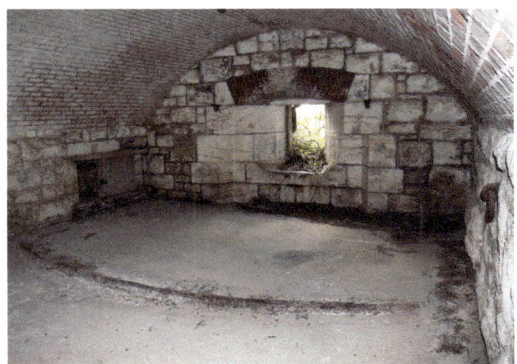 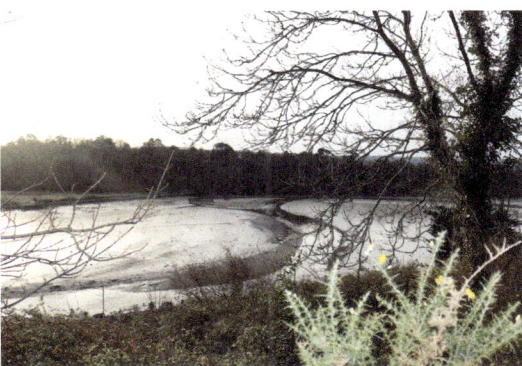

Above left: One of Laira Battery's casemates is still in excellent condition.

Above right: A gunner's view from the casemate.

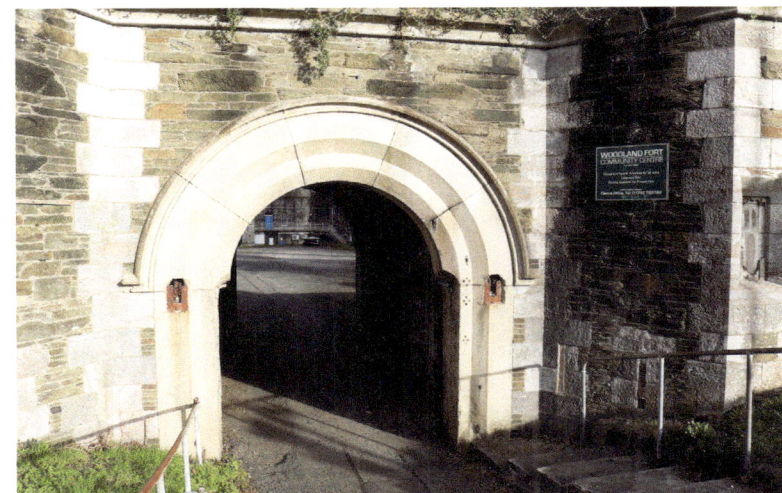

Woodland Fort's gatehouse is still in good order.

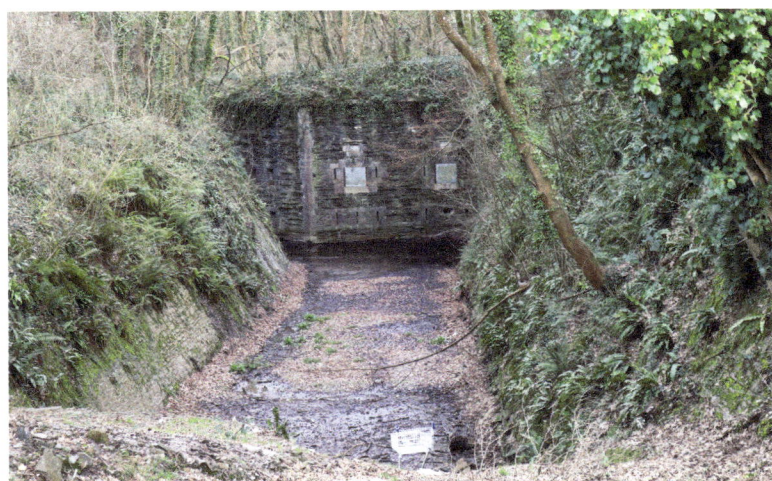

The defensive ditch at Woodland has been partly filled but is still visible.

Plymouth at Work

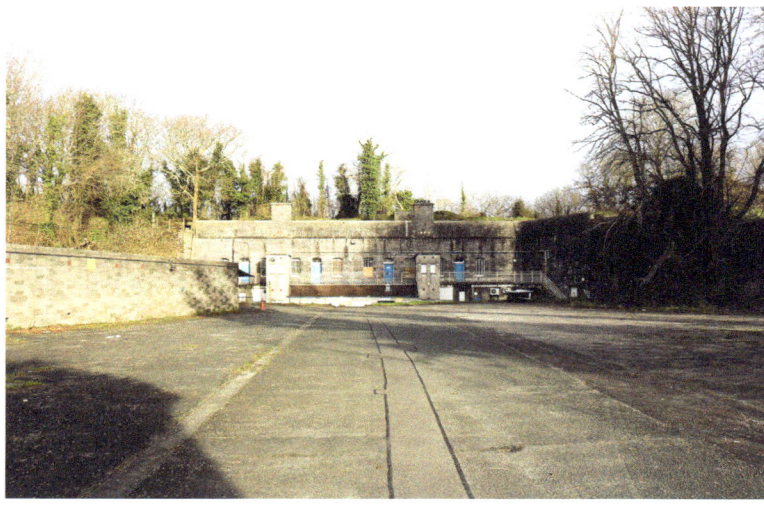

Woodland's accommodation now houses a community centre.

Crownhill Fort, however, is owned by the Landmark Trust, who have restored it superbly and hold occasional public open days during which there are guided tours and displays of gunfire. There is even a working replica of the Moncrieff Disappearing gun! Small businesses occupy the former military buildings surrounding the parade ground and holidaymakers can stay in part of the former officers' quarters on a self-catering basis.

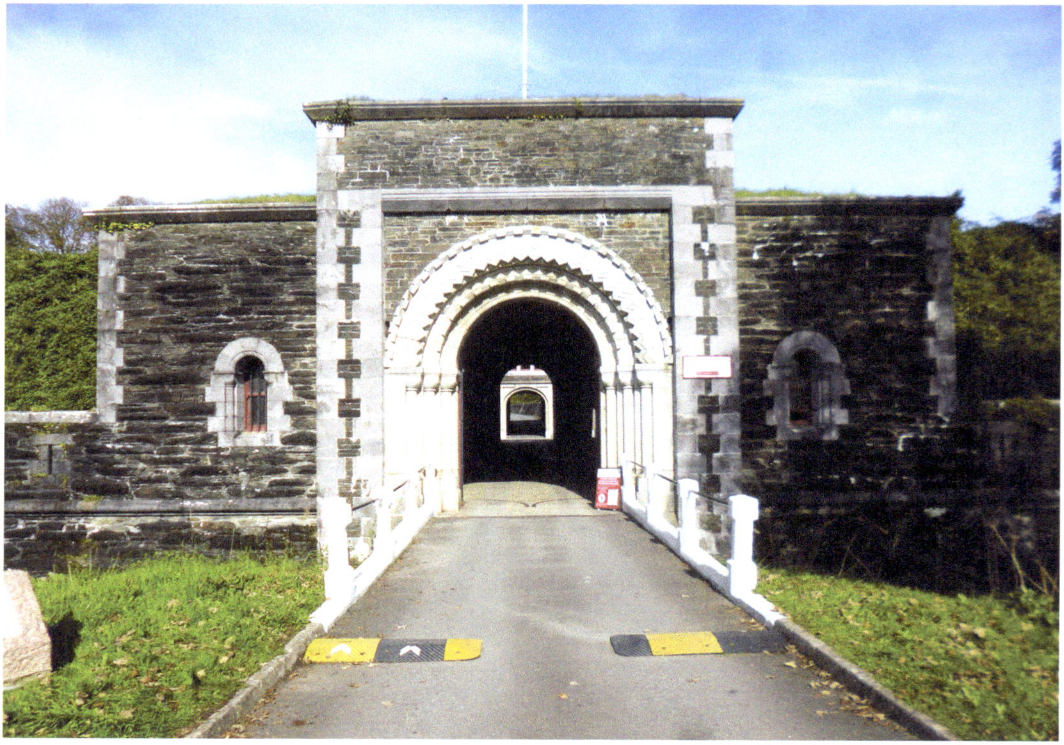

Crownhill gatehouse. (Care of Landmark Trust)

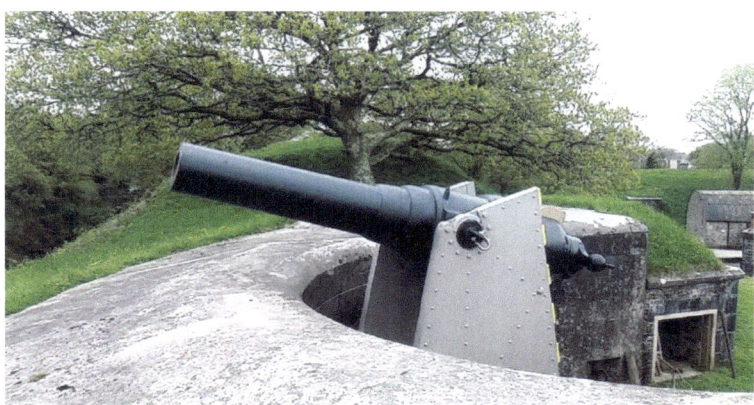

Right: Replica Moncrieff disappearing gun. (Care of Landmark Trust)

Below: Officers' quarters, which can be rented for a stay. (Care of Landmark Trust)

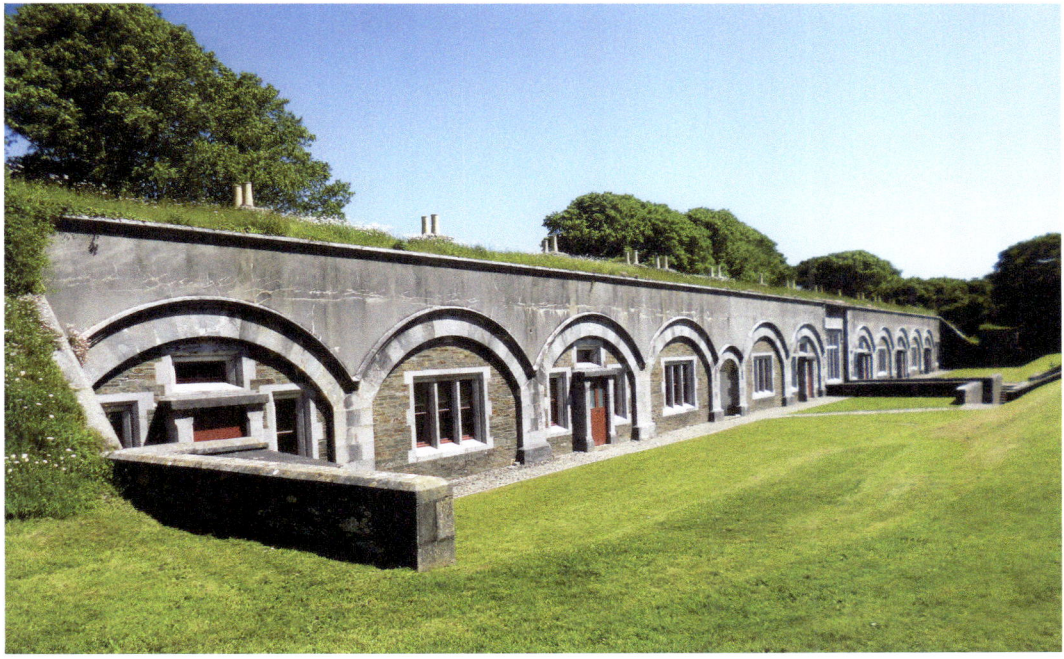

Of these forts and batteries three in the north-east – Fort Austin, Bowden Fort and Forder Battery – never appear in any census between 1881 and 1901. The north-eastern forts were the last to be completed and by that time economies were already needed, not least because there were not sufficient trained soldiers to man them fully. Between the censuses of 1841 and 1901 there are a few oddities that show how sporadically some of the forts were manned. Bluff Battery, which was built in the late eighteenth century as an extension of the old Devonport Lines, appears in the censuses of 1841, 1881 and 1891 although only ever with a caretaker, sometimes even a civilian, with his wife. Woodland Fort appears in 1881 with the only occupants a barrack labourer and his family, nine in total. The following census, 1891, is the only time so far it appears as being manned. There is a different barrack labourer and his wife, a corporal RA, four gunners RA and seventeen boys RA, forty-one people in total. The fact they were using boys to man the fort shows how the economies were biting.

Eggbuckland Fort appears once only, in 1891, and under that name so it is not clear whether it is Eggbuckland Keep or one of the nearby forts – Bowden Fort, Fort Austin, or Forder Battery – which are all within a short distance in Eggbuckland. Working on the assumption that the name is correct and only the military designation is wrong, I would guess at it being Eggbuckland Keep. Whichever it was, there was one civilian family, an army messenger, his wife and three sons. Apart from them they were all unmarried or unaccompanied members of the Devon Regiment under a lieutenant, one sergeant major, one staff sergeant, six colour sergeants, six sergeants, two corporal and sixty-four privates, a total of eighty-five people.

Another part of the Palmerston ring of forts was Drake's Island Fort. A small fort was built in the mid-sixteenth century on the 6-acre island. Being in the centre of Plymouth Sound it protected the dockyard and was, along with the Citadel, one of the most important parts of the defences. Over the next two centuries it was continuously extended with additional gun batteries.

Between 1860 and 1900 it was much strengthened and equipped with twenty-one guns in armoured casemates until the whole island was effectively fortified. During the 1860s, 9- and 10-inch rifled muzzle loader guns (RML) were used and these were upgraded to 11 and 12 inch by the 1880s along with a Brennan torpedo launcher. Before the First World War the armaments were three 6-inch breech loaders and six quick-firing guns. Army use ceased in 1956 and the island is now privately owned and unfortunately not open to the public.

When the First World War broke out in 1914 many of those people who had lived in barracks in and around Plymouth were shipped off to various places; many obviously to France but some went to Egypt and the Near East. Sadly vast numbers were never to

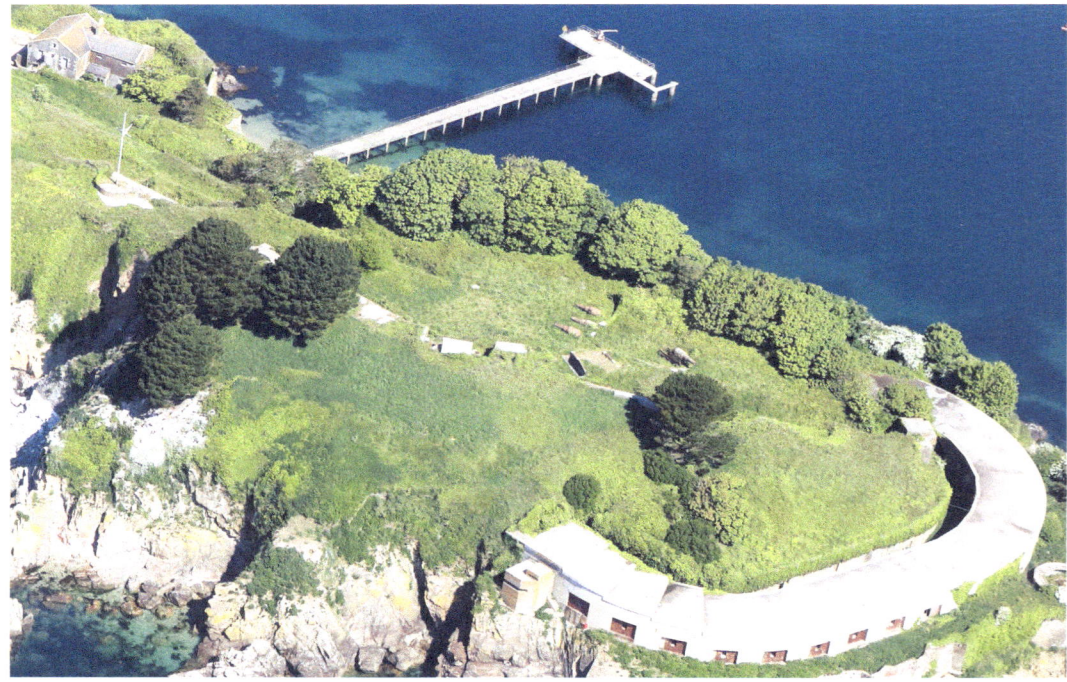

Drake's Island showing RML guns laying on the top.

return. Plymouth also had a huge influx of soldiers, firstly the Canadians who arrived in 1914 on a convoy of thirty-two liners, and later from America.

According to Parliamentary records the total number of personnel in the armed forces in peacetime, between 1901 and 1914, during the interwar years and post-war up until the 1970s varied between roughly 300,000 and 400,000. During the two world wars the numbers obviously increased massively to roughly 4.2 million in the First World War and 4.7 million during the Second. Crispin Gill mentions in his *Plymouth: A New History* that when the Americans entered the war in 1917 they took over the area around Victoria Wharves as a naval base. 'Within weeks two destroyers and sixty submarine chasers were based there, with over 3,000 men working from the port.'

The numbers of armed forces personnel stationed around Plymouth would have followed this trend with the Palmerston forts used as barracks and bases for anti-aircraft guns and barrage balloons during the Second World War.

The Navy had a major presence of course, with ships arriving for repairs and refits and personnel awaiting posting billetted in HMS Drake (as HMS Vivid was by now named).

In the run-up to D-Day Plymouth, along with much of southern England and especially the South Hams, was swamped by British, American and many other nationalities soldiers, awaiting embarkation. After 6 June 1944 the whole area was eerily quiet; they had all vanished.

Stretching my area slightly, during the First World War the Royal Naval Air Service opened a seaplane base at Mount Batten named RNAS Cattewater. It operated seaplanes, which were often hoisted on to Mount Batten pier. After 1918 this became RAF Cattewater, later rebuilt, expanded and renamed RAF Mount Batten from which various RAF and RAAF seaplanes operated between the wars and right up to the end of the Second World War. In fact as a very young child I saw the final flight of a Sunderland from RAF Mount Batten, which according to the website forces-war-records was on 30 January 1957.

This meant that during both world wars Plymouth played host to every branch of the military. The RAF presence disappeared in 1986 when Mount Batten closed, and the constant threat of defence cuts hangs over everything else but at the time of writing Plymouth still plays host to the army in the Citadel, the Royal Marines in Stonehouse and the Royal Navy at HMS Drake. All of the other 1901 barracks except these have gone, including Bull Point Barracks and Ernesettle Fort, which were intended to protect the Armament Depots at Bull Point (now closed) and Ernesettle (now Defence Munitions Plymouth). On the plus side, we now have the Royal Marine base on the shore of Weston Mill lake, north of the dockyard, known as RM Tamar. This is the base for RM amphibious forces known as 1 Assault Group and provides dock space for the amphibious assault ships, HMS *Bulwark*, *Albion* and *Ocean*, plus it permanently houses 300 marines plus others on courses.

Above I mentioned that in the post-war years and up until the 1970s forces personnel numbered around 400,000. Another Parliamentary record shows that current total strength of the armed forces (at October 2017, the latest statistics available) stands at 195,730, of which 147,520 are regular forces, the rest mainly reserves. It should come as no surprise that there are threats to sell off the Royal Citadel and Stonehouse Barracks. The dockyard has receded up into North Yard and competes for civilian contracts as well as Royal Navy ones to keep it afloat. Princess Yachts now owns South Yard; who knows, one day they may own the whole dockyard if the Navy shrinks any further. It also wouldn't surprise me to find that both the Royal Citadel and Stonehouse Barracks have been sold off for that great current boom industry in Plymouth – student accommodation!

What a sad end that would be to a once proud military city.

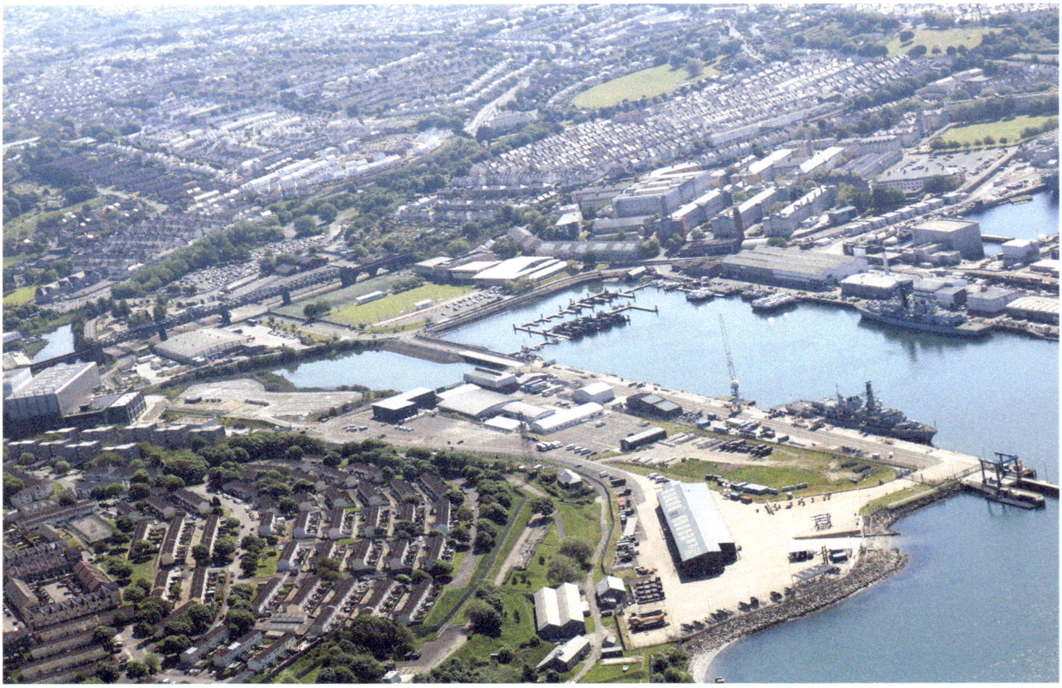

Above: RM Tamar.

Below: RM Tamar from the south.

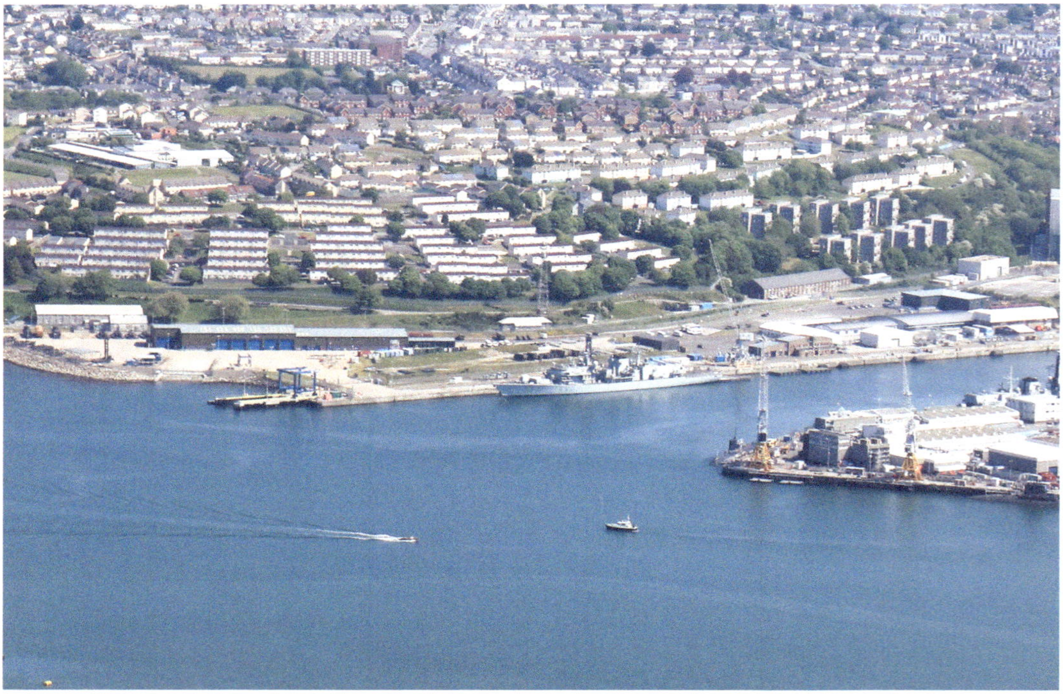